I0878546

The Canadian Department of Justice and the Completion of Confederation, 1867-78

Jonathan Swainger

The Canadian Department of Justice and the Completion of Confederation, 1867-78

UBC Press · Vancouver · Toronto

Printed in Canada on acid-free paper ∞

ISBN 0-7748-0792-X
ISBN 0-7748-0793-8

Canadian Cataloguing in Publication Data

Swainger, Jonathan Scott, 1962-
The Canadian Department of Justice and the completion of confederation, 1867-78

Includes bibliographical references and index.
ISBN 0-7748-0792-X (bound)
ISBN 0-7748-0793-8 (pbk.)

1. Canada. Dept. of Justice – History. 2. Canada – Politics and government – 1867-1896.* 3. Justice, Administration of – Canada – History. I. Title.

KE4752.S92 2000 353.4'0971'09034 C00-910442-9
KF5107.S92 2000

This book has been published with the help of a grant from the Humanities and Social Sciences Federation of Canada, using funds provided by the Social Sciences and Humanities Research Council of Canada.

UBC Press acknowledges the financial support of the Government of Canada through the Book Publishing Industry Development Program (BPIDP) for our publishing activities.
Canadä

We also gratefully acknowledge the support of the Canada Council for the Arts for our publishing program, as well as the support of the British Columbia Arts Council.

UBC Press
University of British Columbia
2029 West Mall, Vancouver, BC V6T 1Z2
(604) 822-5959
Fax: (604) 822-6083
E-mail: info@ubcpress.ubc.ca
www.ubcpress.ubc.ca

Contents

Acknowledgments

The completion of this research has been a long time in coming and, not surprisingly, the debts accumulated along the way are considerable. As an undergraduate at the University of Lethbridge, I had splendid professors. To Raymond Huel, William Baker, and James Tagg, I express my sincere gratitude for the start you provided and the support and encouragement that is still offered. When obtaining my master's degree at the University of Calgary, I had the pleasure of working with Louis Knafla who has, from the first day we met, been an unwavering supporter and friend. My doctoral advisor and friend, David H. Flaherty, has been and continues to be a valuable source of advice and assistance. My debts to David will never be repaid. My friend and colleague Gordon Martel, of the University of Northern British Columbia, has provided wise counsel in all things academic and scholarly while also setting a sterling example of what it means to be a historian.

In revising my dissertation, I benefited from the criticism and suggestions of John Weaver, Paul Romney, Louis Knafla, and Don Spanner. Collectively and individually, their comments have improved the shape and clarity of this work. Of course, they bear no responsibility for the fact I did not always pay heed to their advice. Others have lent assistance in a variety of ways. My thanks to Drs. Martin Goldbach and Libardo Melendez for their considerable skills when I needed open-heart surgery in London, Ontario. Also to Steve Thorlakson of Fort St. John, British Columbia, who has been generous with his time and experience in helping get my feet on the ground at the outset of my career. Thanks also to Laura Macleod, formerly of the University of British Columbia Press, for her patience and gentle persistence, and to Jean Wilson for taking this project on in midstream. And without the consistent assistance and good humour of Joanne Matthews and Lorraine Prafke of the University of Northern British Columbia Library and Jan Johnson, now at the University of Manitoba, tracking down the final pieces to this research project would have been a much more grueling process.

I would like to acknowledge the financial support provided by the Social Sciences and Humanities Research Council, which funded my research as a doctoral student at the University of Western Ontario. I also wish to thank that institution generally, and the Faculty of Graduate Studies and the History Department specifically, for the research funding I received while a student. The Osgoode Society for Canadian Legal History and the University of Northern British Columbia also provided financial support during the redrafting stage and for that, I am grateful.

It is a great pleasure to thank those friends and family who have lived with the project for these past years. Don Spanner was not only a friend and colleague at Western but, in company with his lovely wife Evelyn, was a gem of my years in London; both have remained splendid friends ever since. As a former office mate, Don has heard more about the Department of Justice than anyone deserves and for his friendship, I will be forever grateful. Others at Western also offered support and good humour during my studies; thanks to fellow students Andrew Meeson, Paul Butler, Scott Warwick, Reem Bahdi, Martina Hardwick, Eileen Mak, and Meg Stanley, as well as to Professors Constance Backhouse, Peter Neary, Donald Avery, Roger Hall, and J.C.M. Ogelsby. To those who provided advice, support, criticism, and coffee, I hope that I will be able to respond in kind: Wayne Shirley, Maynard Kolskog, Kemis Switzer, Ben Forster, John McLaren, Hamar Foster, W. Wesley Pue, Peter Oliver, Tina Loo, Carolyn Strange, Sidney Harring, James Snell, Steve Roe, and Nick Petryszak.

My family has witnessed my entire educational career, from its not so impressive beginnings in Rocky Mountain House, Alberta, to my current position at the University of Northern British Columbia. Throughout these years, my mother, Alice Swainger, maintained an unwavering faith in my abilities, and to her I can attribute my own unwillingness to flinch when the challenges mounted. My sisters Deborah and Jennifer have always been supportive. To my in-laws, Honour and William Sauvé, I also wish to offer my thanks, not only for their daughter's hand in marriage but for patience and understanding as I carted Jennifer across Canada in search of archives and teaching opportunities.

Finally, I dedicate this work to Jennifer, my splendid wife and friend, and mother of our two wonderful sons Matthew and Thomas. For without her support and willingness to sacrifice in the countless ways she has in the past and, most certainly did during the completion of this manuscript, I would have been unable and quite unwilling to put in the hours. And thus to Jennifer, a very special thanks for putting up with everything in the hope that someday we might look forward to a summer holiday when I don't bring the computer along and we can enjoy a little quiet time to just relax.

The Canadian Department of Justice and the Completion of Confederation, 1867-78

1
Introduction

Shortly after the new Canadian nation came into existence during the summer of 1867, Prime Minister John A. Macdonald agreed to pay lobbyist George W. Brega for an assortment of clandestine tasks in Washington. Although his primary responsibility was to ascertain the American attitude towards ongoing trade negotiations, he was also paid to investigate the organization of a number of American departments of state, including the attorney general's office. Upon returning to Ottawa, Brega reported his findings to Hewitt Bernard, Macdonald's new brother-in-law and long-time principal secretary. Noting that the report contained "a statement of the duties and functions of the U.S. attorney general," he included a list of the salaries paid the American attorney general and his staff. Brega added a brief commentary on proposed congressional legislation affecting the office: "Congress is about to pass an act by which all law officers in the several Executive Departments, such as the solicitor of the Works Department, solicitor of the Treasury & c are to be placed under the immediate control of the Attorney General, and thus there has been a lack of uniformity in their legal opinions which has led to such embarrassment as to call for the passing of the act in question."[1] While the American legislation languished for two years, Macdonald pressed forward. Within five months, he established the Canadian Department of Justice, on 22 May 1868.[2]

Although the timing of Brega's sojourn and the report that followed suggest that Macdonald copied the American legislation, the events were largely coincidental. Essentially, the American scheme paralleled Macdonald's plan to constitute a Canadian Department of Justice, an innovation consistent with administrative reforms dating back to the early 1840s. The change was also in accord with the prime minister's personal expectations as to the working out of Confederation. And creating a department of state to support the government's legal advisor was a reconciliation between the increasing demands placed upon governments in mid-nineteenth-century North America and the historic functions of the attorney general in Britain.

Finally, the decision in both Canada and the United States to surround the federal government's legal advisor with a bureaucracy revealed a North American confluence of law and politics. These continuities with the past should not, however, overshadow the significance of the departure from former practices. Specifically, while the attorney general's offices in the various British North American colonies before 1867 interacted regularly with the general public, the Department of Justice avoided similar functions after Confederation. As envisioned and created, the department was to be responsible for advising the federal government alone and, as such, revealed the central role that law and legal remedy would play in the statecraft of the post-Confederation era.

The creation of a federal Department of Justice should also be viewed as one aspect of the completion of Confederation, a process that ended in 1878. Arguably, this notion that the years between 1867 and 1878 are best understood in relation to "making a constitution" is a deviation from the traditional periodization of Canadian national history.[3] Essentially, those eleven years after 1867 were the concluding phase of events that, as Ged Martin ably demonstrates, began in 1837.[4] Support for this complementary phase following Martin's period is both empirical and inferential. In this particular instance, the evidence can be broken down into four basic points. Martin's exploration of how the British North American union of 1867 came to pass indicates that, beyond broad jurisdictional contours, little attention had been given to the specifics of the federal government's appearance or internal organization. While it might be expected that the federal government would duplicate most of the offices existing prior to union, this assumption ignores jurisdictional changes as well as the demands of serving a national constituency. As a consequence, one of the pressing demands of the period between 1867 and 1878 was establishing responsibilities within the federal government and, just as importantly, clarifying the relationship between the federal and provincial governments. Creating the Department of Justice was intrinsic to these processes.

Second, the completion of Confederation between 1867 and 1878 also involved the establishment or reconstitution of a number of national or quasi-national institutions. The creation of the North West Mounted Police in 1873, the unveiling of the Supreme Court in 1875, the redrafting of the governor general's instructions between 1875 and 1877, and the centralization of a national penitentiaries system by 1875 were amongst the notable examples. On a different institutional level, these years also witnessed the hardening of political identification and party affiliation in Canada, a development largely the result of the Liberal Party assuming greater stability and permanence.[5] The completion of Confederation imprinted the new nation with the predominance of the Liberal and Conservative parties. Under the banner of the National Policy, the election year of 1878 heralded the Conservative nation-building platform that would frame national political debate for the remainder of the century. And with that platform came the resurrected notion of a transcontinental railway stretching from sea to sea.[6] Therefore, the electoral victory of Macdonald's Conservatives in 1878 signalled both the completion of the institutional structure of Confederation and the beginning of the battle over its practical and philosophic workings.

Third, in the waning days of Alexander Mackenzie's Liberal government, Minister of Justice Toussaint-Antoine-Rodolphe Laflamme introduced a bill abolishing the receiver general's office and recasting the leadership of the Department of Justice.[7] While the absorption of the receiver general's duties within the Ministry of Finance was greeted with general approval, the plan to have two men act separately as attorney general and minister of justice was roundly denounced by the Conservative Opposition. Defended as a reasonable response to the enormous increase in departmental business, the opposition characterized the measure as evidence of governmental ineptitude in handling the nation's legal affairs. Although the bill would die in the Senate, the proposed legislation and the debate it engendered revealed both a parting of the ways concerning the administration of the department and, more importantly, an emergent difference between the two parties and their philosophies of the role of law in governance.[8] As such, these exchanges in April 1878 not only symbolized the final act in the completion of Confederation but also served to foreshadow important aspects of the constitutional clashes to follow.

Finally, as was hinted in the heated words over the proposed bill of 1878, a significant difference surfaced in the approach to governance exhibited during the Conservative and Liberal administrations from 1867 to 1878 as compared with that pursued after Macdonald's return. Notwithstanding the usual fractiousness of public life, before 1878, both parties demonstrated a willingness to accommodate conflicting views and, when prudent, to embrace conciliatory policies when in power.[9] For example, Robert Vipond points out that in the use of disallowance, a contentious issue in the years to follow, there was little disagreement between federal Conservatives and Liberals before 1878. "Indeed," Vipond writes, "the Mackenzie government used the power rather more freely than Macdonald had."[10]

This flexibility was further revealed in the successful reliance, by both Liberal and Conservative administrations, upon unofficial correspondence as a means of eliminating potential points of conflict between the federal and provincial governments. Or, as Garth Stevenson writes of the Conservative leader, "During his first government Macdonald bypassed the formal channels of communication and corresponded directly with most of the provincial premiers regarding questionable legislation."[11] The prevalence of, and preference for, this tactic is attested to by Oliver Mowat's entreaty to fellow Liberal and then Minister of Justice Télesphore Fournier that, rather than unilaterally disallowing provincial legislation, it would be wise to adopt Macdonald's more flexible practices.[12] Four months later, Mowat returned to the topic, asking Edward Blake, "As long as the two governments are in accord," was not "Sir John's plan the better one?"[13] That upon his return to office Sir John was no longer willing to resume his earlier conciliatory approach and replaced it with a more confrontational and less successful method marked 1878 as a pivotal point in the nation's early history.

This change of heart is of crucial importance. In his compelling study of post-Confederation federalism, Robert Vipond accurately points out an apparent difference between Macdonald and the Liberals. Writing of David Mills, crowned by Sir John as "the philosopher from Bothwell," Vipond notes that, "From Mills' perspective, Macdonald behaved as if the highest act of federal statesmanship was to assess the national interest case by case and act accordingly ... The crucial condition of this 'political federalism' was that the federal government have sufficient manoeuvrability to construct the right policy mix to achieve its ends."[14] Mills was correct; this was the Macdonald method of governing, and yet both the Conservatives and the Liberals employed it before 1878. Therefore, while Mills preferred to believe that this was an important distinction between the two parties, a look at the pre-1878 era (and the post-1896 Liberal administration of Wilfrid Laurier) suggests that Mills was only partially correct, at least when it came to his own party.[15] Nevertheless, after 1878, it was Macdonald who, despite the efforts of his colleague Alexander Campbell, abandoned this conciliatory approach towards constitutional disagreements. Campbell's replacement by the more centralist John Thompson did not end these attempts at reconciliation with Ontario, although, admittedly, by 1885 the federal cause had been thoroughly routed.[16]

Not surprisingly, this change in how constitutional and political clashes were handled corresponded to a reappraisal of how the interpretation and application of law would shape Confederation. True to his conservative roots, Macdonald and the Department of Justice he created subscribed to a robust scepticism concerning the reform potential of humankind. Consequently, before 1878, neither Macdonald nor the department placed a great deal of faith in the law, or any other mechanism, to create and sustain fundamental improvement. The best that could be hoped for was that a law, legal interpretation, or judicial ruling would not upset a brokered political understanding. In effect, the department subscribed to a particular "governmentality" wherein it employed tactics rather than law and even used law, and its interpretation, as tactics.[17] It was this use and manipulation of law and legal remedy that underscores the notion that the department actively attempted to govern the law in accordance with federal political interests. Central to this practice was the expectation that "understandings" between gentlemen politicians could dissolve any legal disagreement or conundrum. Politics and policy seemingly governed the law. Admittedly, it was precisely this way of thinking that drove to distraction David Mills and like-minded Liberals. While Mills castigated Macdonald's methods, it would be incorrect to assert that Sir John's approach was devoid of principle or, as some have argued, evidence that Macdonald was essentially a pragmatic opportunist. Rather, as Rod Preece has shown, Macdonald was a Burkean conservative whose scepticism concerning the prudence of broadly conceived fundamental reform coloured every aspect of his life and political career.[18]

Predictably, Macdonald's creation, staffing, and administration of the Department of Justice permeated the office with an approach to law that remained in place even after his departure. That Hewitt Bernard, Macdonald's brother-in-law, remained as deputy minister until 1875 certainly was a factor in reinforcing this scepticism. While Bernard's presence cannot be overlooked, it deserves noting that, although the Liberal ministers in the department were not obliged to maintain Bernard's views, they did.[19] Evidently, the emergent ambit of federal responsibility placed a premium on contextual flexibility at the ministerial level and, as such, discouraged literalism in interpreting and applying the law. Essentially, this approach to governance and constitutional interpretation was as much a reflection of the federal role in completing Confederation as it was a manifestation of Macdonald's own philosophy and method. That we equate this method primarily with Macdonald reflects, in large part, that he was its most charismatic practitioner and devotee. The flaw in this common attribution is that it ceased to be an accurate description of Sir John's approach to constitutional conflict after 1878.

This alteration in Macdonald's approach was extremely significant because the Department of Justice was ill prepared to respond accordingly. Created within an environment framed by scepticism and one in which any problem, legal or otherwise, was made amenable to political solutions, the department proffered advice in the expectation that it was to be the opening gambit in subsequent negotiations. Given the federal inclination towards accommodation during the completion of Confederation, such advice was both sensible and politically astute. Unfortunately, it encouraged unimaginative thinking and what amounted to an air of comfortable indifference within the Department of Justice. Consequently, when Macdonald's return to government in 1878 was accompanied with a steely resistance to any compromise and a corresponding requirement for farsighted and creative legal counsel, the Department of Justice was poorly equipped to answer the call to battle. This failure, it must be noted, was less the department's doing than an unintended product of the environment fostered by the completion of Confederation.

This interpretation of the years from 1867 to 1878 raises a number of enticing possibilities. On the one hand, we have the historical image of John A. Macdonald as the convivial Father of Confederation who, despite a reputation for deal making and tactical delay, steadfastly refused to strike a compromise in the constitutional fracas after 1878. Notwithstanding the claims of ideological liberals such as David Mills, we discover that, in performing the daily business of government, there was not a great deal to distinguish the federal Liberals and Conservatives as the Confederation scheme hardened into shape. And although both the Conservatives and Liberals espoused a faith in the rule of law, their respective governments employed the Department of Justice in a fashion that singed this notion while leaving its body intact. Amid this clashing of ideals, the practical demands of governance, and well-worn historical images, the Department of Justice practised the art of statecraft and endeavoured to govern the law.

My inquiry, therefore, proceeds on two levels. The first concerns the translation, from 1867 to 1878, of legal ideals into meaningful responses to the daily demands of governance. Specifically, how did the federal government and its legal advisor render notions such as the rule of law into practical effect, without either scuttling the ideal in all but form or hobbling governmental initiative with legalism? Not surprisingly, the completion of Confederation required a balancing act between that which was politically desirable and that which was constitutionally permissible. From the perspective of the federal government, this balance was lost after the return of Macdonald and the Conservatives in 1878. The second level is more narrowly concentrated on how the Department of Justice functioned within this sometimes-precarious environment. My interest concerns not only what constituted the department's mandate but also the degree to which there is evidence of a conscious effort to reconcile these responsibilities with perceived legal ideals and political realities. Naturally, there will be occasions when the connection between the daily run of business and the broader philosophic inquiries appears remote at best. But connections were there. The decision to parole a penitentiary inmate, for example, entailed a range of conscious and subconscious views on punishment, penitence, and the likelihood of a legal sanction to reform undesirable behaviour. This determination, as much as those concerned with the constitutionality of a piece of legislation or the suitability of a particular candidate for the bench, was grounded in basic assumptions about the feasibility or desirability of reconciling legal ideals with the demands of daily governance.

The Department and Its Place

Concentrating on the philosophy, function, and actions of the Department of Justice raises both particular and general challenges. One of the greatest difficulties rests with the actual notion of law. Given that the department's mandate is enmeshed with law and legal decision making, it is often assumed that the consequent activities would be concrete and clear cut, since this is a widely held expectation of law's nature. Typically, this perception manifests itself in the belief that a judicial ruling, legal opinion, or legislative statute creates a reality corresponding to the concern at hand.

For example, Parliament passed a variety of acts designed to prevent crimping, the coercive recruitment of individuals for naval service. Upon becoming law, these initiatives were, like all legislation, published in the *Official Gazette* and then specifically circulated to those officials resident where such press gang tactics occurred. But because of personal dispositions, ill will, the economics of sailor-town, and a range of other factors, enforcement was generally ineffective. Even when prosecutions followed arrests, judges sometimes viewed the law in a different light than that initially intended and, as a result, some accused that should have been convicted were, instead, acquitted. Thus, despite having a law with a consequent expectation that "something" had been done about a behaviour that some thought undesirable, crimping continued relatively unabated. Indeed, it was the ascendancy of steam-power vessels that eventually led to the disappearance of crimps.[20] That aside, it is clear the law had not altered social or economic reality. It might be argued that the law failed because of the foibles of those charged with its enforcement. Unfortunately, even on those few occasions when general agreement exists as to the desirability of a law or set of legal reforms and the envisaged ends, it is extremely rare to be able to discern a straight line between intentions and results.[21] As long as human beings share a legal system that depends on the actions of other human beings, we will be confronted with the basic notion that law is, at best, an undependable device for creating a new or improved reality.

Rather than searching for these elusive direct relationships, our time is better spent characterizing the tone or flavour of factors shaping the environment in which law functioned. Such an approach allows us to gauge how economics, politics, personalities, effective planning, and idiosyncratic luck or fortune produced a result approximating or thwarting aspects of the law's intent. Not only does this tack highlight the law as one ingredient within ongoing complex human relationships but, for purposes of uncovering the function of the Department of Justice, our attention is drawn to the means whereby the department, in endeavouring to provide the federal government with legal advice, navigated these changeable seas.

Another challenge concerns the administrative and functional nature of the Department of Justice. The Department of Justice was a primarily administrative office whose tasks "related to the servicing or co-ordinating of the work of other departments"; its work was spread throughout the entire governmental structure and was subsumed in the form and function of other departments.[22] This tendency was exacerbated by an inconsistent reliance on the department for drafting legislation. Despite the express provision that it assume all legal work for the federal government, bills continued to be drafted within other departments and "prepared" by the law clerk for the House of Commons.[23] Given this practice, it is sometimes uncertain when the department actually reviewed, commented upon, or altered prospective legislation.

This service function and the challenges it poses for researchers can also be seen in the relationship between the Department of Justice and the judiciary. Under the jurisdictional divisions of the British North America Act, 1867, the federal government assumed responsibility for appointment and general supervision of members of the bench.[24] While in practice, officials within the department performed this work, all communication between the judiciary and the federal government was routed through the secretary of state. Consequently, the historical paper trail of these communications was housed with the secretary of state, an official whose departmental records have not, in any consistent fashion, survived the ravages of time. While the Department of Justice retained letterpress copies of its outgoing correspondence, a great deal of the incoming correspondence is terribly fragmented. At best, we are left with portions and snippets of the relationship existing between the bench and the Department of Justice.

The staff composition of the department and the wider environment in which it functioned also raises a number of intriguing possibilities. In her study of the American civil service, Cindy Sondik Aron argues that after the Civil War, working in the government was transformed into a respectable occupation for those beginning a career, pursuing stability, or attempting to regain their feet after personal or business failure.[25] While respectability may have been in the offing for some, the suspicion that most government positions were sinecures remained common currency in both the United States and Canada. Further, the passage of various civil service acts in Canada did little to alter popular impressions that the bureaucracy was ridden with opportunists and scoundrels, especially in light of recurring scandals in Ottawa and throughout the service.[26]

Depending on where one looked in the Department of Justice, varying degrees of respectability could be found. For those lacking legal training, a junior clerkship was probably enviable for the status and stability it implied. Arguably, it is at this level within the department, and in the bureaucracy generally, that we are most likely to find those members of the aspiring middle class that Sondik Aron identified in her study.[27] For those with legal training, however, a civil service position created a mixed impression. Government employment for a young lawyer potentially implied a lack of talent or a shortage of desire and skill. On the other hand, a number of deputy ministers and chief clerks such as Hugh Richardson, Zebulon Lash, and Frederick White parlayed government experience into lengthy and sometimes lucrative careers, including positions on the bench. It might be said, therefore, that for those possessing legal training, the Department of Justice offered an opportunity but not a guarantee of success. Notably, it was at the ministerial level, where one might expect to find consistency of character and respectability, that the department was most regularly exposed to scandal. Of the five people acting as minister of justice from 1867 to 1878, only one, Antoine-Aimé Dorion, avoided an occasion wherein professional or personal character became a topic of public attention. Ironically, while most contemporary and historical commentary focused on the shortcomings of civil service officials, the Department of Justice was more often hurt by the actions of its minister.

Therefore, while one scholar of the Department of Justice has asserted that, aside from a few incidents of drunkenness and laxity, the department was well staffed, with people hired for their skills, such a generalization cannot be sustained.[28] Rather, much like the rest of the bureaucracy, the department had its share of mediocrities sprinkled amidst those aspiring to respectable careers. Further, the minister could, on occasion, be rightly charged with failing to provide a sterling example to those around him. As such, it can be acknowledged that as regards the competence of its officials, the department was no better and certainly no worse than the federal bureaucracy was as a whole.

That the department personnel were, as a group, unspectacular might appear somewhat surprising given their collective responsibility for reviewing all legislation and providing the federal government with legal advice. Not only was the composition of the so-called internal service of the department fairly ordinary, the actual number of officials located in Ottawa was quite small. In 1867, the department included nine employees when other departments of state ranged in staff from ten to sixty-one, which meant that other than Education and Indian Affairs, it had the smallest staff of the administrative departments in the internal service.[29] Although the contingent within the Department of Justice would rise to fourteen by 1876, it shrank to ten by the return of Macdonald and the Conservative Party two years later.[30]

The relatively small internal staff suggests a number of inferences. It might be argued that given the number of lawyers available within both the Conservative and Liberal parties, easy access to wide-ranging legal advice was hardly a great concern. The difficulty with such an explanation is that it contradicts the basic rationale for creating a Department of Justice: the desirability of having reference to what appeared to be apolitical legal counsel. Second, the small staff may imply that the drafting, review, and interpretation of governmental policy and legislation were, in the final analysis, relatively unimportant. On the other hand, Macdonald's attempt to centralize the provision of legal advice within the Department of Justice, combined with the ongoing contest over constitutional interpretation, clearly documents the importance of the department's mandate for the federal government. A third possibility suggests that a significant portion of the department's daily business involved fitting all the pegs into all the right holes. For such duties, sterling legal talent was not crucial. Significantly, such a process encouraged mechanistic or literal interpretations of the law that the federal government could then adapt, if necessary, in the search for a functional understanding. Essentially, a cadre of highly skilled legal minds in the department was unnecessary since the federal government approached legal and political disputes with the expectation that an accommodation was always in the offing.

A final challenge that the Department of Justice offers prospective researchers rises from idiosyncratic arrangements for the submission of annual reports to Parliament. Given the department's administrative character, its work was reported upon through other departments of state. For example, when the quality of Quebec's judiciary became a topic of controversy immediately after Confederation, the secretary of state provided Parliament with the record of correspondence, though most had originated in the Department of Justice.[31] While these peculiarities of the paper trail are hardly insurmountable, it is nevertheless impossible to obtain a complete and official record of the department, since only the penitentiaries' branch was obligated to report annually to Parliament. These annual reports are a boon to researchers who focus on penitentiaries and their administration in providing a wealth of information on activities in the external service of the department as opposed to that occurring in the capital. However, they also have the potential to skew any rendering of the department's mandate.

The existence of the penitentiaries' reports combined with the absence of a wider departmental version is doubly problematic. The lure of a written record is considerable, as is the inclination to place a great deal of credence in that record. That there is no corresponding document covering the remainder of the department's activity certainly encourages an emphasis on the one area that can be most easily accessed. Yet, while penitentiary administration and penal reform has attracted a considerable amount of scholarly attention in Canada, the role of the Department of Justice has gone almost unnoticed.[32] Given the literature, one might conclude that the department was wholly occupied with administering the penitentiary system. Consequently, the existence of the penitentiary reports not only can distort the impression of the department's labours but also overshadows the broader administrative context in which penitentiary administration occurred.

The mere existence of the annual reports on the penitentiaries, like any written record surviving the ravages of time, subtly encourages the grateful historian to presume the document's veracity. Obviously, at a time when many scholars are growing increasingly sceptical of accepting any historical artifact at face value, the willingness to uncritically embrace the annual reports or, for that matter, any departmental record, can be rather perilous. In effect, the penitentiary reports are no more likely to reveal the interests and assumptions underlying a particular policy than they could document a direct relationship between that policy and the results that supposedly followed. Therefore, while W.A. Calder is able to discern a pattern of increasing centralization in the administration of Canadian penitentiaries between 1867 and 1899, it is less clear that this apparent tendency actually produced the increased efficiency alleged in the correspondence and reports sustaining Calder's analysis.[33] It is not that Calder's thorough-going and indispensable study is wrong, but rather, that we can no longer let the availability of certain documents shape our analysis of that record.

That the historical record is weighted unevenly, in its substantive content and portrayal of cause and effect, serves to underscore a basic contention of this study. Unravelling the functions of the Department of Justice within the federal government during the completion of Confederation is, by necessity, an inquiry into the nature of contextual forces and an exploration of what exists between the lines, as much as it is founded on the empirical record. Indeed, that an annual report, a departmental memorandum, or a discrete account in private correspondence is at best only one possible version of an event merely confirms an intuitive expectation that any human interaction would necessarily be very elaborate. As such, this book begins with the assertion that those surviving historical documents form only part, albeit an indispensable part, of any effort to reconstruct the approach to law embedded in the department's mandate as legal advisor to the federal government.

The Path Ahead

What follows is an effort to trace the intricate connections between law and politics in the completion of Confederation between 1867 and 1878, and to document how the management of that relationship was the very essence of the department's mandate. A crucial ingredient of this activity was a basic ideological assumption, or worldview, about the nature of law, the character of legal education, and the attributes of those schooled in the law.[34] Specifically, this ideology of law and its corollary, the ideology of the legal profession, posits that law and its practitioners are both "apolitical and necessary."[35] In its widest manifestation, this ideology lent weight to ordinary administrative decisions and practices rendered by and through the department, provided a sometimes unwarranted patina of legitimacy to everything falling within the department's mandate and, most importantly, created an aura of legal objectivity that obscured and disguised the politicized character of law and legal remedy. Undiluted, the ideology of law functioned as a powerful rationalization for the prominence of legally trained individuals within a wide variety of governmental and bureaucratic roles while, at the same time, heralded legal acumen as an art of statecraft.

Yet, despite the centrality of the ideology of law in the department's philosophical make-up, it was but one ingredient. Alloyed to this notion was an equally powerful belief that the completion of the institutional structure of the new nation would be best effected by the federal government's willingness to build compromises in avoidance of conflict; an approach that distinguished the era from 1867 to 1878. This style of governance was not merely the result of a desire to follow the path of least resistance. Rather, it reflected Macdonald's deeply held scepticism concerning the ability of legislation, law, or legal interpretation to effect thoroughgoing reform. The Department of Justice was infused with this scepticism to the degree that, in pursuing its responsibilities, it assumed that most, if not all, quandaries flowing from its mandate could be resolved by political means. In terms of daily problem solving, this philosophy produced a singular method; an assertion that the right of action or inaction rested solely with the federal government and that it also entailed the freedom to reach a compromise, especially with provincial governments. This method of governance succeeded to a degree only so long as the parties remained willing to achieve compromise. Consequently, when the Macdonald government abandoned this approach for a more literalist interpretation of the law and constitution after 1878, it signalled the completion of Confederation and heralded a new age of intergovernmental conflict.

The ideology of law and the practised search for administrative and constitutional accommodations were, therefore, the central components of the art of statecraft within the Department of Justice during the completion of Confederation between 1867 and 1878. On the one hand, the ideology of law and its attendant cache for those with legal training provided a rationalization for vesting the management of the royal prerogative of mercy, the appointment of the judiciary, and the creation of a national penitentiary system with the minister of justice, attorney general, and the Department of Justice. This study reveals, however, that these responsibilities drew more on allusions to specialized legal knowledge or insight than on the necessity of that knowledge per se. As a result, these aspects of the department's mandate could appear to be above the taint of politics while, at the same time, being grounded in the politicized notions of the age. On the other hand, the studied scepticism that questioned the ability of even specialized legal knowledge to bring about fundamental change placed a premium on flexibility and compromise in completing the unfinished aspects of the union scheme. This wariness was particularly evident in the daily administration of departmental business, where the difficulties of time and distance in the latter half of the nineteenth century placed practical limitations on any solutions, legal or otherwise, imposed by Ottawa on the far reaches of the new dominion.

It would be folly to launch into an examination of these complex interrelationships without first setting the stage. Indeed, it is impossible to detail the genesis of how the Department of Justice functioned without touching upon the attorney general's role in colonial British North America. Therefore, Chapter 2 concentrates on the historic office of the attorney general and how it assumed a distinct character in the North American environment. Specifically, while the English office attempted to maintain the veneer of an apolitical legal advisor, the British North American attorney general was, almost from his inception, an overtly political figure who, thanks to the ideology of law and a willing suspension of disbelief, affected an apolitical status. This suspension of disbelief, or fiction, effectively shaped the attorney general's role within the emerging structure of responsible government and subsequent jurisdictional and administrative changes wrought by the Union of 1867. In fact, the fiction was so pervasive that it remained unscathed on each occasion concerns were raised over the increasing political duties heaped upon the attorney general's office; inquiries that failed to reflect upon the politicized nature of law and legal remedy.

Anchored within an historic context, Chapter 3 turns to recreating the manner whereby the Department of Justice functioned from 1867 to 1878. This necessarily involves a broad canvas touching on daily business such as clearing patent applications, approving electoral writs, acknowledging requests for judicial respites, and redirecting misinformed inquiries to more obliging recipients. It will also cast light upon the departmental efforts to manage crises such as a threatened invasion of Cuba launched from Nova Scotia and the 1875 rumours of a Métis uprising in the Northwest. More than any other aspect of its activities, handling the mundane queries of daily business along with the periodic crises demonstrated the department's rooted scepticism of the use of legal remedy. Not only did the law discourage haste, but the department was keenly aware that wielding the law unnecessarily was counterproductive, especially when the passage of time could often dissolve problems or untangle emergencies. Employing the law as a battering ram also failed to engender the jurisdictional flexibility that was required in hammering out the institutional workings of the union. As such, while the ideology of law provided the Department of Justice with a wide field of activity, the completion of Confederation required a deft touch from the federal government's legal advisors, in anticipation of politicized accommodations fashioned by the various levels of government.

Chapter 4 is the first of a series of thematic studies concentrating on how the ideology of law and the search for administrative and legalistic flexibility coloured the department's mandate. Concerned with the prerogative of mercy for both early release from incarceration and the review of capital sentences, this chapter explores appeals to mitigate punishments specified by statute, portrayed against the fiction that as legal advisors, the minister of justice and his supporting staff possessed specialized insight for handling this responsibility. In fact, an examination of the prerogative demonstrates, as Carolyn Strange has so ably documented in her study of the "lottery of death," that the application of capital sentences turned on a wide range of factors, few of which arguably fell within the exclusive purview of those schooled in the law.[36] Indeed, rather than relying upon identifiable legal knowledge in cases where prisoners requested a remission of sentence, the department responded with formulaic calculations of time served and institutionalized rewards for good behaviour in the penitentiary. Nonetheless, entreaties filed on behalf of hopeful prisoners suggest that petitioners believed in both the reform potential of humankind and the possibility of genuine contrition for past crimes, and expected that the department subscribed to such notions as well. The second part of this chapter examines what Edward Blake described as the "awful responsibility" shouldered by the minister of justice in determining whether another human being should be put to death.[37] The case files, ministerial correspondence, and newspaper clippings provide the documentary record of this process and lay bare the tragedy that these cases entailed – tragedy not only in terms of senseless acts of violence but because too often the fateful decision rested largely on a single person whose decision was, in the end, framed by the interests and perspective of one official: the minister of justice.[38]

Flowing in part from the preceding examination of the policies and practices shaping the early release of prisoners, Chapter 5 broadens the inquiry by detailing the department's responsibility for Canadian penitentiaries. Conceived as a natural extension of its mandate as the federal government's legal advisor and thus a product of the ideology of law, the department's creation of a national system of penitentiary administration was more apparent than real. In fact, despite manifestations of centralization and occasional flourishes of rehabilitative zeal, the Department of Justice failed to create a singular penal philosophy and did little to demonstrate that efforts at institutionalized reformation of prisoners produced anything more than rhetoric for public consumption. Indeed, true to the scepticism that Macdonald imprinted on the department, there is little evidence that penitentiaries were viewed, at the ministerial and bureaucratic level, as anything more than warehouses for miscreants. At the same time, this attitude did not necessarily colour the perspectives of individual wardens, and the corresponding lack of symmetry signalled a note of friction between the internal service in Ottawa and those charged with the localized daily administration of Canada's federal penitentiaries. Viewed in this light, the entire project of centralizing the nation's penitentiaries in the name of greater administrative efficiency and consistency, in concert with the supposed uniform application of rehabilitative methods, was but another fiction associated with the Department of Justice. And like the other fictions linked to the department, its administration of penitentiaries was built upon the notion that those schooled in the law possessed specialized knowledge that rendered them better suited to carry out the task. Yet while the immediate results of nationalizing the penitentiary system were less impressive than alleged, the project nonetheless furthered the completion of Confederation in representing what the new nation could accomplish. Indeed, the very fact that *national* standards and practices were at issue was but one aspect of "imagining" a new dominion and a new nationality.[39]

Of all the responsibilities shouldered by the Department of Justice, few taxed the art of statecraft more than did the intriguing and complicated relationship between the federal government and the judiciary. Akin to much of the department's mandate, the challenge of dealing with aspirants to the bench, their supporters, and sitting judges involved navigating a path between the notion that law and its practitioners were apolitical and none-too-subtle assertions that judicial appointments were simple matters of patronage. Specifically, while legal qualifications and partisan advantage certainly shaped the determination of who would be elevated to the bench, the assay of a candidate's antecedents also involved broadly conceived politicized concerns including social, religious, economic, and what might be termed impressionistic ingredients. Indeed, the distinction between partisan and political factors can be seen in Sir John A. Macdonald's claim that party, as opposed to political, considerations never determined who would rise to the bench. As evidence, he would often cite the 1869 appointment of Samuel Blake as a prime example of this equity of opportunity. However, even a cursory examination of the Blake appointment reveals that while narrow partisan advantage could occasionally play second fiddle to politics, judicial appointments nonetheless demonstrated the intersection of law and politics in nineteenth-century Canada and the degree to which that congruence coloured the department's mandate, despite the apolitical façade of law and its practitioners.

This final thematic chapter also concentrates on the Department of Justice and the judiciary, but shifts emphasis to the expectation for, and subsequent creation and staffing of, the Canadian Supreme Court. Given the relationship that existed between the department and the judiciary, it is hardly surprising that political considerations shaped initial conceptions of the Court's role in Confederation as well as subsequent debates and legislative initiatives. There is little question that while Macdonald and the Conservatives were interested in creating the Court, Sir John preferred to have in place an institution that would forward his vision of Confederation. For the Liberals, who succeeded in creating the Court, there are indications that the party leaders envisioned the Court as a principled aspect of national greatness. The irony, of course, was that while Macdonald helped scuttle Liberal plans to construct a Canadian tribunal of last resort, the watered-down Supreme Court proved to be a weak reed in Macdonald's post-1878 battles with the provinces. While it might be too harsh to suggest that the event demonstrates a sharp example of Macdonald being hoist on his own petard, the chain of events documents the unpredictability of political manoeuvres grounded in the legal world.

Arguing that 1878 marked the end of the Confederation era is based, at least partially, on the fact that with Macdonald's return to power, constitutional strife erupted between Ottawa and the provinces. Further, this outbreak of hostilities was clearly a departure from the manner of business for both the Conservative and Liberal administrations during the first eleven years of Confederation. While it hardly needs to be shown that relations soured after 1878, there has been no effort to discern the role of the federal government's legal advisors in this deteriorating state of affairs, and whether, in fact, the Department of Justice played a crucial role at all. It is my contention that, aside from the fundamental questions of constitutional dispute and the relative merit of either the provincial or federal positions, two connected events explain why, at a basic level, the federal government was so ill prepared for the post-1878 litigation. First, the Department of Justice had never been called upon to be either creative or particularly insightful in its legal interpretation. The department's approach, from its inception, had been unimaginative and mechanical in anticipation of politicized accommodations. In the face of the more contextual and dynamic vision advocated by the provinces, this institutionalized federal view was hardly compelling. Second, in directing the federal position from behind the scenes, Macdonald abandoned his earlier willingness to work towards political solutions and adopted a literalist position as the official mindset of the federal government. In departing from past practices, Macdonald distanced himself and his administration from the strategy of office that, during the completion of Confederation, had become the federal approach to governance. My conclusion argues that the provincial victories were not only a consequence of the merit of their arguments and the peculiarities of the Judicial Committee of the Privy Council but, just as importantly, also a result that can be attributed to a style of thinking and approach to law and governance nurtured in the aftermath of responsible government and institutionalized by the federal government during the completion of Confederation from 1867 to 1878.

2
An Apolitical Advisor: The Fiction of the Attorney General

Edmund Morgan's compelling book *Inventing the People: The Rise of Popular Sovereignty in England and America* opens with an assertion that the success of any form of government requires the acceptance of a number of fictions. In democracies, for example, it is necessary for the population to "believe that the people *have* a voice or ... that the representatives of the people *are* the people."[1] While a necessary deception, the fiction "must bear some resemblance to fact. If it strays too far from fact, the willing suspension of disbelief collapses. And conversely it may collapse if facts stray too far from the fiction that we want them to resemble."[2] Morgan was not, of course, referring to the legal fictions whereby the common law historically responded to novel situations falling outside the traditional forms of action or to the crafted narratives identified by Natalie Zemon Davis in her study of "pardon tales" in sixteenth-century France.[3] Nor was he describing a delusion or untruth. Rather, he was concerned with those instances of "make-believe" where we willingly suspend disbelief so that our world conforms "to what we want it to be."[4] Or, from a different perspective, fictions serve to frame uneven relationships as constituting a desirable and natural order of things. Sometimes depicted as "self-evident truths" or practical arrangements advantageous to the public, these rationalizations traced observable contours of political, economic, and social authority in tandem with the subdued means whereby power could be exercised. In this particular instance, a version of Morgan's fiction refers to the illusory contention that the attorney general functioned as an apolitical legal advisor. Indeed, this particular fiction has been an unwavering theme in the history of the attorney general and, with the creation of the Department of Justice, it too came to be served by this specious notion.

The ingredients of this fiction exist as embedded and often untested assumptions about the very essence of law. Its primary source rests in what Harry Arthurs identifies as the basic paradigm shaping the way in which most legal professionals and much of the public regards the law.

> The law is formal; it exists as a thing apart from society, politics, or economics; law has the capacity to achieve, and does achieve, results by encouraging or discouraging behaviour, by attaching specified consequences to behaviour that facilitate it, deter it or undo its harmful effects; law is made and administered by the state; and access to law is provided in courts by legal professionals – lawyers and judges – who invoke a body of authoritative learning in order to argue and decide cases.[5]

This view sustains a layered assertion that law and its practitioners are both "apolitical and necessary."[6] In effect, those who practise or interpret the law benefit from the notion that its ultimate goal is the pursuit of idealized justice. Or, as Robert Gordon writes, from one perspective, "The law ... is an artificial utopia of social harmony, a kind of collectively maintained fantasy of what society would look like if everyone played by the rules."[7] Accepting for a moment that such a utopia is attainable, it is a risky proposition to conflate the law with the ideal of justice, or the practical realities of its daily administration.[8] Essentially, the law or the administration of justice ought not be confused with the pursuit of justice. Yet the very fact that these distinct elements *are* viewed as synonymous is the bone and marrow of the fiction casting the attorney general as an apolitical legal advisor.

It would be disingenuous to suggest that this willing suspension of disbelief was solely the product of those outside of the legal community. As Arthurs points out, the fiction also reflects how the legal profession has viewed itself historically.[9] Common-law training consciously created the ideology of law that claimed those schooled in the law were endowed with highly specialized and ancient knowledge, which, in course, affirmed the status of those who possessed that learning: "The tradition associated law with both science and high culture, and justified the prestige and power of its practitioners. Law was authoritative because [it was] autonomous; and its autonomy derived from two sources, its formality (or technicality) and its antiquity."[10] Although most practitioners would have disavowed such lofty intellectual pretensions and taken refuge in the self-acclaimed role as skilled artisans applying technical rules, this merely substituted one characterization for another. Either way, lawyers were apolitical because, in one instance, they applied ancient principles that theoretically were not coloured by political interests or, in the other, because they pulled levers in a mechanical legal structure.

While it may be imprudent to leap from the ideology of law to that of the illusory attorney general functioning above politics, a link does exist. It entails the assertion that law and politics are so thoroughly intertwined that it is neither practicable nor useful to pull them apart. Such an attempt would only serve to distort and oversimplify the nexus.[11] Legal decisions are by their nature inherently political. Further, the legal profession's desire to deny this indissoluble connection through the benefit of an apolitical veneer is yet another political act. Therefore, when the decision was made in the fifteenth century to secure an additional counsellor to further protect and proliferate the English monarch's interests, the newly minted attorney general assumed the status of a personal advisor to the King, to defend at law, the King's interests.[12]

If the political character of the attorney general's origins and function are so easily revealed, why then is it necessary for the fiction to obscure this basic attribute? The answer lies with the rationale for creating, sustaining, and subscribing to such fictions in the first place; in their broadest sense they act as a palliative for a complex and sometimes frightening world. Essentially, the notion that the law and its practitioners are apolitical and can be the means for the pursuit of either idealized or practical justice is obviously more comforting than the contrary proposition. As such, the community and the profession have both an emotional and pragmatic interest to accept and propagate the fiction. The subsequent "social bargain" asserts that the profession, through and by the application of law, dispassionately shoulders a wide range of activities and behaviours on behalf of the community. In exchange, it acquires both individual autonomy and professional self-governance.[13] For the attorney general, this bargain, with its embedded notion of independence facilitating objectivity in applying impartial law, creates and reifies the notion that both the legal advisor to, and the advice tendered for a government, is necessarily apolitical.

Not surprisingly, we find caveats in this world of law, lawyers, and politics. In this instance, we must be mindful that the ideological assertion that lawyers are apolitical and necessary is not written in stone.[14] Indeed, the measure of a fiction rests in its ability to respond in accordance with changing times and attitudes. Lacking this flexibility, the distance between reality and fiction becomes too great and the fiction collapses. For the attorney general, sustaining the fiction requires avoiding, as much as possible, public behaviour demonstrating or suggesting the confluence of law and politics. This is orchestrated by the deft assertion that the attorney general merely provides the government with a selection of legal or constitutional alternatives, but that the final decision ultimately rests with the politicians. Such adroitness veils the political considerations in determining suitable policy alternatives while affirming, for public consumption, the fictional distinction between legal and political decisions.

Although this fiction has coloured the attorney general's history since its inception, the reforms of mid-nineteenth-century British North America fundamentally reoriented the Canadian office. Administrative innovations such as filing systems that engendered an institutional memory, the notion of governmental possessory rights to departmental records, along with ministerial responsibility, were changes introduced in the wake of Lord Durham's 1839 report on the Canadian political situation. The very idea of political responsibility, both inside the cabinet and to the legislature, raised concerns for the attorney general, such as whether poor legal counsel merited the same consequences as poor political advice.[15] The emergence of individual attorney generals as political leaders served to further muddy the waters. That it remained possible to successfully assert, after the mid-century, that the attorney general functioned as an apolitical legal advisor, even in the face of the evident political role that the office had assumed, was a masterful effort of nurturing the fiction. This effort did not pass entirely unchallenged and on at least five occasions between 1850 and 1878, the attorney general's political character was subjected to scrutiny and public debate.

Indeed, as late as 1863, it was observed that the law officers' departments in Canada West and Canada East shouldered too much political responsibility for the other departments of state while being, on the other hand, rather loosely organized.[16] Although creating the federal Department of Justice in 1868 tightened the administrative organization, the act served to mask these political responsibilities through a reassertion of the fictional attorney general, who merely tendered legal advice. That the attorney general, as the apolitical legal counsel, and the minister of justice, as the political law officer in the cabinet, were to be the same person, required a particularly generous suspension of disbelief. Yet despite its evident implausibility, the fiction remained (and has remained) a central feature of the character of the minister of justice and his or her role in federal statecraft.

Framed in this manner, Chapter 2 outlines the historic office of the attorney general and its evolution in the British North American environment. For while the English office attempted to maintain the veneer of an apolitical legal advisor, the colonial attorney general was, almost from his inception, an overtly political figure who, thanks to the ideology of law and a willing suspension of disbelief, affected an apolitical status. This fiction shaped the attorney general's role within the contours of responsible government and the innovations introduced by the Union of 1867. In fact, the fiction was so pervasive that it remained unscathed on each occasion concerns were raised over the increasing political duties heaped upon the attorney general's office – inquiries that failed to reflect upon the politicized nature of law and legal remedy. Not only did the ideology of law cast the attorney general in a particular light, it would also provide a consequent rationalization for vesting a whole series of duties and responsibilities in the freshly minted Department of Justice within a year of proclaiming the new dominion.

The Politics of Advice

Although it is possible to trace the English attorney general's roots back to the fifteenth century, the administrative changes following the rebellions of 1837-8 set in motion a series of events that recast the office in British North America. True, while the careers of individuals such as Francis Maseres, James Monk, John Beverley Robinson, and Richard Uniacke, Sr., had laid bare the attorney general's inherent political character, the post-rebellion administrative and political reforms raised that character to the forefront of the Canadian office.[17] As Paul Romney argues in his splendid study of the attorney general in Ontario from 1791 to 1899, the effect of responsible government on the law officers was twofold: "The political responsibility of a minister of justice suddenly fell on the Attorney General," and "With it, as an inevitable concomitant of that responsibility, went membership in the cabinet."[18] Romney further argued that although "these developments were unexampled in the history of England and its empire, they were logical consequences of the province's political history and social structure."[19]

Romney's point is well taken, although I hasten to add that the basic paradigm highlighted by Harry Arthurs still shaped the very nature of an attorney general. While local history and social structure provided the attorney general with distinctive regional meaning, that meaning was cast within imbedded notions of law, the legal profession, and the corresponding politics of legal decision making; all were crucial components of the ideology of law and its role in shaping the activities of the federal Department of Justice and its role in completing Confederation. Therefore, while the Durham report initiated a series of reforms giving rise to a particular type of attorney general before 1867, and thus lent a specific flavour to the new Department of Justice in 1868, we must be mindful that these developments were nonetheless framed by a parallel and often unarticulated ideological context.

In voicing his concerns and solutions for the political troubles that had beset the Canadas in 1837-8, Lord Durham emphasized a systemic weakness of the two provinces' administrative structures. Specifically, "The Executive Council, the law officers, and whatever heads of departments are known to the administrative system of the Province, were placed in power, without any regard to the wishes of the people or their representatives; nor indeed are there wanting instances in which a mere hostility to the majority of the Assembly elevated the most incompetent persons to posts of honour and trust."[20] He later continued, "Now, I do not at all exaggerate the real state of the case when I assert, that there is no head of any of the most important departments of public business in the Colony."[21] Finally, "Of no one of these departments is there any responsible head, by whose advice the Governor may safely be guided. There are some subordinate and very capable officers in each department, from whom he is, in fact, compelled to get information from time to time. But there is no one to whom he, or the public, can look for the correct management and sound decision on the policy of each of these important departments."[22]

Durham's notion of responsibility raised two specific issues for the attorney generals.[23] Institutionalizing responsibility in the legislative assembly acknowledged that when the attorney generals tendered advice within the cabinet they, along with all members, did so as political creatures. The legalistic character of this advice, however, did nothing to shield the law officers in the assembly. Arguably, the absence of any special standing tacitly admitted the confluence of law and politics. Yet despite ordinary status within the assembly, government decision making provided the attorney generals with the singular position of providing allegedly apolitical legal advice and then, as members of cabinet, voting on political initiatives flowing from that legal advice.[24]

Attendant was a second level of responsibility wherein the attorney generals were to be accountable for sound departmental management and policy. Beyond the subtle distinctions created by political responsibility in the assembly and cabinet, the question of what defined sound management created another set of potential institutional quandaries. Was sound management and policy a wholly internal guideline that, on a practical basis, was concerned with the creation and operation of an administrative structure through which policy decisions could be traced to their origins? Or was this to be a manifestation of the broader political responsibility wherein the attorney general, and the government of which he was a part, were to be politically and legally responsible for the action, or lack of action, from the supporting bureaucracy? Essentially, in assuming the role of political and legal head of his office, did the attorney general obtain full administrative and internal autonomy, or was the whole process to be answerable to Durham's broadly conceived political responsibility?

Sorting out the implications of Durham's suggested reforms fell to Charles Poulett Thomson, who, upon his appointment as governor general of British North America, assumed his peerage as Lord Sydenham. Influenced by Benthamite Utilitarianism, Sydenham embraced centralization and reform in the united Canadas as the key elements in solidifying imperial bonds and preventing further outbreaks of disaffection.[25] Indeed, Sydenham and Colonial Secretary Lord John Russell agreed that a complete reorganization of the local departmental structure needed to occur before any fundamental reordering of colonial government.[26] Following the recommendation set out in Durham's report, Russell further thought it crucial that, "The functions of the department heads should be clearly explained to them and that all were to be directly responsible to the governor for the conduct of public business. Recognizing the importance of unity of command, Russell wanted to provide each department with a responsible ministerial head."[27] Not only would this place the attorney general at the head of his own department, but the direct responsibility of other heads would encourage an increased reliance on the attorney general for guidance in the formulation of a wide range of government initiatives.[28]

The establishment of responsible government, the parallel emergence of political parties, and the coincidence of party leaders being drawn from the legal profession gave rise to yet another change when "it became the practice for the leader of the government party to take the office of the Attorney General."[29] Once again, the attorney general was placed in a position revealing the congruence of law and politics. Considering the genesis of the attorney general, it is clear that responsible government did not create this congruence. Rather, it confirmed that the notion of an apolitical law officer was a fiction. Indeed, as J.E. Hodgetts writes, "*By the time* responsible government had been granted, the offices of the attorney general for Canada East and Canada West had become the centres where parliamentary strategy was planned and major administrative decisions were reached. It was no accident, then, that found the two premiers most frequently operating from these two offices."[30] Indeed, in 1846 it was recognized that the expanding political activities of the attorney generals made it increasingly difficult to perform their traditional legal functions.[31]

Although these elaborations in the stature of the attorney general did not escape criticism, much of the commentary and debate focused on fairly specific concerns. For example, the almost perennial midcentury discussion of the law officers' duties and remuneration only occasionally considered the implications of the congruent legal and political activities.[32] And even when individual members did raise the question, their concerns were framed within the dominant paradigm that the law and its interpretation were apolitical. Thus, rather than wrestling with the question of whether the law was inherently political, critics such as Robert Christie, Lewis Moffat, and John Hillyard Cameron all concentrated on how the political activities of office holders coloured that which normally would be untouched by petty politics and opportunism.[33] This thinking allowed Cameron, for one, to suggest that eliminating the solicitor general's office, creating a cabinet law officer to provide government with advice on policy questions, and restricting the attorney general to nonpolitical legal work would rectify any conflicts concerning legal counsel. Cameron confidently insisted that his reforms provided for the presentation of legal guidance "irrespective of any political bearing."[34]

Not only were the suggestions rejected but the debate provided a forum wherein the attorney general's political aspect was actually extolled. Responding to Cameron's query as to whether an attorney general could provide sound legal and policy advice simultaneously, Attorney General

Robert Baldwin assured the legislative committee that dispensing with the office of attorney general, "as clothed with its present political character ... in a community like ours" would not be "practicable to do so with advantage to the public."[35] Alluding to the circumstances raising men of the bar to political prominence, Baldwin added that the "leading man, of whatever party may be ascendant, will belong to the profession of the Law. In preparing, therefore, the list of an Administration for the consideration of the Representative of the Sovereign, such person will naturally prefer the Office that keeps him, in form at least, connected with his Profession."[36] Portrayed in these terms, Baldwin's description introduced an amended version of the fiction. Rather than simply denying the indissoluble connections between law and politics, he emphasized the public utility and professional advantage of their proximity while, at the same time, stopping short of acknowledging the political essence of the law officer.

The near admission had important consequences for the entire administrative structure of the united Canadas. Consistent with Baldwin's reliance on the utility of the law officers' position, Hodgetts observed the tendency that the law officers came to provide "much of the central co-ordination which was expected of cabinet as a body. Not only were they responsible for directing political strategy in Parliament but also their legal abilities induced other departments to appeal to them for rulings – not always on points of law – which in turn came to be treated as rulings of the whole cabinet."[37] Inasmuch as the development signalled both the prominence of the law officers and the political timidity of their colleagues, it was also rather ironic. While on the one hand it remained necessary to maintain the fiction of law's apolitical character, it had also become convenient for legislators to continually assert the legal character of every decision rather than shoulder the political responsibility for running their respective departments. It was, of course, this exact tendency that compelled D'Arcy McGee to conclude in 1863 that the law officers were assuming too much political responsibility for the other departments.[38]

Although McGee's report was hardly prescriptive, it documented, both consciously and subconsciously, the attorney general's evolution during the previous twenty years. For example, the attempted innovation of registering the various opinions delivered by the two attorney generals was noted as a positive if unevenly executed practice. While the inefficacious policy did not prevent opinions and documents from being carted off, at least it recognized the utility of recording the government's legal memory. In the end, however, McGee was no more able than earlier commentators and critics to move beyond the fictional separation of law and politics: "It seems by no means necessary that references should be constantly made to the Attorney General East or West, on questions of administration as distinguishable from questions of law. That either of the chief law officers may happen to be Premier and, therefore to be consulted on grounds of public policy, cannot of itself relieve the head of any department from his own proper official responsibility."[39]

On the eve of Confederation, therefore, the ideology of law in tandem with the consequences of the Sydenham experiment in responsibility and centralization had placed the attorney general at the forefront of Canadian politics. Criticized on some fronts, the development was especially targeted because it paralleled the attorney general's withdrawal from the courts at the same time the office became synonymous with political leadership. And while commentators circled around the deeper issue, none recognized the futility of criticizing the attorney general for being political. The widespread subscription to the paradigm of law as apolitical and necessary forestalled such an inquiry and ensured that the apolitical attorney general would continue to be a paradox during the completion of Confederation between 1867 and 1878.

A National Department of Justice

Introduced during the first week of May 1868 and receiving royal assent three weeks later, the bill establishing the Department of Justice retained the historic peculiarities of the attorney general's office under new nomenclature.[40] Specifically, the act created a political minister of justice to advise the government in the Privy Council alongside an attorney general to provide legal direction to the departments of state. That a single individual would occupy both roles was a sleight of hand that escaped any discussion in the Commons. Evidently, the pre-Confederation assertion that a person could comment on law or politics without fear of one influencing the other also applied after Confederation to a similar person holding two distinct, if related positions. As John Edwards writes, "It is difficult, however, if not wholly unrealistic, to make such a distinction drawn by the Act of 1868 in circumscribing the advisory role of the Attorney General, qua Attorney General, to that of advising the Heads of Department, as opposed to the Government itself."[41] Although unrealistic, this distinction was nonetheless maintained throughout the act creating the Department of Justice.

Section one of the act brought into existence a department of the civil service called the Department of Justice and created the post of minister of justice, who would manage and direct that department.[42] The ensuing section elaborated the minister's role within the government. Charged with the responsibility of ensuring that "the administration of public affairs is in accordance with the law," the minister also supervised "all matters in connection with the administration of Justice in Canada" not included within provincial jurisdiction.[43] Finally, the minister was to review legislative acts and proceedings of the provincial legislatures, comment on all matters of law referred to the Crown and, finally, assume all other duties assigned by the governor general in Council.

Section three pertained to the responsibilities of the attorney general, as distinct from the minister. The attorney general of Canada was to possess the duties ascribed to the same office in England, while also enjoying the powers and duties of the several provincial attorney generals in the provinces prior to Confederation, so far as they did not conflict with the division of powers under the British North America Act, 1867. Substantively, this meant that the federal attorney general would not supervise the daily administration of criminal law, but would continue to advise the government – a duty shared with the minister of justice. Most importantly, the federal attorney general was entrusted with advising the several heads of departments of the government "upon all matters of Law connected with such Departments."[44] In practice, this meant that the Department of Justice reviewed and approved every piece of federal legislation. Specifically, if the government was to be liable for any action, or could be held accountable for nonaction, the attorney general had to be involved in that determination. Furthermore, in any instance where the government was deemed to be liable, or in litigation where the interests of the federal government or Crown were at stake, the attorney general was to represent those interests. Finally, the attorney general was responsible for the administration of the penitentiaries and prisons of the Dominion; he was charged with the settlement of all instruments issued under the Great Seal of Canada; and he was to be accountable for any additional duties assigned by the governor general.

While the legislation failed to elicit any commentary in Canada, the colonial office was less accommodating. The act's provision that the federal attorney general was to supervise the administration of criminal law caught the attention of those at 14 Downing Street.[45] Their concern focused on whether an expansive reading of the act might allow the attorney general to act in an area that, under section 92 (14) of the British North America Act, was delegated to the provinces. Upon submission to the English law officers, however, it was determined that the Department of Justice Act was consistent with constitutional divisions concerning the administration of justice.[46]

Given the act's content, it is surprising that the colonial office did not raise another query. Aside from questioning the fanciful effort to create the impression of duality in a single office, it is puzzling that the division of responsibilities did not give reason to pause. Specifically, that the minister of justice, who was clearly cast in a political role, would be entrusted with the constitutional review of all provincial legislation seems to be a peculiar choice. To the extent that the fictional division between minister of justice and attorney general could be maintained at all, would it not have been more appropriate for the "apolitical" attorney general to render these highly sensitive and often contentious judgments? However, from the perspective of Sir John A. Macdonald, chief architect of the union scheme and the act creating the department, placing the review of provincial legislation in the hands of the minister of justice made perfect sense. If the completion of Confederation was to be accomplished by building political understandings within the broad contours of the constitution, it was crucial that a political minister of justice be able to round off the edges of strict interpretation. To further this end, two weeks after the Department of Justice Act was passed into law, Macdonald issued a memorandum outlining the terms whereby the minister of justice would reserve or disallow provincial legislation.

The memorandum of 8 June 1868 on reservation and disallowance made three points.[47] First, it was evident that the authority to reserve or disallow was to be used to forward Macdonald's centralist vision of Confederation. Second, the duty of reviewing provincial legislation would place the minister of justice in a quasi-judicial role. Finally, while reservation and disallowance were to be viewed in these terms, it was equally clear that Macdonald remained open to discussions specifying what was practically, as opposed to literally, constitutional.

The most contentious aspect of the memorandum was the minister's prerogative to decide that a provincial enactment was unconstitutional and to then be able to adjudicate the claim. As David Mills, the young reform politician, confided to his diary, declaring a piece of legislation ultra vires "is a judicial determination and should be left to the courts exclusively."[48] Mills concluded that, "Our Court of Error and Appeal should be a Judicial Committee of the Privy Council and then before his Excellency disallowed any Local law they might be called upon to determine judicially whether it is constitutional or not. The Attorney General of the Province being called upon to defend [sic]."[49]

As part of this judicial function, the minister enjoyed considerable latitude in determining what constituted the "interests of the whole Dominion." Given that the minister was to decide, it is evident that this was a political question, despite the constitutional context. The memorandum also cited "cases where the Law and the general interests of the Dominion imperatively demand" disallowance as further grounds for federal action. Although such a decision may initially appear to be one governed by the simple reading of a provincial statute to ascertain its legality and constitutionality, the minister's political inclinations would necessarily have shaped the task. Despite the fiction that legal advice is apolitical, that advice was imbued with the minister's values, just as the law was coloured with the values of those who framed it, or precedents upon which it was based. For the minister, therefore, the task of interpreting the law involved a contest of balancing the letter and spirit of the law with his personal and political interests alongside the broader social, political, and economic environment.

Following in train from the creation of the department and the memorandum on disallowance and reservation, a circular issued by the department on 11 June 1868 reasserted the attorney general's pivotal role in shaping the federal government's legal persona. Consistent with the centralizing flavour of the Sydenham reforms and the Department of Justice Act, the circular specified that the attorney general was charged with advising all departmental heads upon matters of law. Further, the attorney general was "entrusted with the regulation and conduct of all litigation for or against the Crown and any Public department in respect of any subjects within the authority and jurisdiction of the Dominion."[50] Given this responsibility, the various departments were directed to forward a memorandum "of all suits or matters in litigation," as well as the "names and residences of the professional Gentlemen in whose conduct they may have been placed, to enable me [Macdonald] to see that the same are in proper train." Further, Sir John requested that, as cases requiring litigation occurred throughout the federal administration, it be practice to "transmit the same and all necessary documents or instructions to enable me to take such proceedings as may be deemed advisable."

The combined impression of the three initiatives is striking. The act created the peculiar appearance of duality while it confirmed a fictional apolitical attorney general and instituted a political minister of justice to interpret the constitution. Second, the minister was provided a judicial function in tandem with the latitude to foster political understandings as a solvent to constitutional disagreements. Finally, the attorney general was confirmed as *the* authoritative legal voice for the federal government; a particularly advantageous position given the confluence of law and politics in the art statecraft during the completion of Confederation. Thus, as the union scheme of 1867 approached its first birthday, the ideology of law blended with the political environment of the Canadas in the wake of Durham and Sydenham, producing a Department of Justice in which the minister of justice and attorney general were affirmed as the federal government's legal voice. That the act and the initiatives that followed contained a number of vagaries was less important than providing the department with the means to complete that remaining undone in July 1867. To that end, the act, the memorandum, and the circular provided the minister of justice with considerable room to manoeuvre within the general compass of federal responsibility.

Although Macdonald succeeded in reaffirming the fiction, its continuation relied upon a close approximation to reality. This was to be especially challenging given the difficulty of perpetuating the supposed division between minister of justice and attorney general. Since it is unlikely that few would be willing to countenance the artificial duality, Macdonald was obliged to be especially conscientious, at least when it came to his behaviour as the first minister of justice. As much as was possible, his actions needed to correspond to expectations for an apolitical attorney general, as opposed to a political minister of justice. Much to his credit, he generally succeeded during his first term in office. Upon his return to the hustings in the general election of 1872, however, politics tripped up Attorney General Macdonald in what became known as the Pacific Scandal.

Beyond the details of the scandal itself, it is especially notable that from Governor General Lord Dufferin's perspective, the alleged financial indiscretions were particularly fatal for an attorney general. Writing on 19 October 1873 as the scandal erupted, Dufferin asserted that it

> is still an indisputable and patent fact that you and some of your colleagues have been the channels through which extravagant sums of money as derived from a person whom you were negotiating on the part of the Dominion were distributed throughout the constituencies of Ontario and Quebec, and have been applied to purposes forbidden by the statutes ... In acting as you have I am well convinced that you have only followed a traditional practice, and that probably your political opponents have resorted with equal freedom to the same expedients, but *as administrator of justice and the official guardian and protector of the Laws, your responsibilities are exceptional*, and your immediate and personal connection with what has occurred cannot but fatally affect your position as Minister.[51]

While Dufferin's words reflect his own conceptions of propriety as much as they comment upon Macdonald's involvement, they nonetheless hinge on the fiction of the apolitical attorney general. Although there was a genuine flaw in what Dufferin termed "a traditional practice," the perceived misdeed was fatal *because* Macdonald was attorney general. Essentially, Sir John answered to the fictional apolitical attorney general despite the fact that that office was unconnected to the financial irregularities. Ironically, Macdonald imbued the fiction with new credibility by the example of his own personal defeat seventeen days after Dufferin's letter.

Although Alexander Mackenzie's Liberal government swept into office on a wave of moral indignation in 1873, there was little reason to resurrect the pre-Confederation inquiries into the function and place of the attorney general. From the Liberal perspective, the scandal had not revealed the legal advisor's inherent political character but rather that the Conservatives could not be trusted to protect the attorney general's apolitical aura. This declared higher morality, in concert with a commitment to the fiction, was, from a

Liberal perspective, one feature distinguishing them from Macdonald's Conservatives. Given the right circumstances, however, these notions might lead an attorney general to adopt what subsequently emerged as a controversial public stance, in the expectation that Liberal morality shielded the office and entrusted to its occupant a wider field of endeavour. Either naïve or arrogant, the assumption marked the federal Liberals during the completion of Confederation. Considering his exaggerated sense of self-importance, moralistic aspirations, and inclination to overreact to criticism, it is less than surprising that of all the Liberal ministers of justice, it would be Edward Blake who found himself in a predicament questioning his judgment and commitment to maintaining the attorney general's apolitical stature.[52]

Initiated by a Charles Tupper speech delivered in Halifax on 16 November 1875 and then embroidered by Sir John eight days later at a banquet for Thomas White in Montreal, the attack concentrated upon Blake's maintenance of his lucrative private practice while accepting his $7,000-a-year government salary.[53] Macdonald's criticism sharpened the censure: "I do not wish to make his holding Briefs, a ground for attack upon Mr Blake, as being wrong, in itself, but I say as Minister of Justice he ought always be at head-quarters (applause); and I know it took me all my time to perform the duties of my office – when holding that position – faithfully and well." Further, "We find Mr Blake, the Minister of Justice, practising before the Judges he himself nominates, and whose salaries he may recommend to be raised, and whom he promotes from Puisne Judges to Chief Justice, and from Vice Chancellor to Chancellors (Hear, hear). This is the experience we have of their administration of public affairs (Applause)."[54] That the *Toronto Globe* defended the besieged Blake by suggesting he should be better paid for his skills as attorney general caused still more aggravation.[55]

As Blake reminded Mackenzie two days after Macdonald's Montreal speech, accepting the attorney general's post had been contingent on his "intention not wholly to dissociate myself from practice during my tenure of office." From Blake's perspective, a principle was involved. If a lawyer built his practice and was then compelled to abandon it upon elevation to office, a class of dependent public men would be created: a result that Blake described as "highly injurious to the country."[56] For his part, Mackenzie reassured the irascible Blake that their understanding had not been forgotten: "I considered the subject before you joined the Government and as I told you then, came to the conclusion that there was no reason why you should not continue your practice though certain cases would as a matter of course come up which you would not accept a brief in. Judges and lawyers have expressed themselves to me in the strongest possible terms in confirmation of these views within the last few days."[57] After threatening to refuse his public salary, Blake reversed course and resolved to distance himself from private legal business, and the embarrassment passed from the political arena.

The naïveté of the agreement between Mackenzie and Blake, and how it reflected both Liberal self-perception and their faith in the ideology of law, is remarkable. Had a Conservative attorney general, and especially John A. Macdonald, acted in a similar vein, the Liberals would have howled. Yet because as Liberals they drew on a "tradition of respect for the rule of law, popular and individual rights, equality and honesty," they felt entrusted with greater latitude in defining what was appropriate for an attorney general while respecting his apolitical character.[58] The logic was credible only if one was prepared to accept the a priori assertion that liberal ideals necessarily shaped the daily reality of Liberal policy and decision making. Evidently, neither Mackenzie nor Blake considered the possibility that those outside the fold would reject this depiction of Liberal virtue.

Nearing the end of their term, the Liberals acted on their belief that they alone could be trusted to respect the distinctions between the political minister of justice and the apolitical attorney general. Evidently, Blake had long harboured the notion that the department required two leaders and, after having obtained Mackenzie's backing, set about drafting such a reform.[59] Four months after the promise had been made, Blake produced a nine-page memorandum abolishing the receiver general's department and reorganizing the Department of Justice.[60] Blake resigned from office before the measure could be introduced, and so it fell to Toussaint-Antoine-Rodolphe Laflamme to announce Bill 51 regarding the receiver general and attorney general. The substance of the legislation was relatively straightforward; the receiver general's office would be subsumed by the Department of Finance and the Department of Justice would be subdivided into two distinct branches under the supervision of a minister of justice and an attorney general.[61]

The Opposition's attack on Laflamme's bill followed two tacks. Although Peter Mitchell, Independent MP for Northumberland, New Brunswick, accepted the contention that the receiver general's office had become redundant, he objected to a separate office of attorney general since it would further enhance the legal profession's influence in the House. Mitchell took specific offence at seeing "the offices of the country monopolized by the legal sharks of this House."[62] Suggesting that the alleged increase in departmental business was the result of inexperienced ministers, Sir John A. Macdonald resurrected the earlier attack on Blake by suggesting that, "Any Minister of Justice applying himself solely and entirely to the work of his Department could fairly perform it; one man could do it with proper assistance."[63] More importantly, the presence of two legal advisors in cabinet would lead to a division in opinion and perhaps in public responsibility. Such an environment produced "weakness, vacillation, and want of unity of action."[64] In Macdonald's opinion, "You cannot have two chairmen. You cannot have a double-head. There is a three-headed Cerberus; but there cannot be a double-headed Minister of Justice."[65]

Prime Minister Mackenzie reversed Sir John's criticisms by first pointing out that Macdonald "had four members conducting the legal business of Old Canada, and he never objected to the plan then."[66] And regarding the increased business in the Department of Justice, Mackenzie suggested that, "The right hon. gentleman must be aware that the change in the laws, and many other incidents connected with recent legislation, has materially increased the duties. The Hon. member for South Bruce (Mr Blake) had, perhaps, a capacity for work more than any other member of the House, and yet his powers were taxed to the very up most in order to keep up with the duties of office."[67]

Blake then rose in defence of the measure, arguing that no single individual could, under such circumstances, address the queries forwarded to the Department of Justice and attend the requests of members and government departments: "It was surely impossible for any one man, no matter how great his ability, to accomplish, during a session, the whole of the business assigned to him. No man who held a high political position, no matter how great his talent, could succeed in accomplishing all that business."[68] Although passed by the Liberal majority in the Commons, the Conservative-dominated Senate voted against the bill "as a most unnecessary and unwise move."[69]

The Fiction Remains

The bill's defeat signalled an important event for the attorney general. While both parties had subscribed to the fiction of the apolitical attorney general, by 1878, the Liberals had concluded that they alone could be entrusted to protect the ideal and its function for the federal government. From a Liberal perspective, experience demonstrated that the transparent duality of the Department of Justice Act was untenable in Conservative hands. Further, while the Liberals could be trusted with the original form of two offices held by one person, under their leadership, the suggested reform would have no adverse effects and would improve the department's efficiency. Left in its original form and in Conservative hands, the artificial duality would foster inefficiency, the politicization of justice, and, as the Pacific Scandal demonstrated, corruption. That the initiative fell in the Conservative Senate merely confirmed that their party had no respect for the liberal ideal of justice and the rule of law.

Significantly, the parting of ways over the structure of the Department of Justice did not correspond to a fundamental disagreement as to its function. The Liberal bill sought to create the appearance that the attorney general, as a distinct person from the minister of justice, would be uninvolved in "political" decisions. As had occurred on every occasion when the attorney general became a subject of debate since the 1840s, the discussion failed to explore the issue that by determining rights, dividing property, imposing rules, or attempting to create stability, law is inherently political. Doing so under the auspices of an allegedly apolitical attorney general did nothing to change this basic attribute. The disagreement over the proposal revealed that while Conservatives were comfortable with the manoeuvrability provided by blurry distinctions between law and politics, Liberals preferred the illusion of fixed and observable boundaries.

Despite the notable divergence over how the law officer should appear, the fiction of the apolitical attorney general nevertheless remained intact. Given that both parties and most of their members would have subscribed to the basic paradigm of law, an unspoken agreement as to the attorney general's function is neither surprising nor accidental. In practical terms this meant that as attorney general or minister of justice, the government's legal advisor possessed enormous latitude in performing his duties. Nor was this accidental. Little was truly fixed in 1867, and completing the Confederation scheme required interpretative flexibility in what was often a charged political environment. While the federal government expected to be the dominant force in shaping the substance of Confederation after 1867, even at that early date it was perfectly clear that this would not be effected by battering the provinces into submission. Regardless of who held power between 1867 and 1878, this view from Ottawa was remarkably consistent.

Breathing life into the act of union, smoothing over rough spots, and rounding sharp edges were not, however, tasks to be completed with great haste. Feeling a way through the new constitution often required understandings and accommodations born of patience and a willingness to build consensus. This was a process that occurred on a daily basis, as the Department of Justice staff attempted to steer the government through the evolving legal and political relationships of Confederation. Some of these relationships eventually appeared within new national institutions while others took form as the daily methods of governance and statecraft. In the final analysis, while the attorney general was able to effect understandings on a political level, the dynamic within the department itself was necessarily framed by a different context. For while the attorney general or minister of justice could administer the appropriate measure of political solvent to a legal impasse, it was the department's responsibility to map the legal terrain in preparation for such a solution. To be effective, the government's legal advisor required sound intelligence on a given situation, and the departmental staff was charged with that responsibility. Their approach to that task is the subject of the next chapter.

3
The Department of Justice and the Business of Governance

Shortly after Confederation had been proclaimed in early July 1867, Hewitt Bernard wrote Judge James Gowan, an old acquaintance and family friend. Bernard, soon to be deputy minister of justice, described the state of affairs in the capital and noted how his former duties as chief clerk for the attorney general had changed: "One has a larger field to look after, even as a matter of business, – and to be interested in. I feel my official questions are being expanded from the [Upper Canadian] questions to those of the provinces: and one fits imperceptibly into queries of a constitutional character, and the consideration of what belongs to the Genl. and which to the Local Govt."[1] Acknowledging the probable consequences, Bernard continued: "I suppose my hands will be full, that is, if I remain in my present office which I suppose is likely to be the case ... I shall best act by keeping to the Law, if I get that option given to me."[2] Considering his association with Sir John A. Macdonald, the option was hardly in doubt.

Although his duties had assumed a different tenor, Bernard undoubtedly took solace from the fact that, in many ways, Confederation had not altered his routine as Sir John's second. The designation of Ottawa as the new capital for the united provinces in 1858 had long since initiated the transfer of government offices. And thus, when Confederation came to pass, there was scarcely a ripple in departmental business. Mundane tasks intermingled with those heralding the new union. Draft proclamations for the Senate, cabinet, and lieutenant governorships were dispatched along with a patent application for the appropriately patriotic Hallam's New Dominion Churn and Washer.[3] True, as Bernard observed, jurisdictional responsibilities opened up new areas of interest, but, inasmuch as the daily demands continued, there were apparently few novelties to tax the denizens of the attorney general's office.

Although Bernard's confidence was well founded, determining what could be accomplished by the Department of Justice was a complicated matter. On one level and according to the ideology of law, the law could be a formidable device to effect change. However, to the extent that anyone associated with the attorney general's office subscribed to this particular notion, the daily realities of business would have trimmed such grand aspirations. In the first instance, the law did not encourage haste. Legal machinery worked slowly, and there was little reason to quicken the pace if time might provide a solution to many quandaries. Wielding the law unnecessarily was, for the attorney general's office, counterproductive. Further, solving any problem in Canada during the last third of the nineteenth century confronted some basic realities. Telegraphic communication was often indifferent, transportation unreliable, and given the physical expanse of the nation, the autonomy of distance played havoc with attempts at centralized decision making.[4] Given this environment, the best way for the department to remain effective was to recognize and accept the practical limitations of its jurisdictional and administrative reach.

Cast within this light, the contours of how the department ordinarily functioned begins to emerge. It is evident that John Cell's description of the mid-nineteenth-century colonial office is equally applicable to the Department of Justice: "At any given moment there is not so much policy as policy formation, an unsettled and changing set of responses by government to the continual interaction among men, forces, ideas and institutions."[5] And to the extent that a pattern of policy formation existed within the department, it reflected "thousands of tiny contingent practices" shaped by what Robert Gordon describes as "relatively abstract clusters of concepts" constraining the department's collective imagination and field of action.[6] In effect, other than a broadly expressed desire to counter legal notions perceived to be inimical to federal interests, the department did not articulate an exclusive policy or method of business. To the degree that federal interests could be identified, the consequent limits imposed by those notions combined with the indeterminacy of law to confine the department and the advice it provided. The unadorned result was that while the department shouldered the burden of acting in support of the attorney general and minister of justice as the federal government's law officers, its actions amounted to a governmentality that perceived the law as a tactic to be employed to further policy objectives.[7] For the Department of Justice, this was the art of statecraft.

This chapter, which illuminates the department's use of law, legal remedy, and the search for compromise as a manifestation of its own governmentality, proceeds on two interconnected levels. The first concerns how the department responded to both the ordinary press of business as well as to unexpected events and crises. From 1867 to 1878, this involved a disparate assortment of responsibilities, ranging from clearing bonds for government representatives and agents, orchestrating requests for extradition, policing matters, to, as in one instance, preventing the launch of a Cuban invasion from Nova Scotia. A second level concentrates on the broader question of how these activities fit, to the degree they fit at all, into the attorney general's role in the completion of Confederation. Consistent with the contingent nature of policy formation and response, few of the department's mundane responsibilities revealed an obvious relationship with wider political concerns. This is not to say that the department never participated in crucial events but, rather, that the singularity of these occasions testifies to an important achievement. Success in the Department of Justice was measured, in large part, by the degree to which its activities failed to attract attention. For while the ideology of law provided the Department of Justice with a wide field of activity, the completion of Confederation required a deft touch from the federal government's legal advisors, in anticipation of politicized accommodations fashioned by the various levels of government. After all, "One never has more power than when one has so successfully appropriated the symbols of authority that one's actions are not seen as exercises of power at all, but simply as expressions of sound pragmatic common sense."[8]

Prominent Staff and Daily Affairs

Given the human element in framing and interpreting the law, reconstructing a profile of the department's personnel is a crucial aspect in detailing how it functioned. Such an image is especially useful since it was the deputy minister and his supporting clerks who managed the department's daily burden, while the minister necessarily remained aloof from details and intricacies. Therefore, while it is true that federal departments of state in the early years of Confederation "were small enough to enable energetic ministerial heads to attend personally to much of the day-to-day business," the press of events in the Department of Justice placed enormous responsibility upon the deputy minister.[9] In the immediate aftermath of the union, the deputy's supporting staff was almost exclusively English-speaking clerks, a number of whom had worked for the attorney general's office in Upper Canada. A further element of continuity was provided by the necessity of a legal education for the deputy minister and, in time, the chief and senior clerks. This also ensured that while much of the federal bureaucracy was staffed by sinecures, crucial members of the Department of Justice shared the basic skills and education required to perform the duties in a law office.[10]

Admittedly, the role legal education played in the effectiveness of departmental personnel is a complex issue. Passing the bar ensured neither the ability nor the will to become a knowledgeable practitioner or legal advisor. Further, if a young lawyer was especially skilled, it seems unlikely that a career in the bureaucracy would be particularly attractive. On the other hand, the subsequent success enjoyed by former staffers such as Zebulon

Lash and Hugh Richardson suggests that the department was not, by definition, a place for meagre legal talents. It appears that while a keen legal mind could succeed in the department, the relatively mechanical and fairly conservative approach to problem solving was, in the long run, of limited appeal for expansive legal minds. Consequently, while examples of clever thinking within the department exist, a more common image is that of a workmanlike atmosphere staffed by competent, if unspectacular, individuals.

The deputy minister was unquestionably the most important figure in the daily operation of the department. Responsible for the finalization of all opinions, memorandums, edicts, orders, and directives, the deputy was the conduit between the minister and the department, as well as between the department and the federal and provincial bureaucracies. During the completion of Confederation, the department was especially fortunate to have two particularly skilled deputy ministers: Hewitt Bernard and Zebulon Lash. Having served as Macdonald's secretary since 15 February 1858, his chief clerk since 4 March 1859, and less dutifully as his brother-in-law since 16 February 1867, Bernard was named deputy minister of justice by an order-in-council on 29 May 1868, one day after the Department of Justice officially came into existence.[11] The heart of the staff until his retirement because of ill health in 1876, Bernard provided consistency and stability, especially during the early years of the Mackenzie government, when ministers passed through the department at an alarming rate.

When it became clear that Bernard's tenure as deputy was ending, Minister of Justice Edward Blake initiated a search for an appropriate replacement. After making a number of inquiries and discussing the matter with Prime Minister Alexander Mackenzie, on 18 April 1876 Blake offered the position to Zebulon Lash, then a thirty-year-old lawyer practising in Toronto and who lectured in commercial and criminal law for the Law Society of Ontario.[12] Blake prefaced his offer by stating that, "The work is arduous but very pleasant and after attaining familiarity with the general run of the office can be easily managed by a man of energy, system, and powers of organisation."[13] Lash admitted that the offer was a pleasant surprise and the opportunity of working with Blake would have been a great pleasure but monetary considerations and an unwillingness to give up practice compelled him to decline the offer.[14] Blake was undeterred, and by 26 April Lash had relented and telegraphed his acceptance of the position.[15]

By mid-May, an order-in-council authorized Lash's temporary appointment as chief clerk of the Department of Justice until his elevation to deputy minister upon Bernard's formal retirement.[16] The arrangement allowed Bernard to teach Lash the manner of business in the department or, as Bernard wrote, "It is agreed that I shall remain deputy until 1st Sept next in order to supervise the Dept and indoctrinate my successor."[17] What exactly Bernard meant by indoctrination is unclear but, regardless of whether he was content with Lash's mastery of affairs, the reins of power in the Department of Justice passed from Bernard's hands on 1 September 1876. While the work may have indeed been "arduous but very pleasant," it held Lash's interest only until his resignation in late May 1882, when he reentered private practice as a partner in Blake, Lash, Cassels and Holman.[18]

Although the department was expected to provide legal counsel to the federal government, initially there was a surprising absence of legal talent supporting the deputy minister. While persons such as Charles Drinkwater had experience with railway administration and others such as Frederick White brought dedication and commitment, it was not until Hugh Richardson's 26 October 1872 appointment that another employee schooled in the law entered the Department of Justice.[19] Along with the requisite legal education, Richardson evidently fulfilled Sir John's expectation that the addition to the department be "a man of honour."[20]

Fortunately for Lash, by the time he assumed Bernard's place, additional professional men had been added to the department staff. Minister of Justice Télesphore Fournier hired George Duval, a barrister from the province of Quebec, as his private secretary on 28 July 1874.[21] Four months later, Fournier elevated Duval to the position of chief clerk, citing the 12 October 1872 order-in-council recommending that a barrister from the province of Quebec be brought into the department.[22] The appointment of Augustus Power in July 1875 introduced yet another legally trained employee to the department.[23] Power, whose father William P. Power had sat on the Superior Court of Lower Canada, received his legal education at McGill University, where he gained a valuable knowledge of French civil law.[24] Finally, weeks after Lash replaced Bernard as deputy minister, John L.B. Fraser, a young barrister from Osgoode Hall, was added to the staff.[25]

Several impressions emerge even from this brief profile of departmental personnel. From its beginnings, it appears that Hewitt Bernard was effectively *the* Department of Justice. Certainly he would have had benefit of Sir John's legal experience but, on a practical basis, Bernard was very much on his own until 1872. Essentially, the department's legal imagination was limited to what Bernard and Macdonald were willing to envision. Even had both been brilliant legal minds – and there is little evidence to sustain such an attribution – the department was overmatched by the volume and variety of legal issues arising from a new and diverse nation. Bernard admitted as much in his letter to Judge Gowan, wherein the soon-to-be deputy minister acknowledged that he still retained an Upper Canadian perspective on the nation. Further, considering Sir John's inclination to create political understandings and the influence that evidently placed on Bernard, it is hardly surprising that in these early years the department assumed an important place in facilitating such agreements.

Second, the increased presence of legally trained staff combined with the influence of nineteenth-century liberalism introduced an aspect of combative idealism to the department. Whereas Macdonald and Bernard had been content with constructing accommodations, the bureaucratic generation arriving in the mid-1870s was less inclined to pursue the same route. Buoyed by the promise of law's potential to effect positive social, institutional, and economic reform, these young lawyers expected great things of the law and the Department of Justice. This expectation not only led to a greater emphasis on legalistic solutions to the department's business but also created a demand for fighting and winning battles framed by literalist legal thinking at the ministerial level. As the constitutional struggles of the post-1878 era would attest, this was not a particularly successful change of course. This, however, was in the future.

Descriptions of what mid-nineteenth-century attorney generals and their clerks nominally did on a daily basis are relatively common if one looks in the right place. For example, in the legislative inquiry of 1850, the attorney general's duties were outlined as entailing the giving of advice

> upon all legal questions affecting any interest of the Crown, which may be brought under their cognisance, whether by direct reference from the Executive Government or from any Head of a Department. This will embrace cases arising in Customs matters, land matters, matters connected with contracts with Commissioners of Public Works, and matters arising from their own management of Criminal and Revenue cases. They also attend to the criminal duties in Circuit, either in person, by the Solicitor General, or by some other Counsel appointed for that purpose, and more particularly to argue any points of Law whatever that may arise out of criminal cases before the Judges. As far as I can recollect, this will embrace every class of legal duties they perform, except reporting upon Act of Parliament, after they have passed both Houses.[26]

Fourteen years later, D'Arcy McGee further detailed these activities:

> The business of the Department consists in reporting on references from His Excellency the Governor General, made through the various Departments, on matters in which a point of law is involved, in the preparation of drafts of all Proclamations, Commissions, deeds, or official documents issued or granted by the crown, the examinations of all bills introduced into either of the Houses of the Legislature, except the Government measures, and the examination of and comparison, in both languages, of all bills passed by both Houses, and reports thereon to the Governor General, previous to His Giving his sanction thereto.
>
> The business of the Crown Law Department may be distinguished into

two kinds, that which originates with the department itself, and that which is referred to it from other offices.[27]

For its part, the civil service commission of 1868 reported that, "The main business of this Department consists in legal opinions given upon references from the other Departments, which are estimated at about 1200 annually, besides numerous verbal references upon questions of law. It has also to examine the legislation of the Provinces, and the bills brought in by private members, and to draft or devise Government bills."[28] The problem remains that while providing an image of sorts, these descriptions merely depict rather than explain what occurred in practical and intellectual terms. Obtaining an image of that texture requires both a discerning eye and the willingness to acknowledge that while some attributes can be revealed, others will remain unseen.

Viewed abstractly and from a distance, the department's primary function was to regulate access to law or legal remedy. While the ideology of law asserted that the law could be a powerful device, its unfettered use was self-defeating. Thus, in its supporting role behind the attorney general or minister of justice, the department worked to forestall official reliance on the law as an all-purpose and autonomous solvent. At another level, the department managed legal and physical space within the federal regulatory world. This enormous range of responsibility arose from countless federal statutes governing everything from the regulation of trade and commerce, the postal service, fisheries, weights and measures, and patents of invention, amongst other areas specified directly or implied in the 1867 act of union. Akin to its approach to the use of law within the federal government, the department's tack in these far-flung responsibilities was to create regulatory structures that allowed, as David Sugarman points out in another context, the means for the pursuit of individual interests while preventing harmful disputes and litigation.[29] The department's uneven success in these endeavours reveals not only the varied interests at play in a diverse national community but also the indeterminacy of law and legal remedy.

One of the most effective ways to uncover these activities is through the Department of Justice mail registers, which are a barometer of the volume, and the relative complexity of, references.[30] Each piece of incoming correspondence was numbered and the date received entered in the register, along with the correspondent, subject, and all subsequent departmental action. In cases warranting such detail, the clerk would also record the page number from the department's letter books, where copies of outgoing correspondence could be located for future reference. When an inquiry continued beyond the calendar year, the original reference noted the subsequent entry in the following year, a practice that allowed a specific issue to be traced through to its conclusion or back to its origin.

Akin to the generalized descriptions of what the law officers and their supporting staff nominally did, the registers' most striking characteristic is how little they correspond to the statutory mandate of the Department of Justice. The registers reveal that while the department was cast in the role of legal interpreter, much of its time was filled with clerical duties such as filing patents of invention, issuing election writs, remitting sentences, granting leaves to judges, and approving pensions for the families of wounded or deceased militia men. More challenging work involved checking provincial enactments for jurisdictional conflicts, drafting and translating federal legislation, determining the legal boundaries of Rideau Hall estate, reviewing certificates of incorporation, and sorting through the Byzantine history of the Windsor and Annapolis Railway.[31] Constituting Robert Gordon's "thousands of tiny contingent practices," these were the activities that unrelentingly occupied the department and demonstrated that its primary task was to regulate and regularize the law and its use.

The challenge of addressing such a disparate range of topics and concerns is revealed in the ever-increasing workload documented by the registers and letter books. As reported by Edward Blake and Rodolphe Laflamme, the volume of business in the Department of Justice tripled between 1869 and 1877. Both men noted that in 1869 there were 1,693 registered references while in 1877 approximately 5,600 were expected.[32] Even these numbers told only part of the entire story in that they did not reveal the varying amount of labour each reference involved. If the matter was the somewhat routine determination of granting a prisoner remission of sentence, the deputy minister considered whether there were sufficient or appropriate grounds for early release from the penitentiary, then sought the trial judge's notes and commentary, reviewed the convicting evidence, and constructed a brief report for the minister, who advised the governor general in Council.[33] Depending on the mails and the cooperation of the judge involved, the entire matter could be disposed of by a day or two of labour over the course of a few weeks. A more complex issue involved a corresponding amount of work and considerably more time. For example, as part of the lengthy process leading to the codification of criminal law in Canada, in one month Bernard and G.W. Wicksteed compiled, summarized, and reorganized all the criminal statutes in force in the various provinces constituting Canada in 1868. Their working document ran 581 pages in length.[34] Obviously, a task such as this, involving multiple jurisdictions and statutes, was especially taxing. That it was performed in a month-long period in which 110 other requests were handled is compelling testament to the workload that departmental personnel shouldered.[35]

Canal Reserves: Sixty-Six Feet of Latitude

As this broad perspective provides a necessarily generalized impression of the department's activities, a more concentrated view reveals specific examples of how problems were managed. It would not be an exaggeration to suggest that there are thousands of cases and references that might illustrate the intricacies of the department in action. A set of queries arising from legal conflicts over canals, however, has particular appeal for a number of reasons. Canals and the land that abutted them maintained a significant place in the economy of central Canada after 1867. Further, while some were striking examples of engineering innovation, they were by the 1870s fairly commonplace and, unlike railway projects, unlikely to stir great public interest. Essentially, canals were quite ordinary. Yet because these waterways and the reserves running on either side were supposed to be maintained for military or canal purposes alone, they gave rise to a number of interesting legal questions for the Department of Justice. The eventual solutions were in of themselves illuminating examples of how the department practised the art of statecraft.

Constructed between 1826 and 1832 to prevent an American military invasion severing the only transportation link between Upper and Lower Canada, the Rideau Canal from Kingston to Bytown (now Ottawa) never actually served as a military lifeline. Moreover, expectations that the canal would provide a valuable trading route to the American west failed to materialize. As a result, the canal cost more to maintain than the income it generated.[36] Driven by the desire to escape from the financial and military commitments in British North America, the imperial government proposed in the early 1850s that the Canadian government assume responsibility for the Rideau. The Canadians would do so only if the ordnance reserve, the strip of land bordering each side of the canal, was included in the arrangement. The Imperial Board of Ordnance almost scuttled the agreement by suggesting that, "Lands deemed unnecessary for the canal service were to remain at the disposal of the ordnance and when not required for military purposes could be sold with the funds going toward defensive works in the colony."[37] Wishing to use the reserve to generate capital by leases and outright sales, the Canadians balked at the suggestion and held firm that they were to have absolute control of the canals and reserve lands. The British, wanting to rid themselves of these commitments, finally relented and, on 19 June 1856, the Ordnance Estates and Property were transferred to Canadian control.[38]

Once the land was officially vested in the Government of the United Province of Canada, leases, sales, squatters, industry, and adjoining farms quickly eroded the reserve, all wishing to take advantage of easy access to the canal. By the late 1860s and early 1870s, the problem of these encroachments was so great that James B. Slater, superintendent of the Rideau Canal, recommended that no further sales within sixty-six feet of the canal be allowed.[39] Two years later, in response to an inquiry from the minister of public works, Slater reported that the land required by merchants for landing their goods from the canal was already filled by squatters who "have been permitted to occupy until it was required for canal purposes."[40] The difficulty was that four houses, ranging in value from $350 to $500, had been constructed on the reserve. Slater revealed no sympathy for those whose homes were now threatened:

> All these encroachments should be removed as the land is required for the free use and management of the canal, and it is an invariable rule so far as my experience serves, that as soon as any of these people acquire rights, they begin to give trouble for the sake of being bought out ... It is hardly right that proprietors who have given land for Canal purposes should be shut off from the roads and canals by squatters.[41]

These encroachments were especially problematic since some occupants believed, for various reasons, that they were exempt from the restrictions. For example, in August 1872, a Mr. R. Gavin asserted that the usual sixty-six-foot frontage did not apply to him or his land, despite that Nicholas Sparks, the sole owner of the original town-site, had provided the reserve to the city of Ottawa specifically for canal purposes.[42] Gavin's claim was based on a somewhat typical exchange that muddied the status of the canal reserve. Apparently, the land had been initially in the possession of Colonel William Foster Coffin, commissioner of ordnance lands, who had subsequently sold it to Agar Yielding on 1 May 1861.[43] Yielding in turn sold the land to Gavin on 9 October 1867. Then, in 1872, the Minister of Public Works declared the land within the canal reserve. Gavin's defence referred to Colonel Coffin, who asserted that Gavin was justified in denying "the right of the Govt to treat this 66 feet strip [sic] as Canal reserves."

In preparing the Department of Justice opinion for Public Works, Bernard viewed the entire matter as simply as possible. If the sale had been between two individuals, Bernard reasoned, "a Court of Equity on the facts would undoubtedly decree specific performance and would in the absence of ground misrepresentation [sic] or concealment of some material fact by the purchaser, order the vendor to convey what he sold."[44] Therefore, he concluded, "Placing the Govt in the position of a private vendor and in the absence of anything as between individuals would entitle such a vendor to pay the original bargain, I have to express the opinion that Mr. Gavin is entitled to take the stand he does."[45]

The opinion had interesting implications, if the deputy minister was consciously attempting to balance interests. If he was, the harm potentially caused Gavin by upsetting his claim was greater than that expected to "the free use and management of the canal." However, in light of a subsequent opinion given by Bernard in essentially the same circumstances, it appears that there was more at stake in Gavin's case than at first appeared. When Prime Minister Alexander Mackenzie, as Minister of Public Works, forwarded a request to Bernard in June 1874 to issue a land patent for a strip of land falling within the canal reserve, the deputy minister of Justice balked:

> I think it best to represent to you, in the first instance, unofficially, that I think such a grant would be of a rather dangerous character ... I have always had some doubts whether the leases of what are known as Canal lots, to private individuals, could be deemed "purposes of the canal": but there is enough room for some argument that warehouses and stores for commercial purposes may be deemed so to be. And it has always been the custom in those cases, to give leases only as distinguished from absolute transfers, – and those leases, some for definite terms of years and not to be indefinitely renewable.
>
> To grant therefore to private individuals and thereby absolutely to alienate from the Crown and from "purposes of the Canal" any portion of the land freely given by Sparks for such "purposes" only, is I fear a matter which might involve great difficulty ... I suggest therefore for your consideration whether it is not well to abandon such a grant as is contemplated. I do not think that a lease even for term of years would get over the difficulty. And yet I think it would be injudicious publicly to give the reason which guides my views, as the whole question is one which may bear a different interpretation to that which I put on it.[46]

Bernard's language in this unofficial communication with the prime minister was instructive. While acknowledging that he harboured some doubts as to the practice of granting leases, Bernard believed that "there is enough room" in a definition of "canal purposes" to argue that business and industrial encroachments would be permissible. Unconditional grants to private individuals were another matter altogether. Realizing that this uncertainty threatened potentially every sale of reserve land made, Bernard advised Mackenzie to avoid publicizing these views. Essentially, the deputy minister suggested that the matter be left undisturbed and some way be found to lease the land desired, rather than grant an outright patent. Four days later, the Department of Justice authorized a forty-year lease, with a rent of one dollar per year, for the land in question; clearly, both Bernard's opinion and advice advocating discretion had convinced Mackenzie.[47]

These creative manoeuvrings in defining terms such as "canal purposes" were not limited to the Rideau Canal reserve at Ottawa. Requesting the opinion of the Department of Justice in late September 1872, Marine and

Fisheries wished to know if it could lease the Burlington Beach at Hamilton to hotel entrepreneurs, even though the beach was designated as a reserve for canal and fishery purposes.[48] The situation, as described by William Whitcher of Marine and Fisheries, was straightforward. Burlington Beach had been designated before Confederation as a canal and fishing reserve and had since Confederation been passed from the old Department of Crown Lands to the Department of Marine and Fisheries, where it was "disposed of and licensed in stations for fishing purposes."[49] An application had subsequently been made to Marine and Fisheries through D.B. Chisholm, member of Parliament, on behalf of a Hamilton company, to obtain a ninety-nine year lease for a portion of this reserve with intentions of building a public hotel. According to Whitcher, the company wanted to "make other improvements necessary to render it a convenient and healthful resort for the citizens of Hamilton during summer-time for recreational bathing & c."[50] Further, the company was willing to compensate all squatters and fishermen who were occupying the portion of the reserve under consideration.

Whitcher admitted to Bernard that Marine and Fisheries had no objections whatever to the proposal. In fact, "The Minister recognises how very desirable it would be in many respects to convert a very troublesome wasted place, disorderly as regard to some of its occupants, and unsightly as regards to its present appearances, into a respectable establishment and ornamental premises such as the promoters of the scheme intend." The question for Bernard was simple: Could Marine and Fisheries grant a leasehold title or licence of occupation for any other purpose than for what the reserve was specifically designated?

Bernard's response was equally simple: No. For while "the object is admitted to be a desirable one but it is doubted whether or not the Minister of Marine and Fisheries has the power to comply."[51] Citing the act that organized the Department of Marine and Fisheries of Canada, Bernard noted that the management, regulation, and protection of inland fisheries was a responsibility of the department, and that they *did* have the power to "grant licenses of occupation for public lands in connection with fisheries."[52] Clearly, a licence of occupation for a hotel was not within even the broadest construction of the term "fisheries."

All was not lost, however. If the Minister of Public Works were to report that the land was not required for canal purposes, and the Minister of Marine and Fisheries were to do likewise with regard to fisheries, the land would revert to the Province of Ontario, which could then dispose of it in any fashion it thought fit.[53] It seems that since fishermen were in fact using the beach for fishery purposes and the company was willing to buy them out and cover any losses, the proposition that the reserve was no longer needed for fishing purposes was farfetched. By suggesting that the minister could simply decide the reserve was no longer needed for the fishery, Bernard offered a way to strip the term "reserve" of all meaning. Evidently, Bernard's suggestion proved fruitful and an understanding was reached, since four years later, Messrs. Birly and Neville, lessees of the government reserve on Burlington Beach, were asking for clarification on whether they could sell wine and liquor in their establishment. Minister of Justice Edward Blake informed them that wine would be allowable but the sale of "intoxicating liquors at table during meal times" was a question to be determined by local authorities in the corporation within which the property was situated.[54]

In 1872, at the same time that the department was sorting out the meaning of reserve, a vessel called the *Phoenix Banks,* laden with iron ore, sank in the Welland Canal, causing difficulty with passing traffic.[55] James Henry Dickson agreed with the Buffalo Insurance Company, which held the insurance policy on the hull of the vessel, to "raise and remove her at a cost of $1500." During this process, Dickson encountered a number of problems and, as a result, "was put to much more expense than he had anticipated." Eventually, he succeeded in raising the hull and moving it to Port Robinson where, while the canal was closed for the season, the hull was kept afloat by spiles and jackscrews driven into the ground on either side of the vessel.[56] Unfortunately, in preparation for the resumption of traffic in the spring, water was drawn out of the canal, in what would be alleged was "the most unusual manner," and the vessel was left "suspended entirely out of the water." The great weight of the vessel broke the spiles and caused it to fall, seriously damaging her hull. The insurance company, noting the damaged hull, refused to award Dickson the full sum of his agreement and he was therefore compelled to accept only $1,000 "in full satisfaction of his claim against them."

Following this settlement, Dickson alleged losses in late December 1876 of approximately $3,000 as a consequence of the lowering of the water level in the canal where the hull had been suspended. Since the canals and their management were a federal responsibility, he requested compensation from the Government of Canada in a petition of right filed in Chancery. According to Deputy Minister of Justice Zebulon Lash, however, Dickson's application was misguided since the Petition of Right Act specified that petitioners be directed to "the Exchequer Court of Canada" which shall have exclusive original cognizance of such petitions.[57] Despite the petition being redrawn for Exchequer, Lash asserted that no cause for action against the Dominion government existed. The absence of a contract between Dickson and the government, combined with the fact that a petition of right could not provide redress for alleged negligent or improper conduct of Crown employees, was fatal to his claim.[58] Slightly more than two weeks later, the Department of Public Works was assured that the water had not been drained in any unreasonable manner: "The summit level was not lowered more than it was necessary to fill the canal below in order to resume navigation after repairs in the spring, of which the usual notice was given. So that it appears Mr. Dickson has no cause of complaint."[59]

The view adopted by the Department of Justice offers insight into the strategy that it brought to such a case. Obviously, a primary concern was developing a position where the federal government could deny any liability. Thus, Lash approached the question from two perspectives. Since the case, if it were to be heard in court, would be governed by common-law principles in the Court of Exchequer, as opposed to the more flexible forms of equity law, he could frame a response solely in terms of contract. There had been no contract between the federal government and Dickson and, therefore, no legal relationship existed between the two parties. Dickson had merely suspended the vessel in the canal during the off-season. Second, the absence of contract meant that a petition of right could not redress claims based on the negligence of a crown employee. While this second tack was sound reasoning in 1877, a year later, the English House of Lords ruled that, "An action does lie for doing that which the legislature has authorised, if it be done negligently."[60] Therefore, the question in the Dickson case turned on whether the canal master, knowing the vessel was supported by the spiles and buoyed by water, acted negligently despite giving notice of the lowering of the canal level? This question was, however, never considered, as Rodolphe Laflamme, minister of justice, recommended that the governor general's fiat praying that "right be done" should not be granted to Dickson. By steadfastly maintaining that the Dominion government had no responsibility in the matter, the department denied Dickson and his lawyers the governor general's fiat, barring them from bringing a suit in which the government may have been found partially responsible.

Ironically, while the department wrestled with these canal issues, it became apparent in January 1876 that the federal government had been disposing of the canal reserves, defined as ordnance lands, without authority. It seems that these lands, comprising all the fortifications, barracks, military lands and installations, and canals, had been transferred by statute to the Government of the United Provinces of Canada in 1856 but were then vested in the Dominion of Canada merely by an administrative agreement. The federal government had then leased and sold portions of these holdings as if it had the right, when in fact, the absence of statutory provision made such an assumption doubtful. Summarizing the problem for Minister of Justice Edward Blake, Bernard admitted that the titles to the ordnance land "are very much embarrassed by two or three existing plans and by deeds which do not conform to the Registered plan and every day which elapses renders more difficult the tracing out of the errors."[61] When informed again of the problem six months later, Blake turned to Bernard, doubtless with some incredulity, and asked, "Did the question never arise earlier? Has there been no correspondence?" Bernard's response, in light of the history of the canal reserves specifically, was rather elliptical: "The question had not until now, been, I think raised by anyone."[62] Fortunately, the issue of title to the ordnance lands was subsequently addressed by broadly structured statutes that retroactively legitimized all the post-Confederation sales and leases executed by the federal government.[63]

The management of the canals and their reserves stands as an illuminating example of a range of tactics employed within the Department of Justice. In Gavin's case, the government adopted the prudent position of recognizing the legitimacy of his claim and not risking further embarrassment through legal action. When Prime Minister Mackenzie raised the possibility of issuing land patents for a private individual on the reserve, Bernard counselled caution and suggested an understanding rather than drawing attention to the rather murky legal situation. For the entrepreneurs wishing to develop Burlington Beach, Bernard hinted at the means of circumventing the regulations barring the proposed hotel project. And when James Dickson attempted to garner damages from the government for the loss he sustained because of alleged negligence, Lash simply refused to let the matter proceed and advised Minister of Justice Laflamme to reject the petition of right. These methods reveal that in defending what it perceived to be federal interests, the department managed each situation with the desire of making the issue goes away. If a problem was not necessarily solved to everyone's liking, it was usually defused by an accommodation. In the end, the regulation of the canals and their reserves was governed not by statute but by the ability of the Department of Justice to facilitate an understanding.

Crisis Management: The Challenge of Distance and Value of Time

The greatest advantage that the Department of Justice enjoyed in its management of daily business was time. Law and legal interpretation moved slowly, and there was little to be gained, at least from the department's perspective, of speeding up the process. While this pace of business was well suited for the ordinary run of affairs, there were occasions when the department was compelled to gather, analyze, and disseminate information quickly. It was the demand for a quick response shaped solely by immediate circumstances, and not the incident in and of itself, which defined one type of crisis for the department. For example, although the assassination of D'Arcy McGee on 7 April 1868 charged the political environment and besieged the capital, beyond evoking sympathy, regret, and even anger for individual staffers, it was not an administrative crisis for the department.[64] Rather, the investigation that followed became especially noisome when Hewitt Bernard was accused of questionable behaviour over the release of reward money and when Alexander Turner, a key witness, proved to be a thoroughgoing opportunist.[65] Although the accusation against Bernard passed from view, Turner's concerted efforts to garner reward money, reimbursement for lost employment, and finally, assistance in reestablishing himself in France, were both embarrassing and aggravating.[66] Essentially, when a problem that required immediate attention was thrust upon the department, it not only disrupted routine business but, more importantly, limited the department's ability to identify what were, and were not, critical federal interests. Since the department's primary concern was defending those interests, such an occasion was, by definition, a crisis.

A more unsettling type of crisis occurred when the department provided counsel in situations where participants were, by most indications, unlikely to heed any warnings, legal or otherwise. Such events were especially vexatious in that they laid bare the practical limitations of the law. Further, these incidents were often manifestations of more broadly based disputes or concerns, in which the federal government drew upon the law as an opening foray in a struggle where local authority was weak or nonexistent. Not only was the law reduced to the status of a single arrow in the federal quiver, but it provided an opportunity for disaffected individuals or groups to flout legal authority. Given that one ingredient of success for the Department of Justice was a studious avoidance of attention, open disregard for federal authority was obviously a grave concern for practical and philosophical reasons. Thus, despite the possibility of public discomfiture, the department still endeavoured to define and protect federal interests in the midst of events over which it had little, if any, genuine control. While in most cases the department emerged unscathed, these incidents were nonetheless drawn out and sometimes agonizing affairs.

One could hardly fault the Department of Justice for failing to anticipate the three years of aggravation that followed when Cuban republicans, under the leadership of Carlos Manuel de Céspedes, attempted to end Spanish colonial rule in what became the Ten Years War between 1868 and 1878.[67] Indeed, it was only when rumours circulated in July 1869 that Canadian volunteers were being solicited in aid of the insurgency that the department began paying official attention. Yet in hindsight, the context of the Cuban rebellion had all the markings of nineteenth-century Canadian imbroglio. The British demanded that strict neutrality be observed; the Americans sympathized with the republican rebels, while wishing to avoid British ill will in light of outstanding Civil War claims; the Spanish presumed the Canadians would dutifully toe the British line; and the rebels, headquartered in New York, evidently viewed Canada as a lucrative recruiting ground.[68] Navigating through this tangle of external expectations while addressing the pressures and constraints imposed by Canadian interests raised an enormous challenge for the department. In effect, it was no small accomplishment to provide clear and practical legal guidance while hoping nothing disastrous occurred as the Cuban crisis developed, and preventing Canadians volunteers from becoming involved was one such an eventuality to be averted.

Beginning in mid-August 1869 and finally ending in early January 1873, the machinations of the Cuban rebels and their American backers regularly occupied the attention of the Canadian Department of Justice. Its primary concern was the circulation of rumours and intelligence reports that the rebels were planning to outfit and then man their vessels in either New Brunswick or Nova Scotia.[69] Every summer there occurred a flurry of reports that recruiting was underway and that vessels, destined for the Maritimes and then Cuba, were departing American ports. Indeed, by the summer of 1871, it was certain that the rebels were actively soliciting recruits in Montreal.[70] Throughout, there was little the department or the Canadian government could do except reissue warnings about violating the Foreign Enlistment Act and ensure that potential recruits were sufficiently aware of the consequences of their behaviour. Indeed, the first official action by the department was to forward a memorandum to the maritime lieutenant governors directing the strict observance of neutrality towards Spain and Cuba.[71] Yet until one of these rumoured vessels actually entered Canadian waters, the department could do nothing to prevent individual Canadians from being drawn into the Cuban troubles.[72]

All this changed in the summer of 1872. In mid-August, the department received an informant's detailed report of plans to man a vessel of war "at some point on the Bay of Fundy."[73] The same day that this was revealed, Hewitt Bernard, on behalf of the minister of justice, directed the secretary of state to inform the Nova Scotian lieutenant governor of the rebels' plans.[74] Two days later, the department obtained the deposition of John Harrison of New York, who had been part of a contingent sent to Halifax to enlist men, and which revealed that a vessel would be laying in wait for recruits, possibly within a fortnight. By month's end, the rebels' plans to rendezvous in the Bay of Fundy at either Grand Manan or Brier Island were known, and the lieutenant governors of New Brunswick and Nova Scotia were directed, once again, to take all necessary measures to prevent a breach of the Foreign Enlistment Act.[75] Three days later, Bernard reported that the American steamers, the *Northern* and the *Southern,* having set sail for Quebec, were under surveillance.[76] During October, a naval gunboat was actively cruising the Bay of Fundy, dissuading any unlawful activity. The gunboat would not, however, bring the recruits to heel. Rather, it would be sheriff Alexander T. Paul of Charlotte County who, under directions from the lieutenant governor and accompanied by ten hired men, travelled to where the recruits were in hiding and simply ordered them to desist. The anticlimactic arrival of the British gunboat brought the adventure to a close.[77]

In hindsight, Paul had done the recruits a considerable favour. Within days of the sheriff's successful expedition, Spanish authorities captured the rebel vessel *Virginius* and, after a military trial, summarily executed all fifty-three crewmembers on 7 and 8 November 1872. Not only did the executions almost precipitate war between the Spanish and Americans, but it also effected a result that, despite best intentions and efforts, the Canadian Department of Justice could never achieve: it doused the ardour of potential volunteers and recruits. Although the department had failed to prevent recruiting, it had served federal interests by demonstrating, through the issuance of warnings and repeated publication of the Foreign Enlistment Act, that it would not be held accountable for the actions of any Canadians who saw fit to ignore the law.

Given the external forces at play, the Cuban incident was admittedly an awkward event for the department to handle. While the specifics of the situation were unusual, the general challenge of imposing legal notions from Ottawa in the face of distance, incomplete or possibly suspect information, and reliance on local officials, all revealed the indeterminacy of law whenever the department became embroiled in law-and-order issues outside of the capital. Indeed, this is exactly why such involvement was to be avoided; the department simply did not have the means or the jurisdictional authority to participate at such a level. This is also why the acquisition of the North-West Territories gave rise to a whole new assortment of problems for the department. Keeping track of legal business within the federal government was difficult enough without adding the huge prairie expanse. The perils of the situation were made plain when, in the summer of 1875, the department received word that Gabriel Dumont was planning a Métis uprising based at St. Laurent, a Métis community in the North-West Territories.[78]

In fact, the "insurrection" at St. Laurent was wholly created by the confluence of four distinct threads, of which only one the department was partly connected. When, in the absence of effective law enforcement within the community, Dumont had attempted to impose the law of the bison hunt upon the 150 Métis families at St. Laurent, Lawrence Clarke, chief factor of the Hudson's Bay Company in the region, and Chief Commissioner James A. Graham raised the alarm of impending insurrection. Clarke was, for a crucial period, the federal government's primary source of local intelligence. Fearing a repetition of Macdonald's mishandling of Red River, the federal Liberals were inclined to envision the worst in any North-West disturbance.[79]

Believing that trouble was in the making, a detachment of fifty North West Mounted Police was dispatched, only to discover that the insurrection was largely a product of Clarke's overactive imagination. Reporting on the incident, Edward Blake observed that, "There does not appear to have been the slightest foundation for the alarm expressed," and that, "The Lieut. Governor of the N.W. territories should be requested to call on Mr Clarke for any explanation he may have to offer of his conduct."[80] A confidential memorandum drafted shortly after made no effort to conceal Blake's annoyance with the entire affair. In fact, he suggested that the Hudson's Bay Company "was at the bottom of the matter and that it was a delicate plot to create an excitement and if possible prevent the settlement of traders by raising a feeling of insecurity and at the same time obtain the profits from the establishment of a force at the post."[81] Blake had gained some perspective on the matter by 12 October and, somewhat uncharacteristically, offered the novel solution of sending the "enthusiasts ... up to the country for a few months" to rein in their zeal.[82]

A Veneer of Common Sense

While the Cuban affair and the alleged insurrection at St. Laurent were shaped by very different circumstances, they demonstrated how the department responded to the "considerable amount of anxiety" such events produced.[83] Effectively out of touch with developments at points far removed from the capital, the department was limited to acting within its own narrowly defined sense of what entailed federal interests. Given the impossibility of directing a solution from Ottawa, the best the department could offer was by keeping a close watch, a disastrous turn of events might be avoided. Sometimes this worked and sometimes it did not. It is certain, however, that such an environment served to reemphasize the indeterminacy of law as a device for orchestrating specific policy goals. Indeed, considering the state of flux during the completion of Confederation, identifying the short-term results most crucial to the well-being of the union scheme would have been a rare skill. Rather, these crises suggest that from the department's perspective, law and legal interpretation were but one ingredient in a larger process, one in which the most effective legal counsel was that forestalling the imposition of an undesirable political result upon the federal government.

Although the management of daily business worked towards the same end, a more generous time frame provided greater opportunity to manipulate results. This certainly did not ensure federal dominance in any given situation, but it did allow the department to place a reference within a context favourable to federal interests while providing for a more sophisticated depiction of the probable implications flowing from a specific action. Such was the case in Bernard's handling of the difficulties with the ordnance lands along the canals. True, this method of policy formation might be criticized for favouring a defensive posture over that which aggressively defended a well-articulated jurisdictional or interpretative stance. Such a view not only confuses an aggressive posture with intelligence or insight but also fails to account for the considerable value of flexibility in the completion of Confederation. After all, sustaining the union scheme with as little strife as possible was undeniably in the federal government's best interests. To do so while, at the same time, facilitating a regulatory environment where individuals were afforded the opportunity to succeed or fail on their own merits, offered its own rewards.

Admittedly, this approach relied upon both the department's ability to set the ground for an understanding and the willing cooperation of the participants. Once either of these elements was compromised, however, any disagreement could dissipate into a contest of will. If opposed by an individual or company in such a situation, the advantage typically remained with the federal government. Who retained the upper hand if another level of government was involved was less certain. In those instances, the result turned on the specific interests at play, in concert with the indeterminacy of law, as marshalled by the ingenuity and quality of the various legal advisors. Given the risks, such a situation was precisely what the department, as the federal government's legal advisor, worked to avoid.

In the final analysis, the Department of Justice was most effective when it disarmed legalistic or interpretative obstacles to federal interests and policy initiatives. Carried out within a context of completing Confederation, this activity drew heavily on the expectation that the law set the stage for politicized solutions that were usually in the offing. Although this approach might be dismissed as being overly pragmatic or devoid of principle, one hastens to recall Robert Gordon's observation of how significant demonstrations of power can be obscured by the veneer of common sense. That such a veneer could also conceal the department's governmentality and its tactical use of law and legal remedy in support of the federal government's interests was but an additional benefit. Obviously, not all such displays were meant to be discreet or particularly subtle. In fact, there was one responsibility within a broader process which, according to some quarters, required as much public attention as possible. That duty, the management of the royal prerogative of mercy in cases of capital punishment and in requests for early release from penitentiary, could be one of the most wrenching aspects of the department's mandate. And unlike much of the work shouldered in the Department of Justice, the decision of life and death necessarily rested solely with the minister of justice.

4
Advisors to the Crown and the Prerogative of Mercy

One of the Confederation scheme's notable features was the manner in which the framers divided the administration of justice between federal and provincial governments. While responsibility for the criminal law remained in federal hands, the actual administration of the courts and prosecution of crime were left specifically with the provinces.[1] Evidently, this arrangement was intended to maintain national standards in defining what was criminal and how such acts should be punished, while better-informed local authorities were more able to handle the subsequent prosecutions. While this division would prove to work well, colonial office opposition to devolving the royal prerogative to provincial lieutenant governors necessitated federal involvement in respiting the sentences imposed on convicted felons, and in determining who would answer for their capital crimes on the gallows.[2]

From the perspective of the ideology of law and its corollary that those with a legal education possessed specialized knowledge, it might seem natural that given the legal character of administering the royal prerogative, this obligation would fall to the minister of justice and his staff. Indeed, to the extent that advising on the prerogative involved the law or legal interpretation, the department was an obvious choice to shoulder the burden. However, most petitions requesting early release were rather formulaic, raised few legal questions, and thus could be handled in the same fashion as the mundane tasks of daily business in the department. Indeed, there is little to suggest that legal analysis of any sort was involved. The capital cases also reveal that the fateful decision of who was to hang rarely had anything to do with legalistic arguments. More often than not, the decision turned on whether the jury had recommended mercy and on the issues the minister perceived to be at stake. Although the minister of justice and the department were not particularly ill suited to these tasks, nothing suggests that they were especially qualified. In fact, an examination of the prerogative demonstrates, as Carolyn Strange so ably documents in her study of the "lottery of death," that the application of capital sentences turned on a wide range of factors, few of which arguably fell within the exclusive purview of those schooled in the law.[3] Thus, the same rationalization that brought all legalistic concerns within the purview of the apolitical attorney general – the idea that unfettered justice was best served by the minister's management of the royal prerogative – was another wilful suspension of disbelief that, in this instance, provided a patina of weighty deliberation to the remission process while disguising the uneven nature of mercy.

It is especially ironic that the minister and his staff were to act as a font of justice when Sir John A. Macdonald, the primary architect of the British North America Act and of the Department of Justice, had wanted the provinces to retain their colonial responsibilities for remissions and pardons. By all indications, Macdonald preferred that the department be devoted entirely to advising the federal government and not left to deal with trying aspects of the administration of justice. Indeed, given the form and function of the department, designed as it was to advise the federal government alone, responding to the stream of public petitions following from a death sentence and that surfacing in favour of a prisoner's request for early release was rather peculiar. From the department's perspective, not only did advising on the royal prerogative offer few recognizable federal interests to stake, but the duty was hardly amenable to orchestrated understandings between those involved. In fact, one would be hard pressed to measure a greater distance than that between the department's "thousands of tiny contingent practices" and the weighty responsibility of determining whether the law should be allowed to follow its course with a life ending at the end of the hangman's rope.

Managing an Unwanted Responsibility

One of the proposals that the political leaders of British North America agreed upon in the negotiations preceding the act of union was that the provinces retain their colonial responsibility for advising on the royal prerogative. Citing the inconvenience "of the pardoning power being entrusted only to the Governor General," Macdonald and the other British North American delegates pressed "very strongly all the arguments in favour of conferring the power on the Lt. Governors & we pointed out the hardships that would arise."[4] Despite this colonial unanimity, neither Edward Cardwell, colonial secretary in 1864, nor Lord Carnarvon, colonial secretary from 1866 to 1867, agreed that the royal prerogative could be surrendered to the lieutenant governors.[5] According to Cardwell, the reasoned objection was quite simple: "It appears to Her Majesty's Gov't that this duty belongs to the Representative of the Sovereign and could not properly be devolved upon the Lieutenant Governors, who will, under the present scheme, be appointed not directly by the Crown but by the central Government of the United Provinces."[6]

While Macdonald acquiesced to the colonial office's interpretation of both the prerogative powers and the jurisdictional subtleties of the newly minted Confederation, this view failed to rest comfortably with a number of the provincial governments. Although Nova Scotian Attorney General Martin Wilkins' efforts to alter the colonial office's opinion was rebuffed in the early summer of 1868, almost a quarter century later, Ontario Premier and Attorney General Oliver Mowat established that the lieutenant governors possessed full prerogative powers for provincial jurisdictions.[7] This, however, was in the future. In years immediately following the union, both the federal and provincial governments had to accept that the federal government alone would advise the Queen's representative on remissions and pardons.

The actual process of petitioning the governor general in council to invoke the royal prerogative drew upon both formulaic and substantive ingredients.[8] Applications for remission of sentence and pardons were launched wholly on the initiative of the accused or on their behalf by an interested party, whereas in capital cases, the reference was automatic. Petitions often began by praying that the Crown's mercy be delivered upon the accused and his or her long-suffering family. After this formality was fulfilled, the depiction of the supplicant's case was determined largely by a draftsman's perception of what might lead to a favourable response.

Thus, when Mary McGarry petitioned on behalf of her son on 12 December 1867, the application mirrored a common form and tone of such entreaties.[9] In March 1857, when James McGarry was between fourteen and sixteen years of age, he was found guilty before Judge A. McLean and jury of the murder of ten-year-old William Cull. During the trial, attempts were made to demonstrate that McGarry's epileptic fits led to the murder, in that the seizures affected him to such a degree that he was unaccountable for his actions. Although Judge McLean later offered the view that the explanation was unconvincing, the jury recommended mercy after finding McGarry guilty. His sentence was subsequently commuted to life imprisonment and, on 12 December 1867, his mother applied to the governor general in council for a remission of sentence.

The petition recounted the offence and the trial in which her son had been found guilty, sentenced to death, and then commuted to life imprisonment. Mrs. McGarry claimed that during her son's long confinement, he had "never been punished for disobedience or insubordination ... and that he feels so heartfelt sorrow and repentance for the past," despite the deceased Cull having had instigated the fatal encounter. The petition further related that "hundreds of names of the most influential men of the county" supported previous attempts to gain a remission of the sentence. Having expressed the conviction that her son was not the aggressor in the unfortunate incident and that his release was backed by the principal inhabitants of the district, Mary McGarry then made her final plea:

> Your petitioner now infirm in health and advanced in years but with one young son left and in poor and indigent circumstances would most humbly pray and entreat your Excellency to cause enquiry to be made on the subjects contained in the foregoing statements and if not contrary to Justice and the good of Society that your excellency cause the liberation of your Petitioner's said son, that he may once more return to his widowed and unhappy mother.

Despite these pleas, Sir John A. Macdonald dismissed the application tersely, writing, "This case has been considered on several occasions. No new facts are brought forward in this petition and I cannot recommend that the case be re-opened."[10]

The McGarry application of 1867 failed not because its basis was one of emotion but rather because that was its only appeal. Similar pleas also fell on deaf ears. John C. Clifford's application was rejected because pity for his wife and children was "untenable" as grounds for remission.[11] Or, as Hewitt Bernard would write, that Gideon Grotleau had "left a house and wife and youthful family of whom he was the only support and who are now in distressing want" failed to justify executive interference in the original sentence.[12] Eusète Foutaine's petition was also rejected despite his wife and family having been reduced to a state of poverty.[13] Evidently, the Department of Justice was little inclined to be charitable towards such petitions for the simple reason that regardless of a person's family circumstances, the prisoner had been found guilty and the sentence had to be served. These rejections bore the unmistakable tone that had inmates thought of their families before breaking the law, they would not have placed themselves and their loved ones in such disadvantageous positions.

Successful petitions ordinarily followed one of four approaches. The most common tactic flowed from the Penitentiaries Act of 1868, which specified that through "diligence" at work and respect for prison rules, inmates could earn a partial remission of up to five days per month.[14] In 1870, this was altered to specify that such reductions were to be tallied only after the first six months of a sentence had been served.[15] For the Department of Justice, calculating these formulaic reductions was the usual first step in handling legitimate requests for remission. There was nothing automatic about such reductions and, depending on the prisoner's behaviour and diligence, it was entirely possible that only a few days might be shaved off in any given year. Further, applying before half the sentence had been served was a certain recipe for disappointment.[16]

A second and more substantive tactic was to raise a legitimate doubt that justice had been served by the original verdict or sentence. This could be accomplished only by introducing new evidence casting doubt on the convict's guilt or by suggesting that the sentence was not proportionate to the crime. Mrs. McGarry had merely reiterated evidence from the original trial and asserted that it showed that William Cull died while her son was fending off the younger boy's attack. Other than claiming that this was an accurate depiction of the event, McGarry was unable to substantiate the assertion. As a result, the petition was rejected. On the other hand, earlier in 1867, Entichianne Boucher was pardoned after it was successfully demonstrated that she had been deceived into giving false and self-incriminating evidence.[17]

A third tactic was to document that further imprisonment would lead directly to the death or permanent disability of the accused. There existed, however, a fine distinction in such claims. Life in the penitentiary was not intended to be pleasant and, if genuine discomfort and even hardship was produced, such a result was hardly the basis for a remission. For example, when it was reported to Zebulon Lash that convict James Tallon was subject to a disease "of the spinal nervous system of the most serious organic nature," and that further imprisonment "would most certainly bring about his early death," the deputy minister recommended that Tallon be released.[18] However, when an application for remission was forwarded on behalf of convict George Daxon, who was suffering from incurable heart disease, Lash did not respond immediately with the requested remission.[19] Requesting more specific details, Lash asked that the surgeon's certificate concerning the prisoner's health respond "with a view of ascertaining not whether the prisoner is suffering from an incurable disease, but whether in view of the state of his health further confinement in the penitentiary is likely to be attended with fatal consequences to his life."[20] Having been satisfied that imprisonment would shorten Daxon's life, Lash had the prisoner released a month later.

The fourth basis for remission was having performed an extraordinary service while imprisoned. Applications employing this approach were as rare as were the occasions for a prisoner to display such service. However, when a fire broke out at the Kingston Penitentiary and convict Jonathan George "worked admirably" in fighting the blaze, the warden considered these actions deserving of recognition in the consideration of a pardon. In fact, the warden "has no hesitation in saying a more worthy fellow has not been pardoned from the Penitentiary." Since George had already served six-and-a-half years of a seven-year sentence, it was thought he should be granted his remission.[21] On one other occasion, when Eli Bastien helped prevent an escape from St. Vincent de Paul Penitentiary, he was rewarded with a remission of sentence.[22] In both cases, however, the convicts were nearing the end of their imprisonment, and their actions merely provided a justification for early release, as opposed to actually compelling the consideration of an application that might not have occurred otherwise.

Akin to George and Bastien, W.G. Fitzmaurice and James Kerrison received special mention from the directors of penitentiaries in their report for 1874. Evidently, Fitzmaurice and Kerrison had served as orderlies in the penitentiary clinic during a typhoid outbreak. According to the directors, the two inmates "devoted themselves day and night, with a zeal truly heroic, to the care of the fever stricken." Their actions deserved special notice and the directors recommended that both prisoners receive three months' remission for their services. The recounting of the incident ended with "the hope that this act of clemency will be an incentive to others, to emulate the good example set by Fitzmaurice and Kerrison, should the occasion for the display of conduct so laudable at any time unhappily arise."[23]

A final method for obtaining release arose from either unusual events or stipulations to be effected after the release. Ann Connolly obtained a remission only upon the condition that she leave Canada and never return.[24] Henry Smith, George Gustaff, John O'Toole, and S. Cunningham were also given similar instructions as conditions to their receiving remissions.[25] Thomas Connolly's remission was aided by the intercession of his prosecutors, and it was specified that the prisoner be informed of this fact.[26] Henry Allen's release was recommended on 2 September 1874 on the grounds that he apprentice in a trade.[27] Such willingness to make good, however, did not assure a successful request for early release. When Onzième St. Pierre, Joseph Lizotte, Honoré Pin, and Edouard Thibaud volunteered for service with the Second Battalion at Red River, acting Minister of Justice George-Etienne Cartier viewed the offer with a jaundiced eye: "This has already been refused by the Minister of Militia. It would have been obviously bad policy to associate inmates of a prison with the volunteers for the Red River Service."[28]

Given the limited circumstances that could shape a successful petition, it seems unlikely that the process could be initiated with a great deal of hope, unless half the sentence had already been served.[29] Yet regardless of the obstacles and the fairly slim chances, petitioning for a remission or pardon was hardly a wasted effort. As Table 1 reveals, in any given year, a petition had about a 38 percent chance of success.[30] However, when the percentages are ordered in categories of high and low quartiles, the Conservative years of 1870, 1871, and 1872 produced the highest level of remissions, whereas the divided year of 1873 and the Liberal years of 1874 and 1878 produced the lowest percentage of remissions. Indeed, with the exception of 1875, in no year in which the Liberals governed did the rate of remission rise above the twelve-year mean. Apparently, the Liberal ministers of justice believed that serving as much of the sentence assigned by the courts was more likely to produce the desired effect upon the inmate population as a whole.

Table 1

Remissions, 1867-78

Year	Number of applications	Number granted	Percentage
1867	93	33	35.5
1868	121	51	42.2
1869	120	44	36.7
1870	155	70	45.2
1871	214	91	42.5
1872	209	94	45
1873	165	49	29.7
1874	197	65	33
1875	194	80	41.2
1876	263	90	34.2
1877	337	117	34.7
1878	463	150	32.4
Total	2531	934	

Note: Yearly mean: 37.7%

Fortunately for those petitioners who had their applications turned down, rejected prayers did not prejudice future efforts. Fenian prisoner R.B. Lynch requested remission of sentence on at least four occasions following his 1866 conviction and was finally successful in 1871.[31] In some instances, unsuccessful pleas could encourage hope for eventual remission. John Smith and James Ryan were both informed in 1878 that while their current petitions were denied, their chances would improve after serving ten years. For Smith, the news meant he had only two more years before he could genuinely hope for a release, whereas Ryan would have to endure at least another eight years behind bars.[32]

The response to Smith and Ryan, in tandem with the often-repeated counsel that successful applicants had typically served at least half of their time, reinforces the impression that the remission process was fairly mechanical. In most cases, remission was simply the result of quietly serving one's time and observing penitentiary rules. Consequently, penitentiaries were the primary beneficiaries of the promise of remission since such a promise reportedly encouraged "industry and good behaviour" within the inmate population.[33] In turn, this institutional advantage assumed a different face for public consumption. Rather than being acknowledged as a device for managing inmates, remission was presented to the public as an indication of reformation. The inmate who earned remission was, in some reassuringly observable and documented fashion, reformed. For example, Warden John Creighton of Kingston Penitentiary offered his particular notion of reformation through remission: Once an inmate could "perform a day's fair labour, in a workmanlike manner, I would give him that as a task, which he should be required to perform every day, and all he did over should go to the credit of his sentence ... Correct, industrious habits would be formed, and I believe the great majority of prisoners on their release would apply their skill thus obtained to a good purpose."[34]

The promise of early release served two distinct purposes. It effectively provided a means to control inmates by holding out the possibility of a shortened sentence while supporting the inference that those obtaining a remission were reformed and could be released safely back into the community. Therefore, the practice of remitting sentences sustained two distinct if related fictions. Penitentiary officials and the department could point to the system of rewards and punishments, in concert with the use of remissions, as evidence that genuine inmate reform was an integral part of Canadian penitentiaries. For its part, the public could believe that released prisoners were reformed and no longer a threat. Neither assertion could withstand close scrutiny, but acknowledging that penitentiaries were merely warehouses and that released prisoners represented a potential threat was too disturbing. The community needed to believe that the system worked because the alternative was simply unacceptable. In the very least, the department's management of remissions provided an eminently more palatable depiction of penitence and reform.

A Solemn Duty

Although requests for remissions and pardons could be handled mechanically and thus in a manner consistent with how the department solved most problems, advising on the royal prerogative of mercy in capital cases proved more resistant to such methods. In fact, the apparent absence of an accepted formula for weighing the substantive merit of individual capital cases fed upon the assertion that the minister of justice and his supporting staff possessed special attributes qualifying them for the task. Indeed, the ministerial attention suggested that some measure of "justice" was more likely because each case was apparently viewed on its own merits. Unlike remissions, which inferred that a prisoner's reformation could be measured objectively, reviewing capital cases involved the subjective judgment of the minister of justice as a person schooled in the intricacies and subtleties of law. Ironically, it was this level of personal obligation that sustained the idea that justice could be achieved and maintained, a notion that troubled Minister of Justice Edward Blake, who described the capital case deliberations as "a most solemn duty" and "an awful responsibility."[35] It is difficult to avoid the impression that in Blake's case at least, his personal doubts were more deeply felt than was the expectation that an idealized justice was served by his personal involvement.

As gauged by the criminal statutes of the era, post-Confederation Canada was not particularly dependent on capital punishment. Only murder, attempted murder, treason, rape, and carnal knowledge of a female under ten years of age were deemed sufficiently threatening to warrant taking the life of a convicted felon. British Columbia's entry into confederation in 1871 briefly introduced piracy as a capital crime, and Prince Edward Island did the same with burglary when it joined two years later.[36] Even this relatively short list did not reflect the actual reliance on capital punishment. For while cases involving all these offences crossed the minister's desk between 1867 and 1878, only successful prosecutions for murder raised the spectre of fatal consequences for the convict.

The inclusion of rape as a capital offence was a vestige of Canada's colonial past and had been unenforced since the early 1840s. According to John A. Macdonald, this was known generally in the community. Therefore, when Samuel Allen applied for remission because of the mental anguish caused by the death sentence following his conviction, Sir John dismissed the claim in stating: "No one in Canada is now hanged for rape. And every convict knows that well enough to prevent any agony of mind."[37] When asked to elaborate why rapists were never sent to the gallows despite the crime's capital designation, Macdonald replied that:

> We found it necessary, or rather judged it expedient to retain the life penalty principally on account of the influx of blackguards of all kinds from the United States, who can cross and re-cross our border at will and occasionally commit all kinds of outrages. We have thought it well also to continue it on account of the frequency of rape committed by negroes, of whom we have too many in Upper Canada. They are very prone to felonious assaults on white women: if the sentence and imprisonment were not very severe there would be great dread of the people taking the law into their own hands.[38]

While such concerns over the influence of Americans, the sexual threat posed by black men, and the possibility of vigilante violence may have found a receptive audience in Canada in the 1860s and 1870s, the overt conflict between the letter of the law and its enforcement troubled members of the bench. The feelings expressed by Chief Justice W.B. Richards of Ontario were shared by most of his brethren, especially as it pertained to the practice of donning the black cap when delivering capital sentences in rape convictions: "It seems to me very undesirable the public should be accustomed to see so solemn a proceeding gone through within a Court of Justice, where the stern realities of life are supposed to be dealt with, rather than mere forms, where every one present must feel that the passing of the sentence is but a mere form."[39] Given the concern voiced by the judiciary as well as the obvious incongruity, Alexander Mackenzie's Liberal government amended the law and effectively ended the capital designation by allowing judges greater sentencing latitude in cases of rape.[40]

These amendments merely recognized what had been the unofficial practice of commuting automatically all capital offences except murder. As a result, while these other offences were designated as capital crimes and therefore appeared before the minister of justice, their presence served only to skew the public character of capital punishment in Canada. For example, from 1867 to the end of the Mackenzie administration in October 1878, there were a total of 126 capital cases. Of these 126 cases, 89, comprising 70.63 percent, were commuted to a lesser punishment. However, if one eliminates all the cases in which there was a de facto automatic commutation, only 56.47 percent of the cases were reduced. The significance of this difference can be viewed from two perspectives. Either Canada's criminal law was merciful in granting automatic commutation for the majority of its capital crimes or, at best, it offered a convicted murderer a 56 percent chance of escaping the noose. Not surprisingly given the mercurial nature of criminal statistics, a closer examination reveals that even this percent did not reflect the reality of capital punishment.

Five different men held the post of minister of justice from 1867 to October 1878. The longest in office was John A. Macdonald, who occupied the position for five years, while the shortest was Antoine-Aimé Dorion, who was briefly minister at the onset of the Mackenzie government. Macdonald reviewed thirty-six cases of murder during his tenure, sixteen of which he commuted. Dorion considered seven cases and granted clemency to only two, while his replacement, Télesphore Fournier, commuted twelve of the fourteen cases brought to his attention. Edward Blake commuted twelve of twenty cases, while Rodolphe Laflamme mitigated the sentences in six of eight cases. As seen in Table 2, the tendencies among these men are striking. Unlike the pattern of remissions, which revealed that Sir John was consistently more lenient than the Liberal ministers, in capital cases, the Liberals, excepting Dorion, were noticeably more charitable than Macdonald. Even Blake, whose number of reviews most nearly equalled Sir John's, commuted 15 percent more cases. Thus, depending on who the minister of justice was when a case was received, the condemned person had between a 28 and 85 percent chance of commutation. In the very least, the course of justice was uneven.

Table 2

Commutations per minister of justice in murder convictions, 1867-78

Minister	Total cases	Number commuted	Percentage
Macdonald	36	16	44.4
Dorion	7	2	28.6
Fournier	14	12	85.7
Blake	20	12	60
Laflamme	8	6	75
Total	85	48	56.5

Source: Compiled from NAC, RG 13, C1.

A number of explanations for the variations within these statistics are possible. Perhaps the simplest is that Fournier, Laflamme, and, to a certain degree, Blake were less committed to the efficacy of capital punishment than Macdonald and Dorion. Admittedly, this assertion does not mesh well with the remission patterns in which the Conservatives were more generous than the Liberals. The discontinuity may have resulted from the notion that while remissions and petitions for mercy were subsumed under the royal prerogative, the Minister and Department of Justice viewed the two as wholly separate, with each requiring a distinct rationale. Essentially, the grace extended through remission or pardon was substantively different than that bestowed in capital cases.[41] The first professed to measure the suitability of an inmate to reenter society, whereas the second determined if a convict's life should be sacrificed in the name of justice. Cast within this light, Macdonald evidently placed more value on the symbolism of sending someone to the gallows while the Liberals preferred the message that certain and lengthy sentences followed criminal acts.

A second explanation arises from differences in the nature of the cases. During the Liberal years, the insanity defence was far more prominent than it had been under Macdonald. Fournier and Blake were especially sensitized towards these pleas, and both went to considerable lengths to investigate any claim of insanity on behalf of the accused. In contrast, their Liberal colleague Dorion was not particularly receptive to the insanity defence. Marginalia in the first case he reviewed offered the opinion that, "I think that great caution should be used in testing a plea of insanity which is so easily set up." After four examinations by separate doctors, it was concluded that the prisoner James Fox was feigning insanity. Armed with this interpretation, Dorion concluded, "The law should be allowed to take its course."[42] It is also possible that the capital crimes of the Macdonald years were more violent than during the Mackenzie administration and, therefore, more likely to warrant the extreme penalty of law. Yet the exact opposite is the result where the accused was granted clemency in some extremely violent and ferocious crimes during the three years from 1874 to 1877. The rationalization in such cases was that to commit such an offence the prisoner *had* to be insane.

For example, an insanity defence was successful after Christopher Ward murdered his wife Mary on 6 April 1876 and then destroyed their home while attempting to burn her severed head. Reporting on the case to Edward Blake, Dr. Joseph Workman of the Toronto Insane Asylum wrote that, "I am but too well-aware that to adduce, in support of the allegation of insanity, the enormity or ferocity of the acts perpetrated by its subjects is but promptly to evoke the condemnation and disgust of almost the entire community; but with all due deference to enraged public feeling, I would ask why should it be expected that the crimes of the insane should *not* be characterised by unsound ferocity?" Concluding his report, Workman chided the "rabid and bloodthirsty press in Canada" and stated that, "The history of insanity in Canada must be written some day, but no good or honest man can desire that its annals, as those of too many older countries, should show stains which must cause posterity to blush."[43] Yet even the connection between the ferocity of a crime and the possibility of mercy being granted was subject to exceptions. When David Robbins killed his wife Emelina with a mallet and when Michael McConnell killed James Mills with a butcher knife in broad daylight in downtown Hamilton, both were sent to the gallows.[44]

A final explanation, and perhaps the most enlightening, is to be found in the relationship between commutations and jury recommendations for mercy. Concentrating on the eighty-five cases of murder brought to the attention of the ministers of justice, some illuminating trends appear. Table 3 demonstrates that during the period from 1867 to 1878, there was approximately a 51 percent chance of the convicting jury recommending the accused to the mercy of the court. Once the jury recommendation was made, the chances for the accused increased or decreased proportionally. As demonstrated in Tables 4 and 5, when a jury passed a guilty verdict with a recommendation for mercy, 70.83 percent of those cases received a commutation. However, when a guilty verdict was not accompanied with such a recommendation, 72.97 percent of the accused were hanged. Even accounting for the variations between the ministers, a positive recommendation from the jury was a crucial concern for the accused.

We are therefore left with a nuanced impression of the administration of capital cases. While it is certain that the recommendation of the trial jury carried considerable weight, it did not ensure subsequent ministerial action.

Table 3

Jury recommendations for mercy in murder convictions, 1867-78

Minister	Total	With mercy	Without mercy
Macdonald	36	16 (44.4%)	20 (55.6%)
Dorion	7	2 (28.6%)	5 (71.4%)
Fournier	14	11 (78.6%)	3 (21.4%)
Blake	20	9 (45%)	11 (55%)
Laflamme	8	6 (75%)	2 (25%)
Total	85	44 (51.8%)	41 (48.2%)

Source: Compiled from NAC, RG 13, C1.

Table 4

Commutations per minister of justice in murder convictions in relation to jury recommendations for mercy, 1867-78

Minister	Total	With mercy	Without mercy
Macdonald	16	10 (62.5%)	6 (37.5%)
Dorion	2	2 (100%)	0
Fournier	12	10 (83.3%)	2 (16.7%)
Blake	12	7 (58.3%)	5 (41.7%)
Laflamme	6	5 (83.3%)	1 (16.7%)
Total	48	34 (70.8%)	14 (29.2%)

Source: Compiled from NAC, RG 13, C1.

Table 5

Executions per minister of justice in murder convictions in relation to jury recommendations for mercy, 1867-78

Minister	Total	With mercy	Without mercy
Macdonald	20	6 (30%)	14 (37.5%)
Dorion	5	0	5 (100%)
Fournier	2	1 (50%)	1 (50%)
Blake	8	2 (25%)	6 (75%)
Laflamme	2	1 (50%)	1 (50%)
Total	37	10 (27%)	27 (73%)

Source: Compiled from NAC, RG 13, C1.

The two ministers who held office for the longest period, Macdonald and Blake, were the most likely to set aside the recommendation of a jury while, on the other hand, Dorion, Fournier, and Laflamme seldom strayed from the jury's recommendation. Furthermore, although more pleas of insanity were successful during the Mackenzie administration than any other, even here success was uneven. The conclusion from these patterns again points to the idiosyncratic nature of mercy, especially given the dominant role of the minister's personal inclination in the fateful decision. Confronted with the "solemn duty," both Macdonald and Blake proceeded confidently from their own perspectives and understanding of each individual case, whereas others relied on the jury's recommendation.

The confidence displayed by Macdonald and Blake carried a heavy cost. Despite the perceived assurances of a system founded on the processes of trial, jury deliberation, sentencing, and ministerial review, results were not always predictable. Questionable conclusions drawn by ministers who fell victim to the prejudices of the society of which they were a part are easily found in these cases. Sweeping statements made by judges that the victim of a sexual assault was too young to be injured permanently, or that an accused demonstrated intelligence beyond that normally displayed by members of his or her race, or the assumption that indiscretions by a married woman were somehow worse in nature than those of a husband received the minister's concurrence and often informed his actions in deciding the final outcome of a case.[45] Further, as Michael Hindus writes, the entire process of reviewing capital sentences "meant that the ultimate determination of punishment was transformed from the trial judge to the executive" and thus exposed the political context of what was generally perceived as a distinctive legal decision.[46] Shaped in part by such notions and working within an environment charged with the pressure of political and public opinion, the immediacy of sustaining credibility in post-Confederation Canadian society obviously coloured the way in which these decisions were made.

Any one of the capital cases between 1867 and 1878 readily demonstrates the manner in which ministerial notions of grace, public opinion, political gamesmanship, and contemporary notions of right and wrong swirled around these decisions. Each case created newspaper headlines and captured the public attention. On occasion, this attention even flooded across county lines and provincial borders to envelop the nation. Yet for the notoriety that some garnered, each case inevitably boiled down to the basic ingredients of human tragedy. Violent deaths in the wake of alcoholic sprees, the woman who turned to an abortionist only then to die from the procedure, the man who believed his family had been cursed and that he must kill the person responsible, or the misplaced arrogance of an aspirant murderer who felt he or she could simply get away with taking another life all make appearances in these cases. Although any number of cases highlight both the workings of the process of review and the forces shaping the final decision, Elizabeth Workman's case and the trial of Dr. Arthur Davis provide compelling testimony to the centrality of the personal opinions, values, and perceptions of the minister of justice in determining who would answer for their crimes on the gallows. In so doing, they lay bear the fiction that these determinations were the product of specialized knowledge possessed solely by those schooled in the law.

Elizabeth Workman and Jane Gilmour: The System at Work

In the spring of 1873, Elizabeth Workman appeared before Judge Adam Wilson at the Sarnia Assize, charged with the beating death of her fifty-five-year-old husband.[47] The trial revealed that Mrs. Workman had been subjected to a steady stream of verbal, physical, and emotional abuse from her husband, who, it seemed, was prone to alcoholism and extramarital affairs. Evidently at some point before her husband's death, Workman began frequenting Samuel Butler's barbershop, where, it was alleged, she began to have an affair with Butler, a man of colour. On the day before the murder, Mr. Workman bodily removed his wife from the barbershop, and it was then that violent words were exchanged between Butler and Mr. Workman. On the following day, heavy blows were heard coming from the Workman house, and it was asserted that Mrs. Workman was overheard asking her husband "if he had got enough." Although Mr. Workman was still alive after the reported beating, he died the following day. When found, the body showed signs of having been tied to the bed and bearing the marks of a severe beating administered by a mop handle. Mrs. Workman, who had spoken of having given her husband a beating he would not soon forget, was taken into custody immediately. At the subsequent trial she was found guilty of murder, though the jury recommended her to mercy.

Reporting on the trial to John A. Macdonald on 21 March 1873, Judge Wilson drew particular attention to a number of elements in the case and discounted others. He was particularly concerned that there was "some kind of improper intimacy between the woman and Butler."[48] The judge later reiterated this point, suggesting that it explained why Mrs. Workman attacked her husband: "The evidence suggested criminal or improper conduct between the woman and Samuel Butler the coloured man who was tried with her. I mean conduct impeaching her conjugal fidelity and that may have been the motive for her violence – as it may also explain the purpose which she wished to accomplish."[49] While Wilson acknowledged that the Workmans had quarrelled, the husband's abuse was characterized as verbal whereas the wife had physically attacked her husband. Indeed, Wilson was quite determined to highlight any of Elizabeth Workman's supposed flaws while downplaying those of her husband.

Armed with Wilson's report and in direct contrast to numerous and lengthy petitions submitted in Workman's favour, Macdonald decided that Workman must answer for her crime on the gallows. The decision unleashed a renewed flurry of entreaties on Workman's behalf, including a personal plea from Liberal leader Alexander Mackenzie. After acknowledging that the death was horrendous and that the individuals involved came from "a very low class," Mackenzie pressed for mercy, since he believed it clear that the death had not been intended and that defence counsel John Mackenzie had undertaken the case with only a few hours notice.[50] Despite Mackenzie's pleas, in concert with others that continued to arrive, Macdonald remained committed to his chosen course. Writing to Governor General Lord Dufferin on 31 May 1873, Macdonald offered that, "Mr. Mackenzie's appeal is very credible to his humanity, and appears to be dictated by a very sincere conviction on the subject. But your responsibilities and mine in these matters are of course of a more burdensome nature than those of ordinary onlookers."[51] After dismissing Mackenzie's concern, Macdonald continued:

> My respect for human life is such that I should never be prepared to weaken on my own mere motion any of those safeguards by which the Legislature of this country has sought to protect it; nor could I undertake the responsibility of arresting the operation of the law by the exercise of the Queen's Prerogative, except in cases where I have been informed on due authority or have been convinced by patent facts, that a miscarriage of justice has taken place.[52]

Accordingly, Elizabeth Workman was hanged on 19 June 1873.

Workman's case is notable for a variety of reasons. Judge Wilson's emphasis on the alleged relationship between Workman and Butler revealed crucial notions about then-contemporary race and gender relations. Wilson's inferences served as a thinly veiled message indicating what was "really" at stake. Second, the suggestion that the deceased had been an abusive and philandering husband neither provided Workman with licence to act as she did or mitigated the seriousness of the beating. Evidently, while a husband's indiscretions were troubling, they were insignificant as compared with a wife's rumoured behaviour.

Finally, and in specific reference to the office of attorney general and minister of justice, Macdonald's dismissal of Alexander Mackenzie's interest in the case is noteworthy. Obviously, Sir John believed that as a lawyer he possessed special talents and insight for discerning the deeper issues involved in these cases whereas Mackenzie, as an "ordinary onlooker," did not. Macdonald's elaboration of this view, however, did not rest initially on his ability to judge individual cases but, rather, upon a commitment to let the legislated "safeguards" function without interference. It was only when, as a lawyer and legislator, he was convinced that a miscarriage of justice had occurred, that he would intervene in the execution of a court's sentence.

While Macdonald undoubtedly believed that his stated approach maintained a faith in and respect for British constitutional ideals and practice, that belief merely underlined his adherence to the basic paradigm of law. For in asserting that he could choose not to intervene, that choice presupposed the authority to act and, as such, revealed that the decision devolved onto one man and how that man viewed his responsibilities within the context of the times. Even more so than the Elizabeth Workman case, the trial of the abortionists Dr. Arthur P. Davis and his wife Alice Davis for the death of Jane Gilmour in mid-October 1875 demonstrated that, when the decision rested at the minister's feet, the quality of mercy could not be extended to anyone's true satisfaction.

The disappearance of twenty-three-year-old Jane Vaughan Gilmour on 24 July 1875, and the subsequent discovery of her nude body in a crude coffin in the ditch beside Toronto's Bloor Street eight days later, generated considerable discussion in the press. In the week following the discovery, there were eighteen stories, editorials, and letters to the editor in the two main dailies in Toronto, the *Globe* and the *Mail*. The case even compelled the editors of the weekly *Christian Guardian,* "a family paper" which "naturally shrinks" from discussing "some questions of social morality so indelicate, and some forms of sin so suggestive and tainting," to print a column.[53] The lessons of morality that the press saw were plain given that Jane Gilmour had been the daughter of Baptist minister Reverend John Gilmour. For if the child of a minister could succumb to the pleasures of the flesh and then feel compelled to seek an abortionist, perhaps anyone could be tempted.

The preliminary hearing and eventual trial of the Davises laid bare Gilmour's life and inferred that as abortionists, the Davises carried on a thriving trade. Apparently, when Jane became pregnant while working as a domestic, she sought the services of the Davises in Toronto in order to avoid the shame of an unwanted pregnancy.[54] At the trial, Charles Chalk, a storekeeper for the Montreal Telegraph Company, revealed that on the Monday before Gilmour's body was found, he had heard a woman's muffled cries of pain coming from inside the Davises' house. Night watchman Robert Campbell also saw the Davises and a third person load a wagon with a box similar to that in which Gilmour was found. After deliberating over the circumstantial evidence for an hour, the jury returned two guilty verdicts, neither of which was accompanied by a recommendation for mercy.[55]

Predictably, the press covered the trial with excruciating detail. The *Toronto Mail* referred to the Davises' neighbourhood as the "slaughter houses on Scott street" and added that Dr. Davis, who had been long suspected of being involved in the trade, "comes from abortionist stock, his father before him having been a pioneer in the business in Buffalo."[56] For its part, the *Globe* reprinted an article from the *Rochester Express*, noting that the Arthur Davis who had been arrested in Toronto was undoubtedly Paul

Davis, who had fled abortion charges in New York state. Believing the two men to be one and the same, the *Express* concluded with the "hope that the authorities of Toronto will not let up on Davis until he swings from the end of a rope."[57] Running from 14 October to 17 October 1875, the trial occupied much of the two dailies' attention and, when a guilty verdict was returned, both reported with satisfaction the sentence of death.[58] Few newspapers, however, matched the moral rhetoric of the *London Free Press,* which portrayed the conviction as a call to action. The newspaper asserted that in every instance where an abortionist was suspected, "he should be placed under the strictest surveillance, his movements noted, and his antecedents enquired into." Talk of mercy for the condemned was "ill-timed," for "it will be found much easier to prevent this vicious practice from taking root in Canadian soil, than to eradicate the noxious thing after it has acquired strength." Further, "If the verdict be a just one, and if the rigour of the law will assist in stamping out this crime, and in clearing the soil of Canada of such miscreants, then does not the safety of our people, and the clearing of the moral atmosphere of our country demand the execution of the sentence without any mitigation of its severity?"[59]

Consistent with the moralizing tone it had adopted since Gilmour's body was first discovered, the *Globe* saw the death sentences in "this disgusting and terrible case" as befitting an editorial on the lessons to be learned. For those engaged "in the nefarious work which had brought Davis and his wife under the shadow of the gallows," the full and complete punishment of the two would demonstrate the community's desire to rid itself of a crime "which is acknowledged to be praying on the very vitals of society."[60] And for the man who seduced Gilmour, justice demanded that the Crown do its uppermost to "secure the apprehension and conviction of the worst criminal of the three." Finally, the lesson for all women was that each "ought to be her own protector." Reflecting much of contemporary opinion, the *Globe* added that, "There is a time when the first wrong step is taken, and for the taking of it no one can be held so much responsible as she who takes it. But even to avoid disgrace there is no excuse for resort to the abortionist for aid."[61] For society at large, there was also a lesson to be learned. The abortionist, according to the *Globe,* thrived in an atmosphere of indifference. When respectable people countenance a trade, they remove "the barrier to the commission of crime interposed by strong public opinion against it" and are therefore "responsible for the results which follow."[62]

The public response to the trial kept pace with the newspaper coverage. Both the *Globe* and *Mail* reported that huge crowds turned out to witness the proceedings, with the *Mail* adding that besides "a large number of prominent gentlemen and members of the bar ... there was also a considerable sprinkling of ladies among the spectators."[63] Those who took time to correspond with the newspapers generally agreed with the editors' positions. One writer, using the pseudonym of Peona, saw "sharp and summary justice" as the best deterrent to "pseudo-physicians" involved in the abortion trade.[64] A similar letter from "Civis" published in the *Mail* argued that, "The welfare of Canada demands that such men be made quite certain that they carry on their diabolical trade at the never failing peril of their lives."[65] As for those who strayed from the accepted wisdom of the *Mail*, such as "A Lawyer" who questioned the efficacy of capital punishment in deterring crime, or "D," who suggested the services of abortionists would not be needed if Gilmour would have been assured of "charitable secrecy, free from prying eyes and unkind tongues," the editor assured his readers that the newspaper was not responsible for the views expressed by such correspondents.[66] Thus, by the time the case awaited review on Edward Blake's desk, public opinion, as well as the position of the powerful *Globe* newspaper, was clear. To Blake fell the responsibility of separating emotion from law, and in so doing, determine if the Davises would escape from the shadow of the gallows.

The case, in hindsight, appeared deceptively simple. If the Davises had wilfully, with malice aforethought, murdered Jane Gilmour, as the jury had agreed, the Crown should allow the law to take its course. However, if the accused had "feloniously killed and slayed" Gilmour, the verdict should have been manslaughter.[67] The difference was one that weighed heavily in Blake's mind. First of all, he worried that the evidence introduced to demonstrate that an abortion had occurred failed to "show either that the particular acts done in this case as described were likely to produce death or to show generally that an attempt by mechanical means to procure abortion at such a period of gestation was likely to produce death."[68] Had the Davises acted in a manner that would necessarily have led to Gilmour's death, rather than the abortion of her fetus? Furthermore, the Crown's medical evidence seemed "to prove that the death resulted from the violent act of the prisoner deliberately committed for an unlawful purpose but not for the purpose of slaying the deceased."[69] Such a conclusion on Blake's part indicated that while the Davises had broken the law by performing the abortion, they were not murderers because they had not intended to kill Gilmour: there was no guilty mind.

The ease with which the case might have been handled was tempered by the fact that abortion was viewed widely as the scourge of the land. There certainly was no doubt that the popular press was concerned about the perceived increase in abortions. The seriousness of the threat was undoubtedly enhanced by the commutation of the death sentence in a recent controversial case involving Dr. Eric Benzel Sparham and William H. Graves, who were found guilty in the death of Sophia Elizabeth Burnham.[70] Contemporary political opinion, or at least that of John A. Macdonald, agreed that a threat existed. Speaking as a man whose first son died in infancy and whose daughter was hydrocephalic, Sir John believed that the crime of procuring abortion was a practice that "saps the very life blood of a nation and must be put down with a strong hand. My own opinion is that the crime of procuring an abortion is in its consequences on the Public, infinitely greater than rape, and should be dealt with as severely."[71]

For his part, Governor General Lord Dufferin reduced Blake's decision regarding the Davises to a simple factor: "Has the crime of procuring abortion become, or is it becoming, sufficiently rife in Canada, to demand a signal example. If the answer is in the negative, then the absence of malice which we may fairly assume, would I think justify the Executive in satisfying itself with a milder sentence."[72] Despite Dufferin's counsel, performing an abortion was not a capital offence in Canada and, therefore, no matter how prevalent it had become, or how great a threat it was perceived to be, the Davises could not be hanged.

There remained the question of the unknown seducer. Gilmour had worked as a domestic for two families, the Nattrasses and the Clements. Speculating on the age of the fetus when it was aborted, it was rumoured in the press that conception had probably occurred when Gilmour had worked for the Nattrass family. However, Arthur Davis's confession alleged that it had been John Clements and not one of the Nattrasses who delivered Gilmour into his hands in pursuit of an abortion. As a result, Blake was placed in a quandary. Alice Davis's confession failed to provide any information that could convict Clements as an accessory to procurement and, therefore, Arthur's evidence was needed to gain that conviction. While a dying declaration might be taken from Davis before he was sent to the gallows, testimony given after a pardon had been granted would be free from the taint of something acquired through the duress of his situation. Blake concluded that, "If by commuting the sentence of Davis to imprisonment for life the testimony is presented upon which there is a reasonable expectation of convicting Clements the demands of Justice and the views of the more intelligent and reasoning classes of society will be better met than by the execution of Davis and the escape of Clements."[73]

The final pieces of Blake's decision fell into place during the last week of November 1875. Alexander Mackenzie informed him that a personal canvass of legal opinion in Toronto revealed that, "The legal gentlemen were almost unanimous in the expression of grave doubts whether we should execute even the male prisoner; while the opinion was universal that the female prisoner should not be executed."[74] Mackenzie added that, "A considerable number, perhaps the larger number, were half willing that Davis should be executed as an example. But I think I found no one who did not, on considering the matter, express some little doubt even to that, unless it be Mr George Brown."[75] Responding to Mackenzie's letter, Blake wrote that the sentences should be either reprieved or commuted, and he favoured an immediate commutation rather than first reprieving then commuting:

"I dislike what may be said to be trifling with the fate and feelings of an unfortunate wretch for the simple purpose of breaking the ice with the public: in the second place I think it not improbable that the evidence of Davis will have more weight if given after his fate has been determined than if given when as it may be said, his fate is dependent upon his evidence."[76] Consequently, given that the Davises should have been charged with manslaughter rather than murder, and that Arthur Davis's testimony was needed to prosecute John Clements, Blake commuted the sentences to life imprisonment. Disposing of what he had described to Lord Dufferin as "this melancholy business" in such a fashion was agreeable to the governor general, and on 30 November 1875, the *Globe* carried notice of the commutation.[77]

The Liberal government's decision to commute forced the *Globe* to retreat from its earlier position. Citing the desired conviction of Clements as the alleged seducer, the Liberal newspaper argued that by letting the law take its course, the governor general and his advisors could "have secured the adequate punishment of two of the criminals, while they allowed the third and worst of all to escape."[78] The *Globe* assured its readers, however, that the peculiar circumstances of the case were "sufficient to prevent it from being hereafter made a precedent should a case of equal aggravation ever come up."[79]

Not surprisingly, the *Mail* was less charitable in its appraisal of the government's actions. Claiming that Davis should have been hanged, the Conservative newspaper asserted that, "There will still be people to say that the conviction of the seducer is obtained too dearly at the cost of a reprieve to the inhuman wretch DAVIS; and if the case against the man now under arrest should chance to break down – a contingency by no means improbable – the action of the Executive in reprieving Davis will come in for general censure."[80] The unsuccessful prosecution of Clements in late January 1876 provided the *Mail* with an opportunity to repeat these criticisms: "The Minister of Justice might have known that such evidence as [Davis] could give would go a short way with a jury towards the conviction of anyone. The consequences he might have foreseen has [sic] resulted, and a fitting subject has escaped the gallows. The whole business has had a lame and impotent conclusion."[81] For its part, the *Globe* merely recorded Clements' acquittal, adding that the Crown could not be charged with either inefficiency or neglect in the pursuit of justice throughout the entire case.[82] In this final sense, the case proved to be distinctly unsettling for those who had witnessed the twists and turns of this melancholy business.

Justice Sought

Reviewing capital cases and applications for remission was a responsibility that the framers of the British North America Act preferred to leave within provincial jurisdiction. The colonial office and the law officers in London demurred, however, so the obligation remained with the governor general in council. The result was a systemic quirk dividing the daily administration of criminal justice, a provincial responsibility, from the duty of remitting sentences and handling capital cases. Despite the awkwardness of this arrangement, the system of petitions, reports, and departmental review worked tolerably well while reflecting, with some distortion, the contemporary doubts and expectations about crime and the effectiveness of punishment. Given the mechanics of remissions and pardons and the individualistic character of capital cases, the department's oversight of the prerogative could not be credited with ensuring greater justice or equity in these appeals. Rather, the department's involvement was, in its most basic element, another manifestation of the ideology of law and the allied notion that its practitioners were apolitical and necessary.

What is so striking about the means whereby the prerogative was managed is the almost complete absence of an explanatory philosophy for making these decisions. Indeed, beyond the bland assertion that criminals were bad and deserved punishment, there was little apparent effort to justify the department's method other than drawing on the basic fiction that it was best suited for the task. Although wardens and penitentiary inspectors wrote of reformation, there was little apparent agreement as to what such notions constituted or whether the basic idea enjoyed widespread currency at all. Essentially, not only was the department's claim to special insight fictive, but there was evidently little effort to camouflage the ruse. One possible explanation, of which more will be said in the chapter that follows, is that the administration of penitentiaries was primarily constructed to depict a national system rather than to effect a coherent set of ideas as to what that system was supposed to accomplish. Arguably, the appearance that these cases were being dealt with by a process was more important than a substantive indication of how and why the process functioned in the way it did.

The absence of a clearly articulated explanation of how inmate reform was instilled on the one hand, while ensuring that capital crimes were dealt with justly on the other, did not mean that irrationality or brutal indifference drove the process. Rather, it was easier to perceive a rationale at work, or at least believe one existed, if the results fell within the vaguely defined boundaries of what was generally thought to be right or appropriate at any given time. Even if the result of any particular petition or case was a disappointment, it was possible that subsequent decisions would renew the public's faith in the system. Not surprisingly, therefore, the "justice" meted out reflected the assumptions, biases, and idiosyncrasies of nineteenth-century Canada. As a result, there is a wide array of decisions incorporating beliefs about race, gender-roles, and sexuality that, while offensive to some late-twentieth-century sensibilities, were common stock in the 1860s and 1870s. To have expected anything else would be to require the department and its various ministers to have acted as if they were not in the second half of the nineteenth century. That this was effected under the guise of the government's legal advisors merely provided the enterprise with an element of legitimacy that it might not have otherwise enjoyed.

5
Canadian Penitentiaries and the Rhetoric of Nation, Centralization, and Reform

Ten months after assuming the position of warden at Kingston Penitentiary, John Creighton unburdened himself to Sir John A. Macdonald.[1] Writing more as a close acquaintance than as an official answering to the minister of justice, Creighton expressed his personal doubts of his abilities to act as an effective warden at Canada's foremost penal institution. Although Creighton was troubled by his presumed responsibility for making the five or six hundred inmates happier than they had been previously, at its core his unease reflected that, as warden of Kingston, Creighton was in the middle of a basic disagreement as to the practical and symbolic function of the penitentiary in Canadian society.

On the one side, Sir John A. Macdonald subscribed to a no-nonsense approach to crime and punishment. While dismissing Creighton's anxiety that his personal inexperience was a troubling handicap, the minister of justice was more concerned that the warden's "natural kindness of disposition may lead you to forget that the primary object of the Penitentiary is punishment, and the incidental one, reformation."[2] In this regard, Macdonald's view was in accordance with that held by most late-nineteenth-century Canadians.[3] Rather than endeavouring to increase the happiness of the inmates, Sir John offered a more modest goal of making life within the penitentiary "less miserable."[4] Indeed, Macdonald contended that it was possible to make a prison too comfortable and pointed Creighton to *David Copperfield,* where Charles Dickens detailed what both he and Sir John evidently believed to be the overly solicitous nature of the Model Prison.[5]

While Macdonald emphasized the role of punishment, the directors of penitentiaries perennially stressed prisoner reformation as incarceration's ultimate goal. The directors, and later the inspector of penitentiaries, all acknowledged that while some inmates were "insensible to those softening influences which have the effect of subduing and improving those less callous," most were amenable to institutionally directed reformation within the penitentiary system.[6] Consistent reference to the salutary influences of strict discipline, the beneficial opportunity for remission of sentence through good behaviour, and the positive influence of humane prison officials and guards received emphasis throughout these reports, while punishment was often characterized as a necessary evil. As Creighton reported in 1873, "Severity, degradation, and suffering, consequent on conviction for crime, are to some extent necessary; but the rules which govern this institution enable a convict, by good behaviour, to work himself out of that position in a great measure by good conduct and industry. Thus, by stimulated *self-exertion* and *self-restraint,* he is improved, morally and physically."[7]

This lack of accord was partly a consequence of the distinct responsibilities shouldered by the minister as opposed to the directors or the inspector of penitentiaries.[8] Although the minister, as ultimate authority for Canadian penitentiaries could, and did on occasion, initiate investigations of novel penal theories or techniques, supervision of the penitentiary system was but one aspect of his responsibilities; the press of business imposed practical limitations on his substantive involvement in penal issues.[9] Given these practicalities, the effective administration of penitentiaries fell to the directors and, later, the inspector, whose administrative routine engendered a more optimistic outlook on what these institutions could accomplish. Finally, it is important to remember that the minister remained a political figure obliged to defend his record before the voting public. Possessing a reputation for being hard on the criminal class served obvious and considerable political ends.

The discord was not, however, solely the product of the division of labour in overseeing Canadian penitentiaries. These disagreements were, as David Garland has argued, reflections of the ongoing debate within any community concerning the nature of crime and punishment.[10] Not surprisingly, the argument in Canada pursued a variety of different themes. Some believed that, "Crime must be punished in order to strike terror into those who openly brave the mandates of Justice" whereas others placed greater faith "in the effect produced by the hope of recompense, than by the dread of punishment."[11] Another view offered that, "Perhaps it would not be going too far to assert that the kind and considerate treatment which our convicts receive, and the aids furnished them to become self-respecting, self-reliant and industrious, tends as much to produce a salutary change of heart and disposition, as the harsher discipline" administered under the Irish Crofton penal system.[12] The coexistence of these views within the Canadian penitentiary system is compelling evidence that this fundamental debate was alive and well after 1867.

Not surprisingly, the completion of Confederation neither engendered a singular penal philosophy nor did it provide the means to demonstrate that efforts at institutionalized reformation produced anything more than rhetoric for public consumption. It is hardly surprising, then, that despite the increasingly centralized nature of penitentiary administration after the union of 1867, localism still predominated, as the warden's personal outlook coloured the daily routine at most Canadian penitentiaries until 1900.[13] Given this apparent failure to instill a centralized vision and method on the internal workings of the penitentiaries, the question then remains, What effect, if any, did the Department of Justice have on these institutions?

Rather than detailing the actual method whereby prisoner reformation was to be accomplished, the department created the appearance of a centralized system of penal institutions that, by its mere existence, suggested that a penal philosophy was in place. Or, as W.A. Calder asserts, the Department of Justice was most significant "for its attempt to use administrative means to impose centralized control upon the geographically dispersed and parochial institutions of the system."[14] Regular inspections, wardens and prison officials answerable for the performance of their duties, reports on the operation of the penitentiaries annually presented to Parliament, and the federal government periodically espousing an interest in theories of penology implied that a coherent administration of penitentiaries shaped a reformative reality for inmates. In practice, and despite the mountain of statistics weighing down the annual reports, the department devoted most of its energies to cultivating the appearance of this system, while the actual penal philosophy remained a grab bag of expectations, theories, fears, and wishful thinking, harnessed to the hope that "something" would happen to prisoners upon entering the penitentiary's controlled environment.[15] Or, as David Rothman suggests, "It was too easy to succumb to the belief that incarceration in and of itself would accomplish reform."[16]

This dedication to creating a national penal structure also served the department by effectively absolving it from any responsibility for the inmate environment. By shifting this task to the directors and later the inspector of penitentiaries, as well as to the wardens and guards who were to create an appropriate moral atmosphere within the penitentiaries, the department assumed the credit for a national system supposedly protecting citizens from criminals while avoiding the demands of actually managing the inmate populations. Not coincidentally, this penal structure also symbolized what this new Confederation could provide for its citizens. In effect, the image of a *national* system of penitentiaries was an early demonstration of the freshly minted and broadly conceived relationship between the public and the federal government.[17]

Through the nationalization of penitentiaries, the department confirmed its faith in the Lockian notions underlying the institutionalized approach to punishing and reforming inmates. Essentially, human beings were rational creatures capable of making moral choices shaped by the desirability of pleasure and the avoidance of pain; attributes assumed to exist by those hoping to reform criminals. Therefore, the inmates were "free, rational, responsible and self directed" and, thus, the penal institution was to facilitate what most believed would be a self-directed reformation.[18] Or, as Randall McGowen argues, "The prison had become the inescapable centre for the debate about crime ... The reformers had created the belief that the prison was the right way to deal with criminals, and they had produced a regime for gaining control over the individual, a regime that lent itself to both reformist and retributive interpretations."[19] And by endorsing the institutionalization of punishment, the department not only kept Canada apace with developments in Britain and the United States, but it availed itself of a structure wherein ambiguity as to the means and ends of punishment remained intact, unrecognized, and unquestioned.

This ambiguity, in turn, was the product of a variety of factors. Creating a moral environment for the reformation of criminals proved to be an exceedingly difficult undertaking. When J.M. Ferres assumed responsibility for Kingston Penitentiary, he reported that prison officers not only slept on the job but also that some were intoxicated on duty.[20] A similar charge three years later compelled John Creighton to suspend the penitentiary schoolmaster.[21] As W.A. Calder points out, "There is little reason to assume that the idea of a strong reformative example in staff conduct and character was attained."[22] More importantly, the absence of a genuine commitment to rehabilitation normalized a punitive environment that concentrated on inmate characteristics. As such, penal practice "managed" the convict population while failing to recognize penality as a social institution replicating "a whole web of social relations and cultural meanings."[23] By constituting a national penitentiary system as a manifestation of the new nationality, the department adopted the institutionalized approach to criminal behaviour, without confirming its ability to deliver the desire ends. The appearance of a national system was more important than the results it could actually produce. Consistent with the department's responsibility for those law-associated concerns falling within the federal government's jurisdiction, the notion that it was especially well suited to penitentiary administration was a fiction. Conceived as a natural extension of its mandate as the federal government's legal advisor and thus a product of ideology of law, the department's creation of a national system of penitentiaries administration was more apparent than real. Yet while the demonstrable results of nationalizing the penitentiary system were less impressive than alleged, the project nonetheless represented what Confederation could accomplish. Indeed, the very notion of *national* standards and practices corresponded neatly with the broader undertaking of "imagining" a new dominion and nationality.[24]

In a necessary first step towards creating this impression of a national system, the union act of 1867 gathered the institutions at Kingston, Saint

John, and Halifax, along with the Rockwood Lunatic Asylum, under federal jurisdiction.[25] With the completion of Confederation eleven years later, three new penitentiaries had been established, at St. Vincent de Paul in Quebec, Stoney Mountain in Manitoba, and New Westminster in British Columbia. A fourth would be opened at Dorchester, New Brunswick, in 1880, the same year the penitentiaries at Saint John and Halifax were returned to provincial jurisdiction, as had Rockwood asylum been transferred to Ontario in 1877. In effect, while claims to a national penitentiary system in 1867 referred to a system in name only, the decade of the 1870s witnessed a reordering and sorting out of penal institutions under the mandate of nationalization.

Establishing a Federal Presence

Large-scale alterations aside, much of what occupied the Department of Justice and the minister in the immediate aftermath of Confederation concerned demonstrating federal control over the penitentiaries. This was no small feat. In August 1867, a riot at the Halifax Penitentiary threatened to destroy the facility, compelling Lieutenant Governor Sir W.F. Williams to call out the militia and request the appointment of a new warden and turnkey to impose the rules believed to exist at Kingston Penitentiary.[26] The subsequent investigation revealed the Halifax institution to be on the verge of chaos.[27] Ironically, while Kingston was perceived to be the standard by which all Canadian penitentiaries were to be measured, it too was plagued by difficulties until the early 1870s.

Kingston's warden, D.A.E. MacDonell, harboured a well-founded suspicion of the penitentiaries board whom he, quite rightly, understood to be conspiring to effect his removal.[28] As late as mid-October 1867, there is evidence to suggest that the board, and especially Terence O'Neill and J.M Ferres, was actively working to speed MacDonell's resignation, in the hope that one of them might be appointed in his place. Rumours of MacDonell's pending retirement, a direct invitation from Ferres to MacDonell to step down to protect his pension, newspaper stories from unnamed sources, and the circulation of second- and third-hand reports all poisoned the atmosphere between the warden and the board. Throughout it all, Sir John A. Macdonald was privy to much of what was transpiring, though the degree to which he was involved in the skullduggery is unclear.[29]

In the midst of the hostilities, the first systematic change to the operation of Canadian penitentiaries was introduced, in the form of the new Penitentiaries Act.[30] Passed into law on 22 May 1868 – not coincidentally on the same day that the new Department of Justice came into existence – the Penitentiaries Act was a statute rooted in the pre-Confederation debate over the so-called Crofton system, named for Walter Crofton, chairman of the directors of Irish convict prisons from 1854.[31] This system envisioned an environment where punishment, reform, and deterrence were achieved through incremental discipline and rewards. It was expected that prisoners, in the hope of mitigating their conditions of incarceration and possibly gain early release, would participate in their own reform. Championed by E.A. Meredith, who as a member of the Canadian Board of Inspectors authored an early draft of the Penitentiaries act, the Crofton system remained an ever present, if incompletely realized aspect of the Canadian penal structure.[32]

Meredith's enthusiasm for Crofton's notions ensured that the Penitentiaries Act contained aspects of the Irish plan. Prisoners were allowed to earn gratuities for overtime labour, facilities to implement solitary confinement were created, and a strict record of each prisoner's activities, rewards, and punishments were to be kept by the wardens. However, arriving as it did in the midst of MacDonell's conflict with the board, the act's centralizing tone appeared as a rebuke to the Kingston warden. Perceiving such ill intent, MacDonell complained to Sir John six weeks before the legislation passed into law, pointing out that the proposed bill provided the board with even greater authority than had the 1849 Brown Commission and that the warden would no longer sit as a member of the board when it convened at the Kingston penitentiary.[33] While there is little question that the friction between MacDonell and the board coloured the 1868 act, its tone was directly attributable to the Crofton system. The emergent preference for a centralized system of prison management theoretically left little room for the inclinations of individual wardens.[34]

Despite Meredith's hand in shaping the 1868 legislation, the Crofton system was never fully implemented as a guiding philosophy for Canadian penitentiaries. The absence of official sanction by imperial authorities, the popularity of more punitive methods, public concern with the early release of inmates, the cost of constructing appropriate facilities, and resistance to the expenditure of public funds for the so-called criminal class all mitigated against the Crofton system. It is also certain that while the minister of justice was prepared to have Meredith play a role in drafting the new Penitentiaries Act, Macdonald's later correspondence with John Creighton documents the minister's scepticism concerning prisoner reformation under the Crofton system.

The Penitentiaries Act of 1868 and the reformulation of the board of directors to oversee penal policy in Canada failed to end the problems at Kingston or establish a clear program of prisoner management. MacDonell's eventual resignation after twenty-one years of service as warden merely created new friction when James Moylan, who eventually became inspector of penitentiaries, protested that he had not been named MacDonell's replacement. In voicing his displeasure, Moylan warned of dire circumstances from the Irish Canadian electorate.[35] Even worse was the fact that when J.M. Ferres did assume control from the well-liked MacDonell at Kingston on 20 May 1869, the new warden discovered a hostile and chaotic environment functioning without system or reformative philosophy.[36] By early February 1870, exasperation with the state of affairs began to show as Ferres described to Hewitt Bernard the condition of the penitentiary's books: "When Inspector and Director I was, in common with my colleagues, aware that these Books were in a bad state and time after time the attention of the then Warden was called to it, without producing any effect; but I confess I had no idea of the enormous mass of errors, which the examination of them, after my entering on my present duties, exposed."[37] Having alienated much of his staff through his own zealousness, Ferres soon became subjected to rumours and allegations concerning his conduct as warden, but before he could mount a defence, his health collapsed and he died on 21 April 1870.[38]

Filling the warden's office at Kingston with John Creighton after Ferres died marked a subtle departure from previous practice. Creighton's credentials included a life-long friendship with John A. Macdonald and varied careers as a publisher, municipal politician, and police magistrate.[39] In effect, he was an outsider from the small circle of penal reformers in Canada. Fully cognizant that he did not possess Ferres' practical experience or knowledge of penal theory, simple humanitarianism and a desire to be fair with guards, officers, and inmates shaped Creighton's approach.[40] Recorded in the warden's daily journal, a version of Creighton's inaugural address to the inmates sought "God's help to exercise a kindly moral influence amongst them, and use my best exertions to promote their comfort and happiness. That to attain success in that direction they must all aid me, and that the best way to render me assistance was to obey the Rules of the Prison and those who were placed over them that they should do this from principle – not from fear or dread of punishment."[41] Guided more by a personal notion of common sense than by a penal philosophy, the outsider Creighton finally provided the national penitentiary system with stable leadership at its pre-eminent penal institution. By the time of his death in 1884, Creighton had become the model warden for all Canadian penitentiaries.

Settling affairs at Kingston under Creighton's leadership was effected at the same time that the department asserted control over the Maritime penitentiaries. As had been the case at Kingston, the warden's office at both Saint John and Halifax required attention. Although the well-experienced John Quinton administered Saint John Penitentiary, during his twenty-seven years in office, he had never been called upon to provide an annual report.[42] One of the first orders of business was to place Quinton in full control of all aspects of the institution and thus render him accountable for the penitentiary's operation.[43] Quinton proved equal to the task and continued as warden until his retirement on 31 October 1874, when Charles Kitchum replaced him.[44] Circumstances at Halifax were certainly no better, for while order had been reestablished after the riot in August 1867, warden George MacGregor had since died, leaving the penitentiary in the hands "of a young man named Stamper" whose effectiveness was rather limited.[45] Wielding the authority provided by the Penitentiaries Act, the directors placed guard Charles Ross in control of the institution and established the rules by which it would be governed.[46] Ross continued as acting warden until Robert Dunkin assumed the office on 4 November 1870 who, in turn, resigned in favour of John Flinn on 30 June 1875.[47]

The arrival of a new warden provides an intriguing view of how these individuals articulated their respective approaches to punishment and rehabilitation. Wardens were seemingly guided by practical concerns such as the quality of the physical surroundings within the penitentiary, establishing order and discipline (usually by keeping the inmates as busy as possible), and the challenge of administering the institution without losing too much money. Thus, when Dunkin assumed control of Halifax Penitentiary in early November 1870, he reportedly addressed the inmates in stating that he:

> would do all in my power to alleviate their condition as much as possible; that they would always find me of easy access, and ever ready to give patient heed to any reasonable complaints; and that I would think it not only a duty, but a pleasure to contribute to their comforts, as far as the rules of the prison would allow; but I reminded them, at the same time, how much lay in their own power in bringing about this happy state of things, as all depended on how they conducted themselves; for whilst I would encourage, to my utmost, the well-behaved and industrious man, I would as certainly punish, with due severity, the idle and incorrigible offender.[48]

While the influence of the Crofton system can be discerned in Dunkin's statement, his approach was also founded in a desire to establish a reciprocal relationship with his charges. This reciprocity would allow him to administer the penitentiary, while encouraging the inmates to serve out their time as pleasantly as the circumstances permitted. Punishment would be the result of a prisoner's individual failing and not, it was asserted, the whim of guards, the keeper, or the warden.

One year after Dunkin assumed his responsibilities at Halifax, John Creighton initiated his career as the warden at Kingston. Like Dunkin, Creighton addressed the assembled inmates in terms strikingly similar to those employed by his colleague at Halifax:

> I introduced myself to the convicts, and briefly assured them that I would endeavour, by God's help, to exercise a kindly moral influence amongst them, and use my best exertions to promote their comfort and improvement. That, in order to obtain any degree of success in that direction, they must all aid me, and that the best way to render me assistance was to obey the rules of the prison, and those who were placed over them; that they should do this from principle, not from fear of punishment. That I hoped the keeper and guards would treat them fairly, and that the most insignificant convict in the prison would obtain justice at my hands, and always find me ready to redress any real grievance.[49]

Obviously, both wardens were drawing from the same well in their efforts to create workable environments within their institutions. And, in so doing, they placed much of the responsibility for the atmosphere within their penitentiaries squarely upon the inmates. The unmistakable message may well have been consistent with the Crofton system but it was more fundamentally grounded in Christian thought: reap what you shall sow.[50]

This theme in addressing the inmates was continued with the establishment of St. Vincent de Paul Penitentiary when it opened in May 1873. After giving both the staff and prisoners a few days to settle into their new environs, warden F.Z. Tassé encouraged his charges to respect the rules and to act in a polite manner to each other and to the various officials. He then reportedly added that, "There lay within their reach, in accord with what I had just said, efficient means for their rendering prison life as pleasant as possible, even while acting in conformity with the laws which regulated the administration of this great establishment."[51] This, however, would be the last occasion for such an address being recorded. When Charles Kitchum replaced John Quinton, he not did report delivering such an oration, nor did J.A. Ducheseau when he replaced the ailing Tassé, at St. Vincent de Paul on 15 December 1875. And when John Flinn assumed the warden's office at Halifax upon the departure of Robert Dunkin on 1 July 1875, the new warden confined his remarks to pointing out to the prisoners "the particular relationship we bore to each other, and what they had to expect in regard to either reward or punishment, according to their conduct."[52] No such addresses were reported from either Stoney Mountain in Manitoba or from the British Columbia penitentiary once those institutions were established.

The existence and then disappearance of these orations raise a number of questions. Although the wardens evidently delivered these exhortations to their respective inmate populations, it is equally clear that the keepers, guards, directors, the minister of justice, and, by extension, Parliament were also intended audiences. It is also certain that the wardens were, in a fashion, also part of the audience. After all, everyone associated with the penitentiary system needed to be reassured or, perhaps, convinced that providing inmates with the means to shape the nature of their individual terms within a setting characterized by firm but gentle guidance from the warden was an effective means of prisoner rehabilitation. Delivering this message was both an effort to educate prisoners as to how they were to behave and an occasion for the warden to demonstrate that he was, indeed, a modern official whose view of the penitentiary was not grounded wholly or even partly in retributive brutality.

Articulating this message for such a varied constituency was not without its difficulties. Even a cursory review of conditions in Canadian penitentiaries before 1900 documents that allusions to creating an environment of moral rehabilitation, in which inmates were encouraged to take personal responsibility, were without substance. The penitentiary remained a highly regulated and ritualized setting in which prisoners were tutored in unobtrusive obedience in pursuit of early release.[53] As a result, while these orations in the early 1870s were ostensibly directed at the inmates, the physical and psychological surroundings of the penitentiary undoubtedly spoke with greater authority. The same can be said of how these conflicting messages were received by the keepers and guards. While wardens expressed the wishful hope that prison officials would be even-handed with their charges, the daily routine of prison life created a distinctly different reality. Keepers and guards were no more likely to symbolize moral order than would the highly structured pattern of penitentiary life encourage individual responsibility.

If the inmates and guards were not the primary audience for the wardens' orations, preserving these speeches in the annual reports served a wholly different function. By outlining the reciprocity that supposedly existed between the warden and his inmates, these speeches articulated an approach towards prisoner rehabilitation that reified the relationship between the central government, the general public, and the convicts. These reports provided tangible evidence that through the centralization of penitentiaries and the imposition of a reformative regime within prison walls, the newly minted federal government was protecting the public and transforming inmates into responsible and law-abiding citizens. That the reality of convict life fell short of the ideals articulated by the wardens was relatively unimportant in comparison with the necessity of portraying the varied relationships at play.

Given their importance in sustaining a particular vision of what penitentiaries did, why then did these orations disappear from the annual reports? Part of the answer rests in the changes introduced in 1875 by the new Penitentiaries Act.[54] The Penitentiaries Act of 1868 had concentrated administrative authority for prisons with the three appointed directors; the minister of justice was not even mentioned in the legislation. As such, in composing their reports, the wardens felt it necessary to provide statements of principles to the directors, with whom rested the practical authority for administering these institutions. The act of 1875 significantly altered this relationship. Not only did the new legislation specify that the minister of justice exercise "complete administrative power" over Canadian penitentiaries, but the act made the inspector answerable to the minister for the operation of those institutions.[55] While the 1868 act centralized decision-making authority in the directors, the 1875 act shifted responsibility to the inspector and, ultimately, to the minister. Although individual wardens would continue to be crucial figures in shaping the reality of the inmate experience, they no longer took it upon themselves to situate that reality within the broader penological debate.

This shift also affected the content of these reports. The 1875 legislation directed the inspector to provide the minister of justice with a statistical representation of the penitentiaries in operation.[56] While similar data had always played an important function, the new emphasis accorded statistics greater weight than wardens' narratives in depicting the workings of the penitentiary system. Not only did statistics appear more scientific and thus provide the entire system with that veneer, but they offered a higher order of proof in demonstrating the efficiencies of the penitentiary system while reducing crime and punishment into orderly tables and ledgers.[57] Shorn of its human element, the statistics of crime, criminals, punishment, and rehabilitation became manageable; an abstraction that the federally created penitentiary system could control and manipulate. The last thing this system required was wardens' orations reminding listeners and readers of the resolute human reality entailing the inmate experience.

Rhetoric and Reality

Not surprisingly and parallel to these changes within the penitentiary system, there was growing disenchantment with the difficulties of matching practical demands of penitentiary management with theoretical positions on rehabilitation and punishment. While John Creighton, for one, had embraced notions from the Crofton system when he assumed control of Kingston, by 1874 he was expressing grave doubts as to the wisdom of its attendant practice of providing money compensation to prisoners for extra work.[58] Writing to J.G. Moylan, Creighton's scepticism was all too clear: "The gratuity system was introduced as an experiment, borrowed, I suppose, from some philanthropic Prison Reformer. My *practical* experience, however, is that giving any considerable sum of money to a convict on his discharge is so much money thrown away."[59] Indeed, as Moylan observed one year later, while "many writers have furnished theories upon prison discipline and management, very plausible and interesting, but, for the most part, it is found by experience, that the views advanced and the rules set down are, so to speak, local in their tendency and pre-suppose a certain condition of things not always attainable."[60]

The tone of both Creighton's and Moylan's observations is instructive. Both men, the warden of the nation's preeminent penal institution and, the other, the eventual inspector of penitentiaries, harboured unmistakable antagonism towards the supposed supremacy of theory over actual practice in prison management. They were not alone in this view. In his report for 1872, John Quinton of Saint John Penitentiary offered that, "All the fine-spun theories [on prisoner reform] ... divested of verbosity, whittled down to the pith, disclose there but this simple fact after all – that prisoners are men, very much like their brethren in the great mass outside of the prison walls; and to make the best use of them when under restraint, is to treat them as men."[61] Adopting a similar tone and summarizing the state of affairs in Kingston of June 1877, Creighton asserted that, "[It is] unnecessary for me to theorise on the best mode of managing criminals, about which there is very great diversity of opinion. Practical experience and a conscientious and fearless discharge of duty are the best monitors."[62] Or as Moylan observed about those advocating the Crofton system, too often they "will speak as authoritatively, nay, dogmatically on the Crofton or any other system, as if they had been charged with its working for half a lifetime. It will scarcely be credited that some who dogmatize so flippantly on penal systems, have never had an hour's practical experience of their working."[63]

One source of this antagonism was the inability to effectively introduce some of the most basic tenets of prisoner management in Canadian penitentiaries. Overcrowding was a perennial problem at every central and eastern Canadian institution during the eleven years after Confederation. At St. Vincent de Paul, a penitentiary wracked by problems from its inception, it was reported in 1874 that because of severe space shortages, prisoners were sleeping in the corridors.[64] Such melancholy conditions were reported constantly at Saint John, where overcrowding was a concern in 1878, as it had been during every report during the previous six years.[65] Parallel to worries over the number of convicts was the fact that the failure to classify inmates rendered any attempt at rehabilitation unlikely. Described as an "evil" practice allowing "bad men to pollute and degrade their better-inclined fellows" and thus turn penitentiaries into "nurseries of crime," housing long-term prisoners with those serving sentences less than two years was roundly denounced but rarely addressed.[66] While this "system of herding together convicts and short-sentenced prisoners" was especially evident at Saint John and Halifax, only with the establishment of the Central Prison in Toronto did the problem cease to exist at Kingston.[67]

The disappearance of the wardens' exhortations from the annual reports was, therefore, the result of a number of factors. While these individual and collective voices no longer occupied this particular role in the reports, the attempt to place Canadian penal practice in the broader international stream continued nonetheless. After 1875, the responsibility for creating these narratives fell to the inspector of penitentiaries who, as James Moylan admitted, did not have "daily contact with the officers and prisoners."[68] By centralizing penitentiary management in the inspector and the minister of justice and, as a consequence, away from the wardens, the daily conditions of the inmate experience became less important in the overall task of depicting how the system supposedly functioned. In fact, portraying the system as one befitting the entire nation and thus reinforcing the broadly conceived relationship between the general public and the federal government was an end in itself and emerged as the predominant task, as opposed to detailing what was actually accomplished within the nation's prisons.

As this portrait of the Canadian penal system developed during the 1870s, it assumed a number of themes, some of which were contradictory. Not surprisingly in the aftermath of union, one characteristic concentrated on the degree to which Canadian penal practice would chart its own course or echo that set in the United States. There is no question that Canadian officials looked to American prisons for object lessons in what might be effected and avoided. John Creighton used two weeks' holiday leave in 1872 to tour "half a dozen of the more important penitentiaries in the United States."[69] Embracing a none-too-subtle nationalistic aside, James Moylan reported in 1875 that the "occasional inspection" of American facilities provided valuable exposure to different conditions: "By this means our Penitentiary system, though second to none, as already stated, could be still further improved, and the officer making such comparative examination would be rendered more competent to meet the requirements of his position."[70] This goal compelled Moylan to travel to Boston one year later to investigate the plans for the proposed state prison at Concord, at the same time that plans for the new penitentiary at Dorchester were being finalized.[71]

While visits to American penitentiaries were hailed as valuable undertakings, the nascent nationalism revealed in Moylan's assertion was echoed as other Canadians downplayed what could actually be learned. Creighton's tour in 1872 left him unimpressed with what he witnessed. His conclusions were, in a fashion, confirmed that year when prison reformer, Mary Carpenter, spoke in glowing terms of Kingston's inmate population.[72] In his report for 1876, Inspector Moylan thanked Minister of Justice Edward Blake for soliciting a number of reports from American institutions, while dismissing them as "very meagre information of a profitable or practical nature." From Moylan's point of view, visiting American penitentiaries, and especially that one located at Columbus, Ohio, where he could witness its system in action, would be far more beneficial.[73] Two years later, Moylan was again advocating an official visit to American penitentiaries so as to explore those facilities "which have attained celebrity on account of their superior management." At the same time, he reassured the minister that Canadian institutions were still "administered with a commendable degree of zeal and efficiency."[74]

Parallel to the question of American influence and Canadian distinctiveness was the often-tortured debate over the degree to which Canada was in tune with international practice, and especially the Crofton system. One of Moylan's first orders of business as inspector was to assert that with the exception of Crofton, there was "no better system of administration of convict prisons that our own."[75] Perhaps in an effort to press this point further, the 1877 report contained an energetic examination of the Crofton system and its applicability to Canada. Acknowledging that while conditions in the various Canadian institutions had never allowed for the full implementation of the Crofton method, it had been effected "as fully as practicable."[76] Reasons for the incomplete introduction included the cost of building appropriate facilities, especially in light of the then-current economic depression, and the unresolved question of the overall appropriateness of the methods employed under Crofton.

Specifically, Moylan questioned whether the Crofton system was better suited for a region such as Ireland where, he believed, poverty drove many to a life of crime. Such conditions, Moylan offered, did not exist in Canada, where some men and women consciously turned to crime, no matter how irrational the choice. Further, in Canada, where everyone enjoyed liberty and freedom of movement, any amount of confinement, solitary or otherwise, was sure to have a more profound effect than in Ireland, which was, in a manner of speaking, less free. As a result, the phase of solitary confinement at the onset of the Crofton system was unnecessary in Canada. Second, because Canadian inmates were well fed and clothed, they were more amenable to reformation than if conditions were harsh. Farsighted in its approach, the Canadian method acknowledged that most inmates would eventually reenter society. It was poor economy, Moylan opined, to believe that men or women broken in prison could support themselves or their families: "Does the criminal with shattered health and wasted frame, emerge from his prison house a better, a reformed man? Or does he not go forth breathing vengeance, deep and bitter, against the laws and society which subjected him to usage all but inhuman?"[77] Cast in these terms, Moylan declared that, "After much reflection upon the relative merits of the Crofton and our own system, I have reached the conclusion that the former is admirably adapted to the condition of things in Ireland; while the latter is suited to Canada, and, for the reasons stated, is as good as can be looked for, under existing circumstances."[78]

Allied to this examination of Crofton was Moylan's concern with Canada's nonparticipation in international meetings at which penal policy and penitentiary governance were discussed. The complaint was an old one and dated back to 1869 when E.C. Wines, of the Prison Association of New York, invited Canada to send a representative to an international congress on criminal law reform and prison discipline. At the time, Sir John A. Macdonald recommended a representative be sent.[79] Perhaps expecting substantive Canadian involvement, on 9 March 1870, Wines forwarded a copy of the proceedings of an organizational committee meeting from the previous month.[80] Upon realizing that the Canadian Department of Justice was less eager than expected, Wines suggested that E.A. Meredith represent Canada at the National Congress on Penitentiary and Reformatory Discipline to be held in Cincinnati from 12 October to 18 October 1870.[81] This group eventually formed the National Prison Association in the United States.[82] When the first international Penitentiary Congress was organized and scheduled for London in 1872, Sir John did not want the Dominion to incur any expenses and thus no representative was sent.[83] The absence was reportedly conspicuous, since "even Mexico" had sent an official delegate. "In a matter of so much importance, the nonrepresentation of Canada at the London Congress, must be attributed to oversight, or if the matter were considered at all, to a policy of false economy."[84]

Reflecting on Canada's noninvolvement five years later, Moylan thought it useful to meet and discuss penology and, more importantly, to observe practices employed in other jurisdictions. Despite these entreaties, the Department of Justice remained unwilling to finance a delegate. Undeterred, Moylan renewed his efforts in the aftermath of Canada missing the Stockholm Congress in 1878. Claiming that elsewhere it was "the custom of the official appointed by the Government of each State to direct the administration of penal prisons to visit periodically other like institutions, outside the limits of their own jurisdictions," the inspector asked, "Would it not be worth while to make the same experiment in Canada?"[85] Not until the National Prison Association held its annual meeting in Toronto in September 1887 did Canada finally become involved in international discussions.[86]

Yet another aspect of this portrait concerned the unresolved question of whether the system was primarily concerned with punishing or reforming the inmate. This, of course, was the core issue that underlay John Creighton's introspective letter to Sir John A. Macdonald. Unfortunately for Creighton, this dilemma was never truly settled. Sir John believed that punishment was the primary concern while Creighton aspired to effect reform and rehabilitation. And as long as advocacy of Crofton methods remained a rhetorical aspect of Canadian penal practice, the system echoed those reformatory notions. For example, the directors' report for 1872 spoke in glowing terms of how the system of rewards and gratuities, adopted from Crofton, produced "most beneficial results" at Kingston.[87] However, as I have already argued, the passage of time and the failure to effect the organizational and physical changes needed to implement Crofton gave rise to disenchantment and thinly veiled scepticism for theories unattached to practical methods.

The tension became especially apparent after 1875 and Moylan's ascendancy to the inspectorate. In his first report, Moylan argued that an effective penal system was reflected in deterring crime while reformation of inmates was an object to which "we are bound to give our most earnest attention."[88] He did not explain how this precarious balance was to be achieved and, perhaps in accord with the straitened financial times, later added that effecting the means whereby prisoners recoup the cost of their maintenance was also important.[89] In the same report, Moylan then shifted his position in stating that "prisoners are sentenced to undergo punishment" and that it was the duty of prison officials to "reform as well as to punish."[90] The degree to which Moylan was consciously ordering these supposed goals is unclear, but the tension between reformation and punishment remained, to say nothing of the added complication of having the penitentiary system pay for itself.

Revisiting his views a year later, Moylan claimed that, "The sentence that consigns a criminal to the penitentiary including hard labour, which, though technically penal, is really industrial in character."[91] Adopting renewed enthusiasm in his report for 1877, the inspector reasserted the primacy of reformation and described it as "the cardinal object to be effected in our penal institutions" and that it is "above and beyond every consideration."[92] Putting aside Moylan's somewhat inconsistent advocacy for prisoner reformation, the problem remained that punitive conditions within Canadian penitentiaries spoke with greater authority than did the inspector. While these institutions were less than barbaric, they were still harsh, ritualized environments in which surviving with one's physical and mental health intact was an achievement in of itself. Essentially, the rhetoric of rehabilitation and reformation was for outside consumption to reassure the general public that the federal government was looking out after the new nation's best interests.

The advocacy of system, uniformity, and national standards was the final theme constituting the Canadian penal system as it existed by the late 1870s. Although the acts of 1868 and 1875 effected different ends, their symbolic contribution reconfirmed that the administration of Canadian penitentiaries was to be systematic and that it conformed to a uniform national standard. Akin to the growing reliance on statistics to demonstrate the method of prisoner reformation, allusions to centralization suggested that the penal system harnessed "its resources in the manner which it considers most rational and efficient."[93] Not surprisingly, introducing and articulating the substance of such a standard, in concert with its corresponding rhetoric, was a gradual affair. As such, the directors' report for 1871 looked forward to the day when the Maritime penitentiaries would be brought into uniformity with the rest of the Dominion or, if the truth were told, in line with Kingston Penitentiary.[94] The same expectation was held out for Manitoba and British Columbia, where the inspectors predicted that, "Doubtless the Department of Justice will, ere long, make provision for the introduction of the system which has been found so beneficial in the other Provinces of the Dominion."[95] By Moylan's first report as inspector, the system had been introduced or at least it had made its presence felt: "During the period which has elapsed since (at the time of Confederation) the penitentiaries were brought under a uniform plan of management" in which the "Minister of Justice is the supreme head."[96] This supposed uniformity was demonstrated in one instance by the introduction of the system of gratuities and good conduct marks at Halifax in 1875 admittedly long after it had been implemented elsewhere.[97]

Rhetoric aside, Canadian geography and the persistence of lingering localism mitigated against seamless centralization. Even fairly mundane managerial practice such as forwarding accounts through the Department of Justice in Ottawa before being paid out at Manitoba was not yet established routine in 1875.[98] Obviously, the warden retained a great deal of autonomy, even after the increased centralization of the 1875 legislation, since inspections were reduced for reasons of economy. Reminiscent of the challenge faced by the Department of Justice in managing crises far removed from the capital, the best that could be hoped was that wardens at distant penitentiaries acted wisely and that most difficulties would, in a fashion, solve themselves. Such situations proved to be unavoidable and thus unsettling, for, as Moylan wrote of the situation of Stoney Mountain, "The great distance of this Penitentiary from the centre of Administration, and from the source of the advice and information which must be sometimes required, cannot but prove embarrassing to the Warden."[99] Potentially embarrassing to the warden perhaps but also threatening to the rhetoric of system and the symbolic function it served.

The Veneer of Centralization

Although these themes detailing Canadian penal practice during the completion of Confederation were sometimes contradictory, this rhetoric of centralization and uniformity was especially ambiguous. It was not that the advocates of centralization did not believe in the undertaking but that their intended meaning was probably less grandiose than initial impressions might suggest. Specifically, it was possible to extol the virtues of centralization while still expecting that the daily administration of business at the penitentiaries would remain chiefly in the warden's hands. Indeed, heralding centralization and uniformity did not necessarily define exactly what was being made uniform and centralized. W.A. Calder's dissertation on the Canadian penitentiary system from 1867 to 1899 demonstrates that the administrative and financial relationship between Ottawa and the various penitentiaries grew to be controlled and directed from the centre by the close of the century. The management of penitentiaries as part of the institutional structure of the federal government came to be, not surprisingly, governed from the capital. This, of course, is wholly consistent with the argument that the Department of Justice was primarily concerned with creating a system of penitentiary administration. Or, perhaps more accurately, the appearance of such a system. Calder's research also documents the almost complete failure to impose a national scheme of prisoner rehabilitation and reform in Canadian penitentiaries, in large part, I would argue, because of the indifference on the part of the Department of Justice. For capital-bound bureaucrats, their concern was with the institutional relationship between the penitentiaries and Ottawa, not with the management of their respective inmate populations. After all, to the extent that the department was established in support of the federal government's legal advisor, forays into the details of prisoner management would be an unproductive departure from more pressing responsibilities. Running the penitentiaries could be left to the inspector and the wardens.

Further, given the realities of communication and transportation during the eleven years after Confederation, one would be hard pressed to argue that control from the centre was possible, let alone unifying, efficient, or effective. Filing reports, keeping accounts, and letting contracts in the proscribed fashion were activities to be dictated from the centre; handling the inmate population required an immediate presence that simply was not possible from Ottawa. If in England of the 1870s, "ties of familiarity and sentiment between local officials and their prisoners" worked against the uniformity and centralization of a national penitentiary system, one could hardly expect different results in the more expansive Canadian nation.[100] This practical brake on centralization undoubtedly fed into the lingering localism that Calder has also identified.

Therefore, just like the language of prisoner rehabilitation, the reality behind the rhetoric of nationalizing the penitentiary system was less expansive than initial impressions suggest. While neither commitment achieved complete success, they nonetheless created an impression that was significantly greater than the sum of their parts. Nationalizing the penitentiaries sprung from arguments that championed greater efficiency, national standards, and uniformity. It also resonated with the nascent relationship between the new federal government and the citizenry of this new nation. The rhetoric of this national system, extolling theories and methods of prisoner reform, reinforced the sense that these changes, in the wake of Confederation, rendered the new dominion a safer place for all citizens. Admittedly, left unconnected, neither the language of centralization nor that of prisoner rehabilitation could sustain prolonged scrutiny. But together, like the other fictions swirling about the Department of Justice, they assumed a veneer of credibility in the aftermath of union.

By the completion of Confederation in 1878, the administration of Canadian penitentiaries had been structurally reorganized while being exposed to the push and pull of the intellectual and practical demands of prisoner reform. For its part, the Department of Justice had participated begrudgingly in discussions of rehabilitation and sought instead to dedicate its energy to constructing a system of penitentiaries befitting the new dominion. Or, more specifically, to creating a system that promoted "a particular image of the state and of its authority, and of its relationship to offenders and other citizens."[101]

To return, then, to John Creighton's missive to Sir John A. Macdonald in late October 1871. In light of what transpired between 1867 and 1878, it appears as if the old friends were talking about two distinctly different things when the warden questioned his suitability for the post he occupied. Creighton, having found himself in the midst of Canada's foremost penal institution, was practically and symbolically immersed in the debates of reformation, punishment, and rehabilitation. Surrounded by the walls of Kingston, he could not but help to see his immediate challenge as one completely imbued with the prisoner population. Creighton's was an inmate-management problem. For his part, Sir John was untroubled by the realities of the prison population and could concentrate on how the actual existence of that collection of humanity reflected his broader project, that of forging a new dominion. The solution to Creighton's self-doubt was, aside from the demands of friendship, significantly less important in Macdonald's mind than was the fact that the warden's concern reflected the federal government at work. That any warden of a federally supervised penitentiary would voice concerns about his own effectiveness not only implied the existence of a standard by which his performance would be measured but, more generally, that Kingston, and indeed the entire penal structure, *would* be effective, and *would* serve national interests. In effect, just as the wardens' exhortations to the various inmate populations attempted to create a reciprocal relationship while addressing a much broader audience on a variety of levels, the department's effort to create a national penitentiary system was as much about envisioning and constructing a nation of new relationships and obligations as it was about crime, punishment, and reformation.

6
The Department of Justice and the Judiciary

Of all the relationships and responsibilities involving the Department of Justice, few were more complicated and intriguing than that with members of the bench. After all, the core assumption underpinning the notion of an attorney general was the assertion that law and its practitioners were apolitical and able to provide legal counsel without the taint of politics. The judiciary, as the pinnacle of the legal profession, was also cast in this light and, therefore, elevation to the bench was to be based upon professional qualification and not partisan advantage or favour. This, at least, was the argument as it was framed by the ideology of law.

Similar notions shaped expectations as to the role that the judiciary should play within the Canadian legal and political world. Many mid- and late-nineteenth-century observers adhered to what J.A.G. Griffiths describes as the traditional view of the judiciary's function – one concerned with deciding disputes "in accordance with the law and with impartiality." And in this sense, impartiality meant "not merely an absence of personal bias or prejudice in the judge but also the exclusion of 'irrelevant' considerations such as his political or religious views."[1] Others contended that the judiciary was "one of the principal organs of a democratic society without whom government could be carried on only with great difficulty. The essence of their function is the maintenance of law and order and the judges are seen as a mediating influence."[2] Whether perceived as impartial arbiters or restrained but active forces of mediation, most expected that the judiciary would remain above the cut and thrust of partisan life.

Translating these expectations into practice in the aftermath of the union of 1867 was, like much of what the Department of Justice shouldered, an inexact art of statecraft. Commenting upon the situation he discerned in post-Confederation New Brunswick, David Bell succinctly identifies an environment existing throughout the new dominion: "Late

19th-century judges were victims of their time. It was their misfortune to be the first generation of conspicuously partisan appointees to the bench. They were called on, for the first time in our legal tradition, to make necessarily controversial pronouncements in the constitutional field, and to resolve election disputes under a federal franchise law that positively invited partisan suspicions."[3] Drawn against such a setting, almost any judicial appointment could be suspect and any ruling exposed to political critique. As a consequence, selecting candidates for the bench required a subtle touch, capable of gauging the legal, social, and intellectual measure of potential candidates, in concert with a broadly construed sense of their individual inclinations and repute. Essentially, "all the troubles of judge making" were, indeed, very political.[4] And, as events revealed, no occasion presented the Department of Justice with a greater challenge than the creation and staffing of the Canadian Supreme Court in the latter half of 1875. For while it had been envisioned by John A. Macdonald as yet another stay in his centralized structure of Confederation, the Court was brought to life by Alexander Mackenzie's Liberals, who believed that an autonomous Supreme Court was the birthright of a new nation.[5] Neither aspiration was to survive the completion of Confederation.

For the denizens of the Department of Justice, managing relations with aspirants to the bench, their supporters, and sitting judges involved navigating a course between partisanship, the politics of public appointments, professional qualification, and the sensibilities of those schooled in the law. As such, portraying judicial appointments and relations with the judiciary as simple matters of partisanship badly distorts the difficulties involved. And despite the notion that, as the government's legal advisor, the minister of justice and, more practically, the Department of Justice were especially well placed to manage these relations because the law and its practitioners were involved, the attribution was rarely reflected in the daily tasks of dealing with members of the bench. Indeed, to that extent, the substance of its involvement with the judiciary is yet another manifestation of how the ideology of law shaped both the reality and fiction of the department's responsibilities as the government legal advisor.

Relations with the Bench

Contact between the Department of Justice and sitting judges or aspirants to the bench assumed two general forms: official communication and private personal correspondence. The first category included all manner of administrative business, including dealing with entreaties soliciting a judicial appointment or promotion, requests for leave, applications for temporary replacements or assistance, queries concerning travelling expenses and salaries, submissions of trial notes in capital cases, and inquiries about retirement options. These communications were typically routed through the secretary of state and dispensed with varying degrees of ease, depending on the personalities and substantive issues involved. Much of this correspondence was handled by the deputy minister of justice or the chief clerk, though there were inevitably cases requiring the minister of justice to intercede, usually because the judge or the applicant to the bench was especially bumptious. The latter included occasions such as the exhausting four-year struggle to compel Quebec judge Peter Winter to take up official residence at Percé on the Gaspé Peninsula, or the complicated manoeuvrings surrounding Judge Samuel Cornwallis Monk's application for leave in the midst of the attempted renovation of the Quebec bench.[6]

The second category of communication, that of private correspondence addressed directly to the minister, often involved the potentially volatile mixture of official business with expectations of personal consideration or obligation. Rooted in a political setting where favours and concessions were traded with alacrity, these private entreaties and not so subtle reminders of thinly veiled obligations were a constant reminder of the confluence of law and politics in Canadian public life.[7] The authors of these letters often learned, however, that despite having secured promises and commitments from public figures in pursuit of support on the hustings, obtaining satisfaction after the contest had been won was an entirely different matter. It was not that party leaders routinely failed to honour promises but, rather, that in the settling of affairs, there was an inevitable sorting out and ordering of obligations. This fact of political life was a hard lesson for J.W. Carmichael, who, after forwarding his recommendation that James Fogo be appointed to the vacant judgeship for Pictou and Cumberland county in Nova Scotia on 31 March 1876, was passed over in favour of the Halifax-based interests of A.G. Jones.[8] The promised "right" to advise on an appointment was no guarantee that such advice would rank above other more pressing and, perhaps, more valued commitments.

This private correspondence was not limited to that directed at the minister in search of favour or consideration. Private and confidential communication between the minister of justice and sitting judges was also penned at Ottawa, though the contact was often more circuitous in its delivery. John A. Macdonald's attempt to reach Judge William Badgley of Quebec's Superior Court, for example, was delivered by a number of intermediaries; the Honourable J.J.C. Abbott, Judge J.A. Berthelot, and George-E. Cartier.[9] The effort eventually proved successful, and Badgley, citing declining health, resigned from the bench and escaped escalating public criticism directed at Quebec's judiciary. Similar efforts were made by Edward Blake to orchestrate a series of resignations in preparation for the reformation of the Quebec's provincial bench in 1876, though the Liberals enjoyed uneven success in reaching the desired result, despite a number of sitting judges offering to resign.[10] Too often the troublesome judges remained while the conscientious ones wished to make room to speed desired reforms.

A great deal of this unofficial correspondence between the minister of justice, sitting judges, and the Department of Justice involved subtle inquiries and the cultivation of appropriate relationships as a precursor to a person's nomination to the bench. C.E. Church, for example, assured Alexander Mackenzie that B. DesBusay was a fit candidate for the bench and that "he has strong claims in the Reform party having been in public life for a number of years and always a consistent supporter of our side in politics."[11] Basically, a potential judge had to be a known quantity before he would be elevated, and an unstated aspect of character was the understanding that regardless of partisan considerations, it benefited neither the judge nor the government if a member of the bench proved to be, for any number of reasons, an embarrassment. The absence of such an accord lead to the difficulties that Macdonald perceived in Nova Scotia, where the "Judges cling to the Bench so pertinaciously. In England no Judge would be so wanting in self respect as to hold Office if he was aware that age or physical infirmity prevented him from performing his duties efficiently."[12] To avoid similar embarrassments, inquiries were necessary to ascertain whether a candidate was the right type of person. For example, in considering Robert P. Jellet for the vacant judgeship in Prince Edward County in Ontario, Sir John A. wrote Mackenzie Bowell about a number of rumours. Writing with amusing, if unintended, irony, Macdonald noted that there were objections in Prince Edward to Jellet's "habits and style of life. A Judge should be an example to Society among whom he presides. What are the facts about Jellet? They say that he is fond of wine and women; haunts billiard rooms and commits all kinds of enormities. This kind of thing may do for politicians, but it will not do for judges."[13] The fortuitous announcement of Jellet's marriage to the third daughter of the late Reverend John Grier convinced Sir John that Jellet's excesses had come to an end and thus rendered his appointment safe.[14]

Although this unofficial correspondence barely concealed the political undertone of the inquiries, neither the Liberals nor the Conservatives fully acknowledged the degree to which such considerations shaped judicial appointments. As with the rhetoric surrounding the fiction of the apolitical attorney general, there was political capital in portraying the process of judge making as occurring above the fray. Consequently, it is quite possible to discern various possibilities in the rhetoric of elevations to the bench. John A. Macdonald, for example, claimed he had "always held that Judicial Offices stand on quite a different footing from all others, that fitness with respect to the Bench must be the first and chief consideration, and that no political exigency however great would warrant the Government in appointing an unfit man to be a Judge."[15] Fitness, of course, was a mercurial quality and its assay no simple matter. Sharpening his explanation a year later in response to T.W. Anglin, Sir John defended what he believed to be a "true constitutional principle":

> Whenever an Office is vacant it belongs to the party supporting the Government if within that party there can be found a person competent to perform the duties. Responsible Government cannot be carried on any other principle. I am not careful however, what a man's political antecedents have been, if I am satisfied that he is really and bona fide a friend of the Government at the time of the appointment. My principle is, reward your friends and do not buy your enemies.[16]

Obviously, partisan considerations exerted an influence with Macdonald. In concert with other necessary ingredients they could tip the balance, but party alone would not sustain an appointment.

Aside from the understandable aversion to undermining the Bench through the impression that judicial seats were merely sinecures, the disinclination to place too much emphasis on a candidate's political pedigree served a pragmatic function. Not only did it discourage those who aspired to a judicial position solely by right of political service, but it also laid the groundwork for those rare instances when an appointment did cross political lines. Indeed, it was just such an occasion that Macdonald referred to constantly as evidence of this own nonpartisan appointment of judges. Not surprisingly, even this often-cited appointment of Samuel Hume Blake as vice-chancellor for Ontario in 1869 was not the altruistic demonstration that Macdonald portrayed. In fact, the rarity of the gesture, combined with the extraordinary intrigue preceding it, confirms the highly politicized environment encasing all judicial appointments, regardless of allusions to constitutional principle.

All the Troubles of Judge Making

The lengthy chain of events leading to S.H. Blake's appointment as vice-chancellor for Ontario began in mid-February 1868, when Chief Justice W.H. Draper applied for a leave of absence from Ontario's Queen's Bench while tendering his resignation in anticipation of an appointment to the provincial Court of Error and Appeal.[17] Although John A. Macdonald evidently felt that Chancellor P.M. VanKoughnet would be a fitting replacement for Draper, the chief justice thought that while able, the chancellor was probably unwilling. Consistent with the artifice of judicial nominations, Draper believed that VanKoughnet "would like to have the Chief Justiceship offered to him because that would give him the opportunity to reject it."[18]

By March, the rumour mill indicated that despite Draper's suspicions, VanKoughnet was poised to accept the chief justiceship and present Macdonald with the challenge of filling the soon-to-be vacant chancellorship.[19] VanKoughnet was still intent on replacing Draper a month later and suggested that Edward Blake would be a worthy replacement, though Draper thought that Blake's youth or political inclinations rendered such an eventuality doubtful.[20] By July, the entire scheme had unravelled, in part because VanKoughnet decided to "stand committed" with Vice-Chancellors Oliver Mowat and John G. Spragge.[21] In Macdonald's eyes, Mowat and Spragge were responsible for upsetting the well-laid plans: "It is too bad that the interests of Justice should be sacrificed on account of the selfish vanity of Mowat and Spragge, who, although they have no chance of being Chancellors themselves would desire to keep VanKoughnet where he is, rather than have a new Chancellor appointed over their heads."[22]

Five weeks later, the minister of justice broached the matter again with VanKoughnet, noting that if he transferred to Queen's Bench, Edward Blake reportedly was inclined to accept the chancellorship but was consulting with other parties – probably his father and law partners.[23] The question was, however, moot. On 9 November, VanKoughnet confirmed his decision to remain where he was and, as Macdonald wrote Blake, "On public grounds I regret this much, as with your help we could have made a good Court of Equity and the Common Law Bench would have been strengthened by VanKoughnet's accession to it. However, it cannot be helped. I have done everything in my power to keep up the efficiency of the Bench, but have thus far been thwarted."[24] Unable to get VanKoughnet to replace Draper on the Queen's Bench, Sir John turned to Chief Justice William Buell Richards of Common Pleas to assume the chief justiceship of both Queen's Bench and Upper Canada. Justice Hagerty of Queen's Bench ascended to the chief justiceship of common pleas in Richard's place, Justice Adam Wilson filled Hagerty's vacated seat, and John W. Gwynne was appointed to Common Pleas to replace Wilson.[25]

As events turned out, however, the question was not settled. VanKoughnet's untimely death on 7 November 1869 once again threw Macdonald "into all the troubles of judge-making" and, as had occurred in 1868, he thought of Blake to fill the chancellor's seat.[26] Sir John admitted, "I feel to a certain extent committed as to Blake. Had VanKoughnet decided upon accepting the Chief Justiceship last year, Blake would have had the offer of the Chancellorship beyond a doubt. I told him confidentially that I would make him the offer if the vacancy occurred."[27] Despite feeling compelled to renew the offer, Blake's politics rendered the appointment difficult: "It is an unfortunate as well as a singular coincidence that the Members of the Equity Bar are very nearly all Grits."[28]

Not only was Blake's nomination difficult with Conservative friends, but it also provided the Opposition press with an opportunity to portray the offer as motivated by a desire to remove "a formidable political rival."[29] Wishing to avoid the spectacle of "every Grit newspaper in Western Canada" writing that Blake had "patriotically sacrificed his own interests by refusing the Office and remaining true to his Country and his party," Macdonald asked that Judge Morrison confidentially ascertain Blake's feelings about the chancellorship. The position was his if he wanted it, but if not, "It should be considered between us as if the offer were not made."[30]

Subsequent correspondence with Morrison revealed that Blake was not particularly inclined to cooperate with Macdonald's wishes. Sir John was, he admitted to Morrison, a "good deal" disappointed with Blake:

> I think he ought to have met the matter in the same spirit in which I made the offer, and which he admits ... It is all very well for him to say that he will justify the offer in case I am attacked, but there would be no occasion for the attack if he would accept my suggestion, – that unless he accepted, it should be considered that no offer was ever made. Under no circumstances can he lose by this arrangement, while by an other I may be prejudiced and the Government as well.[31]

After twelve days of hearing nothing, Sir John implored Morrison: "Pray tell me what 'demon of silence' has taken possession of you." Would Blake take the seat and "relieve me of the possibility of being subjected to the charge of endeavouring to withdraw a political opponent by an appointment?"[32] If not, the vacancy in Chancery had to be filled immediately, and Macdonald needed time to choose his next appointee.

One week later, the matter was finally settled as Blake declined to accept a seat on the equity bench, and J.G. Spragge, who Macdonald had thought was "not of heavy enough metal to preside in the Court," was given the opportunity.[33] To fill Spragge's place as vice-chancellor, the minister of justice nominated S.H. Strong, who "was pointed out by every leading practitioner at the Equity Bar, without reference to politics, as being the man for the vacancy."[34] It is possible that Strong received the seat, in part, because of his labours drafting Macdonald's first Supreme Court bill. Although Macdonald regretted that Blake had been unable to accept a position on the bench, he assured Judge Morrison that such feelings were of a strictly "professional" nature: "His remaining in the House is rather a service to us. It is important to have gentlemen in the Opposition, as in Government, and there is not a single one answering that description on the left of the Speaker's Chair with the exception of Blake himself."[35]

There the matter sat until 1872, when Oliver Mowat submitted his resignation as vice-chancellor. Displeased with having been passed over for judicial promotion and presented with the opportunity of reentering political life in the wake of Edward Blake's withdrawal from the Ontario premier's office, Mowat stepped down from the bench and back into the fray. Forwarding his unofficial resignation to Macdonald on 23 October 1872, Mowat received a terse acknowledgment forty-eight hours later: "I have transferred your letter to the Secretary of State to submit to His Excellency the Governor General. I have no doubt he accepted as a matter of course."[36] Two days later, Macdonald penned Mowat a lengthier and more revealing response:

> My feelings on learning of your return to political life are of a composite character. I am glad, for the sake of Ontario, that you have assumed your present position. With all your political sins you will impart a respectability to the Local Government which it much wanted, and the Country will have confidence that you will set your face against the courser forms of jobbery which were infecting our country from our proximity to the United States.
>
> At the same time I may venture to say that I regret to see you imitating the American system of judges returning to political life, after having accepted the legal monk hood of the Bench. It is not likely to be extensively followed, the precedent is a bad one, but practically it will not do much mischief. However, you have made the plunge, and there is an end of it.[37]

These twin themes of Americanizing the bench and rejecting the legal "monk hood" came to occupy a prominent place in Sir John's subsequent correspondence detailing "this escapade of Mowat's."[38]

The minister of justice asked both Chief Justice Draper and Chancellor Spragge for suggestions on who might fill the Mowat vacancy, with the notable proviso that Conservative candidates were preferable.[39] Sir John noted that Adam Crooks and Thomas Moss had been suggested but thought that the "Grits would not allow Crooks to go, even if I wanted him for the vice-Chancellorship," and Moss "is too young and too ambitious to shelve himself at present."[40] A month after Mowat's unofficial resignation, it was evident that Edward Blake's brother Samuel – yet another Grit from the equity bar – was to be offered the position.[41] By the end of November, Macdonald nominated the younger Blake, four days after Mowat's resignation was accepted.[42]

As Macdonald admitted to T.C. Patteson of the *Toronto Mail,* Samuel Blake was hardly a popular choice to replace Mowat: "I can quite understand that it is a bitter pill for our Conservative friends to swallow. As S.H. Blake is not held socially in esteem he has no friends on our side."[43] Despite the discomfort flowing from placing so prominent a Liberal on the bench, Macdonald still saw some good in the appointment.[44] Writing to Chief Justice

Morris of Manitoba, Macdonald observed that, in general terms, "By some strange accident all the Common Law Lawyers are Conservatives while the Equity are Grit. Blake will make a good Judge, and I think it is rather a good stroke for the Government to show to the country that the efficiency of the Bench is the first consideration, irrespective of politics."[45] And as he assured D'Arcy Boulton, "Had there been a good Conservative practitioner who could have done the duty as well, he would certainly have been preferred."[46]

The almost five years between W.H. Draper's resignation from Queen's Bench and Samuel Blake's nomination as vice-chancellor provide a compelling demonstration of the political and legal reality behind Sir John A. Macdonald's true constitutional principle. A fit candidate from within the party drew differently than a qualified candidate from across the floor. All things being equal, or nearly equal, Conservatives were always preferable. The challenge, as demonstrated in Macdonald's approaches to the Blake brothers, rested in those rare instances where a plausible fit from within the party simply could not be found. Rather than grumble over the choice he was compelled to make, Macdonald remained true to his witticism that a good carpenter can work with indifferent tools and would long refer to the Blake appointment as a compelling example of his own nonpartisanship in raising judges to the bench.[47] The exception, of course, proved to be the rule, and the elevation of Samuel Blake is an almost singular instance of Macdonald placing a Liberal on the bench. However, while Sir John's reputation for partisanship was well earned, any other approach would have been quixotic in the least. And, while they came to assume their own view of judicial patronage, the Liberals were never outdone in looking after their own, especially when a seat on the bench was in the offing.

Gestures and the Judiciary

Authoring a response to an inquiry from F. Bechard, Edward Blake offered a Macdonaldian perspective of the necessary political and professional temper for those pursuing judicial elevation during the Liberal years. Reflecting upon his own tenure as minister of justice, Blake suggested that it had been his "especial duty ... to take care that no man is appointed to the vacancy who is not thoroughly competent to fill the position. In selecting from amongst those who may fulfil this condition, the Government must of course rely largely upon the advice of those of its friends who from local knowledge and intimate political connection have the best means of deciding upon the political aspect of the question."[48] A year later, Blake confirmed these views during a political picnic at Teeswater, Ontario, but added a slightly different consideration:

> The man who is appointed a judge, and as such may at any time hold in his hands the fate, whether as fortune, freedom, or good name, of any one of

> us, this man holds his office by a tenure practically not far removed from life. He may be a blessing, but again he may be a curse, to his country for twenty or thirty years; and therefore it is a most sacred duty on the part of a Government to search for the very best men to administer these tremendous responsibilities.[49]

Although Blake relied upon similar rhetoric to that used by Macdonald, the language from the Teeswater speech acknowledged the existence of a judicial legacy for the Canadian public. Although it is true that the Mackenzie administration's early practice in appointing judges had followed that of Macdonald's, the creation and staffing of the Canadian Supreme Court placed the nomination of judges into a more expansive perspective. It cannot be argued that the Liberals experienced anything approaching an epiphany with judicial appointments. Rather, the fight for the Supreme Court, and especially the battle over clause 47 and the unsuccessful attempt to end appeals to the Judicial Committee of the Privy Council, cast all judicial nominations into sharper relief. The light was, however, uneven in its strength. As such, the Liberals continued to place party members on the bench as a matter of true constitutional principle while, at the same time, wondering about the implications of such a practice.[50] In the least, raising new judges to the bench was no longer merely an exercise in rewarding qualified party members: it suggested national implications and an implied responsibility for engendering a well-respected and learned judiciary.

This realization hardly made judicial appointments less complicated affairs. As Gordon Stewart succinctly points out, patronage was both the glue and the grease of party politics; abandoning the use of judicial seats to honour and reward service was simply not practical, especially in the aftermath of Confederation, when the federal government was deprived of a whole class of positions and sinecures.[51] Although Stewart accurately identifies the political ingredient in judicial appointments, he understates the complexity of these decisions, even if the governing party did reward its own. The vexatious nature of these appointments was especially trying for the Liberal leadership, which twisted itself in knots attempting to placate and reward long-serving and loyal members. Consistent with party-building strategies of the period, these attempts also served Opposition ends by actually fostering disharmony within Liberal ranks. The most striking instance of these unintended results occurred with the elevation of Antoine-Aimé Dorion and the strained offer of a judicial seat to Rodolphe Laflamme. In the very least, these cases demonstrate that, within the context of Confederation-era public life, giving heed to partisan debts was not always politically astute.

A.A. Dorion was offered Quebec's chief justiceship less than one year after the Liberals formed the government in the wake of the Pacific Scandal ousting Macdonald's Conservatives. Although Mackenzie wished that Dorion, his first minister of justice, would decline the immediate position on the bench with the understanding that a seat on the proposed Supreme Court awaited him, he also counselled his Quebec lieutenant "to consider solely his own interests."[52] Relating the exchange to Edward Blake, Mackenzie admitted that Dorion's departure would be painful, though, "It would be still more painful to me after years to know that I would be blamed for doing him a personal wrong by not acting properly when I had the power."[53] Dorion accepted Mackenzie's nomination, and, in turn, the Liberals were deprived of much-valued Quebec leadership.

Despite Mackenzie's desire to ensure his old comrade the security of the bench, the Dorion appointment was ill conceived. With three full years remaining in the government's mandate, other opportunities to reward the Rouge leader would certainly occur. For example, appointing someone such as Télesphore Fournier to Quebec's chief justiceship and then raising him to the proposed Supreme Court, in order to make room for Dorion, was the more astute move. Further, considering that Dorion, before the union of 1867, had opposed the notion of a Canadian Supreme Court, believing such a tribunal would be an "interference of the General Government" with the laws of Lower Canada, the offer of a seat on that court was nonsensical and hardly a compelling temptation to remain in active politics.[54] In fact, a number of party leaders, including Dorion himself, doubted his suitability for the Supreme Court.[55]

Finally, the notion that Dorion was "entitled to the first offer," regardless of his supposed intent to accept or reject it, laid bare the choreographed intersection of political life and judicial appointments. Some evidently expected that the offer acknowledged Dorion's legal talent and political contributions while, at the same time, encouraged him to remain on the hustings with the understanding of a secure judicial seat in the not-too-distant future. Indicative of a party wishing to reward those who had fought the hard battles while encouraging such individuals to remain in harness, these gestures and the vaguely articulated expectation underlying them created and then exacerbated tensions within the party. In accepting the elevation, Dorion did what was personally and professionally reasonable and politically lamentable. Strong Quebec lieutenants were a rare commodity, and losing one as able as Dorion without an obvious and proven successor to assume his place was, as the Conservatives learned in the aftermath of George-Etienne Cartier's death, a risky venture. Yet in the rush to take early advantage of the power of appointment and the opportunity to pay political debts, the Liberals raised Dorion to the bench. As Mackenzie's biographer Dale Thomson summarizes, the move was "an irreparable loss."[56]

Naming Dorion as Quebec's chief justice echoed throughout the remaining years of Mackenzie's administration. Télesphore Fournier replaced

Dorion in the Department of Justice, to eventually step aside for the recalcitrant Edward Blake. Almost immediately after accepting the post, Blake set about the task of staffing the newly created Supreme Court, an undertaking that necessitated a renewed inquiry of Dorion's expectations which, in turn, impinged upon Rodolphe Laflamme's desire for judicial promotion. As with Dorion's initial appointment, the possibility of raising Laflamme to the bench was not to be determined solely as a reward for party service but also turned on whether such an acknowledgement was prudent, given the political state of affairs. While the Liberals had stumbled in executing the manoeuvres surrounding Dorion's elevation, they had learned their lesson by the autumn of 1875.

Compressed into an exchange of letters during a two-week period, articulating a strategy for dealing with Laflamme's judicial aspirations was basically the work of Alexander Mackenzie, Edward Blake, and Luther Holton. Writing on 11 September, Blake stressed that, "Laflamme should be made aware of the universal feeling that he was the fittest man to take one of the vacant judgeships and that our hesitation arises not merely from losing a seat but from the conviction that Laflamme was still more necessary to his country in the House than on the Bench."[57] Appealing both to ego and political duty, Blake wanted Laflamme placed "in a position to refuse a judgeship even if he in common with his friends thought that public duty required him to refuse it." Summarizing the situation a day later, Holton emphasized that while he would be "delighted to see Laflamme appointed Judge," Prime Minister Mackenzie had intimated that with Fournier's impending appointment to the Supreme Court and the recent collapse of Félix Geoffrien's health, Laflamme "could not be spared from the House and might very soon be wanted in the Cabinet."[58] As a consequence, Holton acknowledged candidly that, "It may sometime be expedient to offer an important man a place with the hope or the understanding that he will disclaim but the compliment is to say the least required."

Perhaps having in mind the handling of Dorion's elevation in 1874, Holton preferred a more straightforward tack be set to deal with Laflamme:

> It seems to me you have to make up your minds whether the interests of the party require Laflamme's presence in the House or not. If you think they do and another equally eligible judge can be found, would it not be better to say to him frankly "We should all be delighted to offer you a position on the Bench if you could be spared from Political life, but we do not think you can be without serious detriment."[59]

Just as important was the news that despite Blake's claim that Laflamme's candidacy enjoyed universal support, considerable political and legal opposition existed. According to Lucius Huntington, another prominent Quebec

Liberal, it was rumoured that if choosing between Fournier and Laflamme for membership on the Court, "It is quite probable that the sympathies of the members of the Court from other provinces would be with Fournier."[60] In Huntington's opinion, intimating this "might perhaps remove an obstacle in the way of Laflamme's coming to the decision we desire."[61]

The manoeuvring and posturing proved successful. Laflamme informed Mackenzie on 22 September that while appreciative of the offer to sit on the Supreme Court, a position which friends advised him to accept, he could not abandon the party. "I feel somewhat as a soldier leaving the army in wartime, and in a struggle not of the most cheering prospects as to result and I made up my mind notwithstanding all the personal advantages, to decline."[62] Laflamme eventually regretted his decision when on the eve of the 1878 federal election he was overlooked as a replacement for Justice Taschereau on the Supreme Court. The snub, probably sparked by a lacklustre performance as minister of justice in the final parliamentary session, ignited a heated missive from Laflamme to Mackenzie. Writing eight days before the Liberals officially relinquished office, the minister of justice and aspirant judge felt no rein to his anger: "I wish you however to understand that I have suffered enough indignity to allow me to abstain from further participation in the deliberations of the Council and will await only to convey such information as may be required or complete any business not yet closed from my department."[63]

By the time Laflamme suffered his perceived humiliation at the hands of Alexander Mackenzie, the party and its various ministers of justice had experienced a great deal in handling members of the judiciary and judicial appointments. Consistent with the evolution of Liberal thinking of all patronage appointments, a measure of unease had crept into a practice that unflinchingly pursued party interests with scant regard for broader virtues. Although this realization was barely broached by 1878, it had, nonetheless, tinged the appointment of judges to the Supreme Court in late 1875. As minister of justice, Edward Blake recognized that as the nation moved from the completion of Confederation to sorting out the workings of the union act in a new era of nation building, the Court would confront myriad legal and political challenges – challenges that would test the Court's legal acumen along with its ability to gauge a nascent national character. These judges could not be of ordinary timbre. The question, of course, was whether Blake would successfully draw upon the best of Canadian legal talent or if circumstances would prune his options in naming a great court for a great nation.

Envisioning a Supreme Court

Locating the creation of Canada's Supreme Court within the inter–play between the Department of Justice and the judiciary uncovers an illuminating episode in completing the institutional structure of confederation. The Court's genesis is a sharp example of how the act of union sustained strikingly dissimilar expectations and how, in working out the Confederation scheme, both the Conservatives and the Liberals failed to realize their aspirations for such a court. However, rather than retell the story that has been told elsewhere, I will concentrate on highlighting the basic assumption underlying Sir John A. Macdonald's abortive attempts to create a Supreme Court in 1869 and 1870 and then upon the distinctive thinking sustaining the successful Liberal effort of 1875.[64] Not surprisingly, a certain symmetry between these attempts to form a court and each party's approach to the judiciary as a whole is discernible. After repeated failures to construct a tribunal to act as yet another stay in his highly centralized vision of Confederation, Sir John A. Macdonald abandoned the exercise in October 1871 with the prediction that, "It will probably be some years before we have a Dominion Court of Appeal."[65] For the Liberals, who came to view the Supreme Court as a powerful symbolic and tangible demonstration of national stature and autonomy, the Court's creation and staffing proved to be a disheartening reminder of inelastic ties to England and the brackish mixture of parochialism, professional achievement, ego, and public stature shaping the temperamental world of the judiciary in nineteenth-century Canada. Court building was not for the faint of heart, and the high expectations of both political parties were dulled in the process. In the very least, the undertaking documented the unpredictability of politically inspired manoeuvres executed in the legal world.

Sir John A. Macdonald's original Supreme Court bill was drafted during the winter of 1868-9 by S.H. Strong, soon to be named vice-chancellor of Ontario and eventually raised to the Supreme Court upon its founding in 1875.[66] Modelled loosely on the United States Supreme Court, the proposed Canadian version was granted an expansive mandate with exclusive jurisdiction in constitutional litigation, cases challenging federal revenue laws, suits involving either the provincial and federal governments, treaty litigation, and any cases where legislation provided for hearings before the Court.[67] When cases involved citizens of different provinces or foreign states, the Court held concurrent jurisdiction with provincial tribunals.[68] Having encouraged the construction of a court matching his vision of governance in the new dominion one year after both the Department of Justice Act and the Penitentiaries Act had received royal assent, Macdonald took another step in the completion of Confederation by giving the House notice of his bill creating the Canadian Supreme Court.

Once introduced on 21 May 1869, the bill vanished from the legislative agenda. Although he would later claim that this abortive first attempt had been "more for the purpose of suggestion and consideration, than for a final measure," the judicial responses to the draft bill revealed that Strong and Macdonald had badly miscalculated.[69] That said, there is nothing to support Ian Bushnell's contention that Macdonald was less than serious in presenting this proposal to the House.[70] Why then did the bill disappear with such speed? Despite a fairly short two-month session in the House, the momentum of Macdonald's political life in the early spring and summer of 1869 surely could have carried the bill some distance. After all, Hudson's Bay Company officials had finally agreed to relinquish control over Rupert's Land, delegates arrived in Ottawa from Newfoundland to discuss entry into Confederation, and the possibility of British Columbia joining the new union had increased considerably.

These successes, however, did not extend to Macdonald's private life. His wife, Agnes, having almost died giving birth to their daughter Mary, was only beginning to recover in April, and by the summer, Mary was diagnosed as hydrocephalic. During these same months, Macdonald learned from Hugh Allan, ship owner and president of the Merchants' Bank, that the claims against Sir John stemming from the failure of the Commercial Bank totalled just over $79,599. Further, despite a brief holiday in Portland, Maine, in late August, Macdonald returned to Ottawa and summarily launched into a drinking binge. And while he would right himself, in early winter, word had been received that the transfer of Rupert's Land had gone terribly wrong, and a new and very pressing crisis was soon at hand.[71]

Ultimately, the tone of the judicial responses to the circulation of the Supreme Court bill in early June sealed the legislation's fate.[72] Although some judges declined the opportunity to comment upon the proposed court, two of the responses received in September were unequivocal. A missive from Oliver Mowat, then vice-chancellor of Ontario, voiced the most persistent concern in questioning the original jurisdiction for the Court. Mowat pointed out that, "You have the power of disallowing provincial statutes; you appoint the Provincial Governors, and you appoint also the Provincial Judges. The reasons therefore for which it was necessary in certain cases to have original jurisdiction to the Supreme Court in the United States are entirely inappropriate to our nation."[73] Allied to Mowat's objection was a broader question of whether section 101 of the British North America Act authorizing "the Establishment of any additional Court for the better Administration of the Laws of Canada" meant that such a court, once constituted, could pass judgment on provincial enactments. As Vice-Chancellor Spragge of Ontario noted, "There is of course a good deal of Provincial law which is not the *law of Canada*."[74]

Echoing Mowat and Spragge, in February 1870, Chief Justice Ritchie of New Brunswick levelled a withering attack on the rationale underpinning the entire Supreme Court scheme: "By what authority then does this Act give exclusive original jurisdiction in causes at Law and in Equity, in matters touching the local laws of the Provinces respectively, as distinguished from the Dominion Laws, or 'the Laws of Canada?' Or, touching property or civil rights in the Provinces? Or, by what authority does it interfere with the administration of Justice in the Province?"[75] Future Supreme Court Chief Justice W.B. Richards continued the onslaught. Writing in April, three weeks after Macdonald introduced his second Supreme Court bill, Richards stated that he believed authority over provincial matters could be established only by provincial legislation and that Parliament could not create concurrent jurisdiction when the British North America Act provided for exclusive provincial control: "The right of the Crown as the fountain of justice to review the discussions of many of its Courts is a very different thing from the Dominion Parliament assuming this right to pass a law giving the power to a court of its own creation to draw to it the proceedings of other tribunals on matters not at all within their jurisdiction for the purpose of reviewing those proceedings."[76]

With or without Richards' late contribution, there was no question that from a judicial perspective, the first Supreme Court bill was an undiluted failure. To the extent that Macdonald has actually intended to generate discussion, the uproar over the bill certainly was not to his liking. Undaunted but enlightened by the strong expression of judicial opinion, Macdonald introduced his second Supreme Court bill on 18 March 1870. This second bill incorporated many of the criticisms that he had received, especially those referring to a reduced original jurisdiction, now including only Dominion revenue laws, extradition, and government reference cases.[77] Describing the proposed legislation on 18 March 1870, Sir John acknowledged the "suggestions and criticisms of the different Benches in the Dominion," and then claimed that the original measure had been submitted to Parliament "more for the purpose of suggestion and consideration, than for a final measure."[78] Circumstances, however, would once again conspire against Macdonald's plans.

The second Supreme Court bill, like the first, also failed. Although Macdonald was intent on getting "the Bill passed in some shape so as to organise the Court," fate dealt his plans a final blow when, less than two months after he had introduced it, he collapsed in his office with a near fatal attack of gallstones. His recuperation in Charlottetown removed him from political life for four months.[79] Control of the party fell into the hands of George-Etienne Cartier, who, along with many of his French Canadian colleagues on both sides of the House, was unenthusiastic about constituting a Dominion court of appeal that offered few explicit guarantees for the sanctity of French civil law in Quebec.[80] Macdonald's collapse, the subsequent passing of leadership to Cartier, and the resistance of Quebec and the Maritimes meant that the Supreme Court would once again fall from the political agenda. Three days after Macdonald collapsed, Cartier, citing the lateness of the session, withdrew the bill.[81]

Although most people who have studied the origins of the Supreme Court point to the resistance of Quebec as the prime factor in the legislative retreat, well-articulated and stern opposition was also voiced by a number of prominent Ontario judges. Further, this resistance was not monolithic. The concern from Quebec's legal profession and judiciary tended to concentrate on the absence of substantive protection for French civil law, whereas opinion from Ontario and the Maritimes questioned the federal government's jurisdiction to create a court for dealing with matters falling within provincial jurisdiction.[82] While Quebec's concerns could, theoretically, be addressed, the resolute opposition to the actual idea of a court was obviously more intractable. Indeed, as David Mills' scathing attack of mid-March 1870 revealed, in some quarters, there was no common ground on which to construct a court.

Although eventually named a minister of justice and a member of the Supreme Court, in mid-March 1870 David Mills was a Reform politician only beginning to make his way in Canadian public life.[83] While somewhat of a political novice, Mills was unflinching in his criticism of Macdonald's proposed legislation. Not only were the bill's basic assumptions unconstitutional, but the unlimited appellate jurisdiction was unwarranted and "forbidden by the nature of our government." According to Mills, Macdonald was evidently driven by a desire to vest the Supreme Court with "the appellate powers now possessed by the Judicial Committee of the Privy Council":[84]

> This provision is another instance of the common error of being misled by an apparent analogy where no real analogy exists. The appellate jurisdiction of the JC of PC is an incident, or, at all events, has been made an incident, of our Colonial condition; our powers are not complementary to those of the Imperial authorities, but derivative and subordinate, which is not the relation of any Province to Canada. The provinces obtain their powers from an Imperial source. Their powers are complementary and not subordinate; it follows therefore, that appellate judicial powers, would vest partly in the Supreme Court of Canada and partly in each province as the legislature of the province might determine.[85]

Not only had the prime minister subscribed to a "common error," but also he failed to appreciate the true nature of the British North America Act.

Mills was not finished: "The relation of England to her colonies is not, then, the relation of Canada to the included provinces. The supreme authority in England is *Parliament*; – the supreme authority in Canada is the *Constitution*, and you can no more centre, ultimately, all judicial authority in one court, than you can centre all legislative authority in the Canadian Parliament."[86] To Macdonald, who believed that "the General

Government assumes towards the local governments precisely the same position as the Imperial Government holds with respect to each of the colonies," Mills was uttering heresy.[87] Echoing the concerns of other correspondents, Mills concluded with the warning, "Create this unlimited appellate power, and litigation will, in all cases, be made costly. The rich can ruin the poor. The whole of our jurisprudence will be converted into an Egyptian labyrinth into which many may enter, but from which few can depart."[88]

The judicial opposition's sustained pressure to water down his Supreme Court proposals and personal crises all conspired against Macdonald. More pointed was the fact that, given his inability to forge a court with a role consistent with his own view of the constitution, Macdonald lost interest in the enterprise. Although referring only to the failure of the 1869 initiative, Bushnell's depiction of Macdonald's approach towards the Court, as well as the rationale for abandoning the scheme, is thoroughly convincing: "If there was to be a very limited constitutional role for the court and the appellate jurisdiction was to be considered somewhat minor, and since the original jurisdiction, the key part of his plan, had been rejected, there was no hurry to reintroduce a measure to establish the Court. There thus seemed to be no compelling need for it to exist as far as Macdonald and his party were concerned."[89] Unless the Court assumed the requisite place within his constitutional vision and thus contributed to the completion of his version of Confederation, the construction of such a tribunal was simply too bothersome. By October 1871 and his return to active political life, Macdonald had placed the project on the shelf.[90]

Creating a Supreme Court

The arrival of Alexander Mackenzie's Liberal government resurrected plans for a Supreme Court. It was not until February 1875, however, that a measure was introduced by Minister of Justice Télesphore Fournier, who shepherded the bill through the House, where the proposal was acknowledged to be essentially the same bill Macdonald had backed in 1870.[91] The Liberals, however, had learned from the two Conservative attempts. Noting the public desire that "there should be some court which would settle the extent of the powers of the Local Legislatures when these powers were in dispute," Fournier acknowledged the federal government's inability to confer such a jurisdiction on the Supreme Court.[92] Rather than press Macdonald's claim that the federal government possessed the authority to invest the Court with that jurisdiction, Fournier announced that given the "inability then to prepare a clause which could constitutionally confer the power of trying such cases upon the court directly he had resorted to the expedient of providing that, by the consent of the Provincial Government concerned, decisions given by the Supreme Court would have their effect in the cases mentioned."[93]

Implicit in the Liberal approach was recognition that if the decisions of the Court were to be respected, its legitimacy could not be subject to constant debate. While the Conservatives sought to impose the Court on the country and the provincial governments, the Liberals wanted to weave it into the Canadian political structure. Therein lay a fundamental difference between the two parties. The Supreme Court, by its very nature the highest court in the land, had to be seen as an integral component of the new nation's life. As a corollary, it was not surprising that the Liberals embarked on the first attempt to end Canadian appeals to the Privy Council in England. Defending this decision, Rodolphe Laflamme, future minister of justice, announced in stirring nationalistic tones:

> We are laying the foundations of a great country and are preparing to establish a nation in Canada. We are preparing for the future. We have formed laws which meet our wants and which suit our peculiar circumstances, and those laws were not and could not be the same as those of England; and on the question of interpretation, the judicial atmosphere in which the English Judges lived was different from that in which dwelt the judges who were born and brought up in Canada and were acquainted with the wants of this country.[94]

For the Liberals, a self-assured Supreme Court acting as the definitive Canadian legal tribunal was the birthright of the new nation.

The battle to limit Canadian appeals to the Judicial Committee of the Privy Council began tentatively with Fournier's admission that, "He wished to see the practice put to an end altogether."[95] Despite this desire, a provision ending such appeals was omitted in anticipation of the expected unveiling of English legislation creating a Supreme Court of Judicature to replace the Judicial Committee of the Privy Council.[96] Even the appearance that the Liberals were contemplating a termination of appeals to England compelled Macdonald to rise in defence of what he termed, "The right of every Canadian, as of every other British subject, to appeal to the Court of the highest jurisdiction ... It seemed to him that it would be severing one of the links between this country and the Mother Country if the right of appeal were cut off ruthlessly."[97] Undoubtedly, Macdonald's outburst contained a generous measure of theatre. For while the Conservative leader zealously and publicly defended the right of every British citizen to bring a grievance to the foot of the throne, in private he admitted that the right was "a mere sentiment," though "none the less powerful for that."[98]

Until Aemilius Irving of Hamilton proposed his amendment on 30 March 1875, ending appeals had been referred to only in passing. Claiming little more than an opportunity to spice up a dull session, the Irving amendment ignited a fiery debate in proposing to end appeals to "any Court of Appeal established by the Parliament of Great Britain ... saving any right which Her Majesty may be graciously pleased to exercise as her royal prerogative."[99] As time would reveal, the amendment actually did little since appeals based on the royal prerogative were specifically retained, whereas appeals by legislative right to an English appeal court were to be eliminated. Such subtleties, despite their centrality to the entire debate, failed to make any headway. Battle lines were soon drawn. Those who favoured an end to appeals subscribed to a burgeoning sense of Canadian nationhood, while those opposed saw the nation's identity tied inextricably to England and the Crown. Perhaps sensing an opportunity to revive his career, Sir John A. Macdonald led the rush of those criticizing the measure as the "first step towards the severance of the Dominion from the Mother Country."[100] Placed into the context of the times, a contest on these terms was not to be won by the few who saw Canada as more than adjunct to the British Empire. Given the mathematics of responsible government, however, the Liberal bill creating the Court, including clause 47 limiting appeals, was carried by a vote of 112 to 40. A tie vote to strike Irving's amendment was lost in the Senate, and the entire question passed from Canadian control.

Having created the Supreme Court, Mackenzie's Liberals were thus confronted with two final obstacles: obtaining royal assent and then appointing suitable members to the new tribunal. Handled in tandem, neither proved to be free from complication. As a preliminary to grappling with these concerns, Edward Blake replaced Télesphore Fournier as minister of justice, in anticipation of Fournier's elevation to the Supreme Court. His departure and the plans for judicial promotion indicated that while the Liberals were increasingly uneasy with the practice, they remained willing to reward party service with a seat on the bench. After all, given Fournier's involvement in a drunken brawl in late November 1874, his qualification to provide high moral leadership from the bench was, to say the least, suspect.[101] On a more positive note, Blake's arrival ensured that the department's business, including the finalization of the Court's creation, would be pressed with energy and dedication.

Appointed in May 1875, Blake insisted that nominees for the Court be pursued and that the Court bill receive royal assent as quickly as possible, despite mounting concerns from the Colonial Office during the summer of 1875.[102] Misunderstandings on how to proceed developed, as Mackenzie believed the Court could be established despite those doubts, while imperial officials believed that some resolution was needed beforehand. Informed by Mackenzie that "the old war horse" Lieutenant Governor Sir O'Grady Haly, who was acting as administrator in Lord Dufferin's absence, wished to delay appointing the judges and establishing the Court, Blake was adamant: "To pause now would be ruinous. If judges not appointed or if bill afterwards disallowed I must resign."[103] Although wary of proceeding, Colonial

Secretary Lord Carnarvon relented with the stipulation that if clause 47 was subsequently determined to be unconstitutional, it would be altered though the Supreme Court act would remain in force.

Having averted a disastrous setback at the hands of the Colonial Office, Blake then set about the task of constituting the Supreme Court.[104] Not surprisingly, political considerations shaped this process, although Blake endeavoured to distinguish himself from past practice. Since Fournier's appointment was assured, Blake was concerned with filling five seats on the bench. That William Henry of Nova Scotia was appointed to the Supreme Court was enough to turn heads; that he was Blake's first nominee would have befuddled most onlookers and even appears to have even caught Henry unawares.[105] Although the Henry appointment seemed peculiar to some, given the tangled world of judicial patronage in Nova Scotia, it is entirely probable that he was chosen precisely because he was the least offensive candidate available.[106]

Without question, the greatest challenge confronting Blake about the Court's legitimacy involved seating the two Ontario judges. Since his first choice for chief justice was then chief justice of Quebec, A.A. Dorion, whose acceptance was unlikely, it was obvious that the chief justice for the Court would have to come from Ontario.[107] Although Blake was almost unanimously hailed as the best candidate to occupy this role on the Court, an appointment that would certainly fulfil long-standing family aspirations, he was reticent about leaving political life.[108] The next candidate and ranking Ontario judge was William Draper, chief justice of the Court of Error and Appeal. Draper's well-known Conservative leanings, advanced age, and pending retirement, however, rendered his appointment untenable. After Draper was William Buell Richards, who was on friendly terms with Mackenzie but linked in Blake's mind to the internecine warfare within the upper ranks of Ontario's judiciary, a state of affairs existing since at least the late 1860s.[109] Despite Blake's doubts, he offered the position to Richards who, while admitting failing health, accepted the appointment as the Supreme Court's first chief justice.[110] The second Ontario seat went to the bilingual former Vice-Chancellor Henry Strong, then sitting on Ontario's Supreme Court, who, although having drafted the flawed original Supreme Court bill, was nonetheless widely respected by the legal profession.[111] Save for an overgenerous sense of self-importance and a gruff and argumentative personality, Strong proved to be a valuable asset to a court requiring legal acumen and broad experience.[112]

As the Ontario seats were finalized, Blake settled the second position representing the three Maritime provinces. In naming New Brunswick's William Johnstone Ritchie, who, it will be recalled, authored a strenuous critique of Macdonald's initial attempt to constitute the tribunal, Blake nominated a man who emerged as one of the Court's strongest members.[113]

The appointment proved to be especially fortuitous given that Richards' ill health limited his effectiveness and compelled Ritchie to unofficially perform as chief justice until named to the position in early January 1879.[114] Ritchie's appointment left only the final Quebec position to be filled. Once Rodolphe Laflamme's judicial aspirations were quenched with the promise that, in due course, his time would come, the position was offered to Jean-Thomas Taschereau, who was well known to be unenthusiastic about the opportunity and concomitant relocation to Ottawa. Expecting that Taschereau would decline, Blake was prepared to turn to Louis-Victor Sicotte, a long-time Reform/Liberal politician who was then sitting on Quebec's Superior Court as the judge for Saint-Hyacinthe.[115] Taschereau surprised Blake in accepting the position and, in so doing, completed the Court's judicial membership.[116]

Situating the Court and its personnel within the context of Confederation-era politics is a complicated affair. At the time, Luther Holton believed that Blake had made a mess of the judicial appointments by creating a "thoroughly Tory" court. He was especially piqued that Strong, a Conservative, had been favoured over Liberal Thomas Moss, who Blake had appointed instead to Ontario's Court of Error and Appeal on 8 October 1875.[117] Although Holton's opinion sprung in part from a deteriorating relationship with Blake, the assessment is still intriguing. His expectation that the Court *would be* Liberal represents similar thinking to Sir John A. Macdonald's "true constitutional principle" of rewarding friends and not buying enemies. At the same time, Blake's correspondence reveals he was committed to constituting a reasonably nonpartisan and professionally respected Bench. Locating some middle ground between the expectations voiced by Holton and the possibilities considered by Blake proved, however, to be impossible. Fournier's reserved seat, the offer to Laflamme, the half-hearted invitation to Taschereau, and even the ill-considered but professionally sound invitation to Richards were certainly shaped by political choreography. Strong's appointment also carried the advantage of appearing nonpartisan, though his professional standing was unassailable. As such, half the Court, including the unhealthy Richards, along with Ritchie and Strong, enjoyed "very respectable judicial credentials," whereas the other half of Fournier, Taschereau, and Henry "were far less impressive."[118]

Caught between the tradition of appointing judicial personnel from within party ranks and Blake's desire to constitute a court befitting a great nation, the Liberals did neither. What was produced was a hybrid of sorts. And while the court that emerged was balanced, it was not so in the sense described by Gordon Bale in his biography of Ritchie.[119] Rather, the Court's equilibrium reflected a juxtaposition of professional standing with the politicized rituals of public life. Predictably, the result was a mediocre and sometimes fractious court producing only occasional demonstrations befitting the title supreme. Denied ultimate authority and saddled with uneven legal talent, the Court was unable to author its own supremacy and thus settled into the role its detractors would allege, that of an intermediate and inconvenient tribunal lacking stature and professional respect along with a well-defined and accepted function.[120] Still, creating the Court was a notable accomplishment. That it became entangled in the complex artistry of statecraft and the choreography of judicial appointments only serves to confirm that it was inextricably bound to the completion of Confederation.

For Blake, of course, the task remained unfinished and would remain so until he crossed the Atlantic to lay the case for clause 47 before the Colonial Office. Although setting out with intentions of mounting a staunch defence of the clause, Blake's memorandum on ending appeals is, in hindsight, problematic. His argument acknowledged that appeals fell into two categories: those defined by statute and those by the royal prerogative. As worded, clause 47 ended statutory appeals but recognized that appeals based on the royal prerogative were retained.[121] Therefore, while the great majority of his discussion urged the termination of appeals to England as a right consistent with Canada's condition as a sovereign nation, Blake recognized that as worded, the Supreme Court bill did not rule out all appeals. In fact, on the fourth page of a thirty-nine-page handwritten opinion, Blake acknowledged that ending appeals to nonprerogative courts was without substance, since appeal to the Crown as a matter of the royal prerogative was specifically retained.[122] Although the memorandum delineates the arguments in favour of ending appeals as a matter of principle, it confirmed Blake's recognition that clause 47 was suspect. While he had written in accordance with what he hoped "would be and ought to be the true Canadian sentiment," the memorandum and the subsequent events in Britain reveal that by early October 1875, Blake knew the clause accomplished very little indeed.[123] He was openly arguing this position by May 1876 and left for England knowing that the Canadian case for ending appeals could not be based on clause 47. What had begun as a struggle over principle and Canadian sovereignty had precipitated into a flurry of paper over an empty clause.

The parliamentary session ended and having dealt with departmental business, Blake launched his mission to England on 3 June 1876.[124] In many ways, the whole rationale behind the trip was ill suited to Blake's vision of Canada's place in the world. Travelling to England to plead the nation's case as if she were a mere colony was humiliating. Knowing that Canada's position regarding the Supreme Court bill was sure to fail made Blake's journey even less palatable. Finally, having to lobby and participate in the niceties of empire politics was an almost insurmountable task for the reticent Blake. Still, after a number of preliminary meetings with Lord

Carnarvon and Robert G.W. Herbert, permanent undersecretary at the Colonial Office, it was agreed that the Supreme Court act would be left intact but that in practice clause 47 had no effect. At his meeting with Lord Cairns on 5 July, Blake confirmed that the clause was without force and arranged for a dispatch noting that the Supreme Court bill would be allowed to stand.[125] Having accomplished his task, Blake set about his return to Canada and a resumption of responsibilities as minister of justice.

Patronage of a Higher Order

As it turned out, the creation of the Supreme Court was both a high and low point for the Mackenzie administration. The debate over the Court, and especially clause 47, suggested just how far some Liberals were prepared to press the rhetoric of a distinct Canadian national identity, apart from that of the British Empire. At the same time, the real effect of the Court's creation was, in terms of such an identity, almost meaningless. And further, the selection of the Court's personnel demonstrated that the pull of politics and public life proved greater than Liberal virtues in managing judicial appointments. As Frank Underhill suggested, creating the Court had been a hollow victory for the Liberal government.[126]

On another level, the entire process of bringing the Court to life symbolized the interaction between contemporary politics, the Canadian Department of Justice, and the judiciary. Judge-making was very political; court-making even more so. Yet despite the obvious character of these appointments, the ministers of justice denied consistently that such considerations played a role in determining who would rise to the bench. Maintaining the fiction of law and its practitioners as being apolitical was evidently of a higher order than acknowledging the obvious. This resilient artifice is intriguing, in part because it was so transparent. Indeed, the allusion to nonpartisanship and its practised avoidance was elevated by Macdonald to constitutional principle and then touted as a tangible demonstration of the nation's British heritage. It was, of course, this same heritage that hobbled the Liberal aspirations to set the footings for a distinctive Canadian jurisprudence formed, in part, by an autonomous Supreme Court. Denied this opportunity and nurtured in an environment favouring appearance over substance and gestures over merit, the Canadian judicial culture that hardened into shape during the completion of Confederation was politicized, parochial, and prone to outbursts of pique over real and imagined slights to professional standing and stature.

Gauging how deeply this culture coloured public perceptions of the judiciary is not easily effected. Complaints of the quality of Quebec's judiciary, the judicial crisis in New Brunswick, the thinly veiled strife amongst senior judges in Ontario, and the uncertain beginnings of the Supreme Court were all grist for the mill of professional and public opinion during these years.

Yet in all, only the difficulties in Quebec and New Brunswick garnered sustained public comment and, on those occasions, criticism was often aimed at the inability or apparent unwillingness of provincial and federal authorities to put the judicial house in order. Only with rare exception were individual judges exposed to scorn. The judiciary, it appears, remained relatively anonymous and untouched by public critique.

Far away from newspaper columns, fundraising dinners, and other public events, individual ministers subscribed to their own measure of Canada's bench. Quite clearly, some held the judiciary in high esteem, believing it to be the crowning achievement for a career in law and politics. After all, Dorion accepted promotion within a year of being elected, Fournier orchestrated his own elevation to the Supreme Court, and Laflamme turned down judicial office only upon the promise that a subsequent position on the bench would be his. Conversely, neither Macdonald nor Blake coveted elevation. Offered judicial robes on numerous occasions, Blake always demurred. And while the notion of Macdonald as a judge is, in hindsight, rather peculiar, on a number of occasions his name was urged for a position on the bench.[127] Like Blake, Macdonald was uninterested. Indeed, when the idea was pressed that he should consider the chief justiceship of the Supreme Court, Sir John dismissed the suggestion with the retort that he "would rather be a dead premier than a live chief justice."[128] Another version of the story has Macdonald claiming he would as soon go to hell than become chief justice.[129] Evidently, the appeal of judicial preferment was not equally shared; for Macdonald and Blake, the attraction of active political life remained too great.

Although the rhetoric circling judicial office was never on level with reality, appointments to the bench did constitute something quite different than did other forms of political patronage. As such, once elevated, judges were unlike other public figures, though the expectations entailing that difference varied according to the individual acting as minister of justice. So while Macdonald howled when Oliver Mowat violated the "monk hood" of the bench and returned to active politics, Sir John was evidently untroubled when he orchestrated John Thompson's return from the bench to political life in 1885.[130] What had been an abomination in one instance was politically expedient in another. Such were the thin distinctions of the relationship between the Department of Justice and the judiciary; distinctions borne out of "true constitutional principle," the art of statecraft, and the confluence of law and politics in the completion of Confederation.

7
Conclusion

The triumphal return to power of the Conservatives on 17 September 1878 marked both a new beginning for Sir John A. Macdonald and an end to the Confederation era. For Macdonald, who had almost died in 1870, had seriously considered retirement shortly thereafter, and had left office in disgrace in the wake of the Pacific Scandal, the electoral victory of 1878 remains the most impressive political recovery in our nation's history. Just months away from his sixty-fourth birthday, Macdonald, who had already occupied a prominent place in Canadian affairs for twenty years before the union of 1867, was about to embark on his second full term as the nation's prime minister. However, the Macdonald of 1878 was "strangely unlike the self-effacing, repentant, ageing man" who had been pushed from office five years earlier.[1] For at least a year he had been notably more combative, and the electoral victory offered both redemption and another opportunity to champion his vision of Canada: "The second chance would be the last chance. It had come late. It could not be, in the nature of things, as favourable a chance as the first. But it would be the last opportunity he would ever get."[2]

That Macdonald was willing and able to reenter the fray did not mean that he could pick up where he had so inelegantly left off in 1873. The five years of Alexander Mackenzie's Liberal government had completed much of what had been left undone. The federal departmental, penal, and judicial structure flowing from the union scheme were in place and functioning by 1878. The Maritimes had been integrated into a broader national community, the North West Mounted Police were asserting Canadian sovereignty over the interior, the treaty process with the Aboriginal peoples of the Canadian prairies had been undertaken, and despite rumblings in the summer of 1875, the Métis had apparently resettled in the distant northwest. As the nation physically expanded from the Atlantic to the Pacific, the distinct identities of the two national political parties had hardened into shape, in part over fundamental disagreements concerning railway construction. So too were future constitutional battles rumoured, as a number of disquieting points of jurisdictional conflict had surfaced in the eleven years since 1867. The stage had been set for the next phase of the nation-building enterprise; a period of grand railway projects and almost twenty years of constitutional strife. The years from union to 1878 had completed Confederation; the almost two decades after would reveal how the union would work in practice. For Macdonald and the nation, that which followed 1878 would be very different from that which went before.

The Constitutional Battle

Aside from the constitutional rumblings, there were other indications of the sea of change to occur after 1878. One, as Peter Waite gently acknowledges, was that Macdonald "was now becoming more and more closed in, natural enough for his age, but nevertheless effectively imprisoned, in a sense, by his old circle of friends and associates."[3] Paired with this closing in and allied to the sense that this would be his final chance, Macdonald proved to be less willing to brook any opposition to either the style or substance of his governance. This was nowhere more apparent than in Macdonald's attitude towards Ontario's premier Oliver Mowat, with whom, according to Donald Creighton, Macdonald "always found it a positive pleasure to do battle."[4] Creighton may well have been accurate in his assessment, but, as time would reveal, there would be precious little pleasure for Macdonald in these engagements with Mowat. Indeed, Mowat seemed to be a solvent for all the attributes and talents that had been central to Macdonald's career. As Mowat's biographer A. Margaret Evans points out, Macdonald's "famous bonhomie, his skill in the management of men, his powers of conciliation, were not evinced where the provincialist premier was concerned."[5] For by the time Macdonald realized that Mowat was deadly serious and "would not be intimidated," the course could not be altered; Sir John was locked in a battle that successive rulings of the Judicial Committee of the Privy Council indicated he could not win.[6]

Although scholars have detailed the constitutional turmoil between Macdonald and Mowat, they have tended to concentrate on why Mowat emerged victorious, rather than on why Macdonald adopted the tactics he did. The emphasis is unsurprising since, more often than not, victors write the history. However, unanswered questions concerning Macdonald's tactics remain. Specifically, why did Macdonald, whose entire career avoided "strident convictions," suddenly became so utterly inflexible in these contests with Mowat after 1878?[7] After all, it was Mowat who, only three years earlier, suggested to Edward Blake that Macdonald's method of dealing with questionable legislation through consultation was preferable to simply striking out that which was alleged to be unconstitutional.[8] Indeed, Blake's predecessor in the Department of Justice, Télesphore Fournier, had adopted the latter course with Ontario's legislation concerning escheats and forfeitures.[9] Abandoning a method both tried and true was not something Macdonald did, yet that was exactly what occurred upon his return to office in 1878.

Creighton's biography of Macdonald pins the animosity on two basic points: Sir John fought as he did because "Mowat was combating the ideal of a great united Dominion with provincial rights and territorial aggrandisement."[10] Essentially, Mowat was undoing what Macdonald believed he had constructed. Further, with the passage of time and the accumulation of conflict and ill will, Macdonald simply disliked Mowat, the "little tyrant" who once deserved to have his chops slapped.[11] Although the perceived threat to the Dominion speaks to Macdonald's motivation, he had regularly counselled others to avoid nursing grudges. Arguably this was no ordinary disagreement, and perhaps the gravity of the situation enhanced a personal stake in the outcome. However, the amount of personal antagonism existing between the two men aggravated a more fundamental and perhaps systemic conflict.

For while personality conflicts played a role in exacerbating these constitutional battles, such considerations ought not detract from a more thoroughgoing inquiry. For example, although most of the conflicts were framed by the years of Macdonald's return in 1878 and his death in 1891, and thus depicted as a contest between Macdonald and Mowat, the dispute over escheats and forfeitures began during the Liberal administration of Alexander Mackenzie. Instead of exploring other possibilities, the presence of Hewitt Bernard as deputy minister of justice has provided a convenient, if not altogether compelling, explanation for the jurisdictional dispute.[12] The apparent source of this interpretation is none other than Oliver Mowat, who specifically and disingenuously blamed Bernard for Fournier's ex parte opinion, striking down Ontario's legislation.[13] If Fournier subscribed to Mowat's position, surely the minister of justice was of stout enough fibre to stand up to his deputy minister rather than cave in on an issue of constitutional interpretation. Yet rather than consider the implications of Fournier actually believing that Ontario's legislation was unconstitutional, it was easier to perceive a Macdonaldian conspiracy with Sir John directing events through Bernard, his brother-in-law and accomplice.[14]

Emphasizing Bernard's role and his connection to Macdonald substitutes personal intrigue for an explanation grounded in how the department functioned. Given the department's method of dealing with conflicts, Bernard's memorandum was merely an opening gambit in the type of unofficial constitutional negotiation that had successfully occurred since 1867. The process went awry when Fournier simply accepted Bernard's position as being sound from a federal point of view, rather than bringing the matter to Mowat's unofficial attention. After all, while Mowat quite rightly believed that Ontario's position was correct, he was equally annoyed that Fournier concurred with Bernard before discussing the matter. That the federal Department of Justice subscribed to a contrary position on the legislation was to be expected; it was the refusal to discuss the question that Mowat found especially galling.

Therefore, the disagreement between the Dominion and Ontario positions on escheats and forfeitures was genuine in how it reflected the federal practice of countering all opinions, legal and otherwise, that threatened federal preeminence. This general approach was pursued by the department, regardless of which political party was in power. That the skirmish over escheat and forfeitures degenerated into a genuine constitutional clash was not the product of Macdonaldian intrigues. Rather, it flowed from the dynamics inherent to the union scheme, the department's role as legal advisor to the federal government, and the abandonment of unofficial communications that had defused these situations in the past. The retreat to literalism in reading the constitution sacrificed the critical flexibility that the federal government required to manage its arena of activity. The contrast is striking; while the federal government assumed this literalist approach in these clashes with Ontario, the province championed a view demanding "a very large, liberal and comprehensive interpretation."[15] Finally, this stubborn reading of the constitution was also a marked departure from the sceptical notions infusing the very origins of the department. Rather than applying the law with the expectation that outstanding disagreements could be dissolved by understandings between gentleman politicians, the department was now being asked to provide the exact, unequivocal, and unassailable meaning of constitution. For the collection of individuals whom the department could attract, such an expectation was with the exception of a notable few, rather steep.

Cast within this light, and completely distinct from the actual merits of the positions adopted by either side in the various contests, the federal approach in these constitutional battles was hobbled by a complicated amalgam of centralist principles, political notions, abandoned expectations, and personal antagonisms. As a consequence, the federal position after 1878 was out-marshalled by Mowat, not only because the provincialist case was on a firmer footing but because Macdonald badly miscalculated the situation, did not truly possess the means within the Department of Justice to fight aggressively, and, finally, was personally unwilling to sit down with Mowat and hammer out a compromise. Indeed, as early as 1881, Macdonald was unwilling to personally discuss the boundary between Ontario and Manitoba with Mowat, who was also becoming increasingly belligerent.[16]

Events seemingly conspired against the federal cause. Although Macdonald was obviously directing the federal charge, Minister of Justice James

MacDonald was of indifferent mettle. Appointed in the wake of the 1878 victory, MacDonald was the "uninspired but judicious Nova Scotian" whom Sir Hector Langevin later dismissed as "an utter failure in federal politics."[17] Building the federal case in these clashes required myriad talents, and MacDonald did not fit the bill. Fortunately for the federal cause, MacDonald's term would be brief, lasting only until May 1881, when he was rewarded for his service to the country by the appointment as Nova Scotia's chief justice. Into his place stepped Sir Alexander Campbell, a long-time associate and occasional business partner of Sir John's. Hardly a newcomer to federal politics, Campbell had been appointed to the Senate by Macdonald on 23 October 1867, from where he supervised the post office throughout Macdonald's first term.[18] Although more likely to hold Sir John's attention than did MacDonald, Campbell was no more able to compel the prime minister to alter his course in refusing to speak with Mowat. Obviously, the die had been cast.

One of the few bright spots for the federal cause was the presence of the department's deputy minister, Zebulon Lash. Just as Hewitt Bernard had eased the transition from the Conservatives to the Liberals in 1873, Lash was there to reverse the process in 1878. Despite recognized political differences with the incoming Conservatives, Lash was willing and welcomed to stay in the department. Although an increase in salary promised by outgoing Minister of Justice Laflamme was not forthcoming, Lash nonetheless received both a financial and professional boost by his appointment "as counsel in cases in which the Government is interested."[19] As a result, it would be Lash who would argue the federal case in *Mercer* v. *the Attorney General for Ontario* before the Canadian Supreme Court and eventually before the Judicial Committee of the Privy Council (JCPC). Although Lash's argument before the Supreme Court secured a federal victory in the winter of 1881, the result was overturned on appeal to the JCPC in the summer of 1883.[20]

By the time the verdict was reversed, Lash had parted company with the Department of Justice. The departure was the product of a number of factors. For a practitioner of his skill, lucrative opportunities existed elsewhere. Indeed, upon his resignation from the department, Lash became a partner in Edward Blake's law firm. More immediately, Lash's relationship with incoming minister Alexander Campbell had gotten off to a rocky start, when the two disagreed over the constitutional question of whether the governor general necessarily had to consult with his ministers. In an opinion dated 3 May 1881, Lash argued that the governor was restricted by the advice of his ministers, while Campbell did not share this opinion. Although James MacDonald was still officially minister of justice at the time, the initial "A" on the memorandum challenging Lash's position reveals that the disagreement had occurred with Alexander Campbell.[21] Lash would remain one year and two days after Campbell's appointment as minister of justice.

Lash's departure was a telling indication of the dire straits in which the Department of Justice and the federal government found themselves. The nadir was, however, yet to come. Although the cases that followed the Manitoba boundary hearing before the JCPC were, in their own way, compelling indications of how badly the federal cause had fared, the defeat over the boundary was perhaps the worst. Argued by Dalton McCarthy, viewed by many as the next in line for the Conservative Party's leadership, the federal side was thoroughly dismantled by Oliver Mowat's arguments and evidence.[22] Mowat's preparation reflected a dispute that had been over a decade in the making, while the federal side appeared utterly disorganized. In comparison to Mowat's presentation, "The lack of preparation on the Manitoba-Dominion side was a striking contrast."[23] The federal side had been simply out-marshalled.

It would take the ministerial terms of Alexander Campbell and John Thompson before relations between the federal government and the Province of Ontario returned to some semblance of civility. Although Campbell's tenure witnessed a number of constitutional defeats for the federal cause, not only did he espouse greater sympathy for Ontario, but these cases had not been of his making and were carried forth despite his objections. Further, as Garth Stevenson points out in his splendid study of federal-provincial relations, Campbell's diplomacy "helped to maintain the necessary degree of co-operation between the dominion and the largest province, despite the mutual hostility of the two leaders."[24] Ironically, given the awkwardness of Thompson's arrival in Ottawa and the unseating of Campbell from the Department of Justice, it would be Thompson who would complete Campbell's work and reestablish a genuine working relationship between the department and Ontario.[25]

Although Thompson was more of a centralist than Campbell was, he was certainly less strident than Macdonald. More importantly, Thompson was uninterested in fighting with Ontario merely on the grounds that a jurisdictional line had been crossed. Further, he was also intelligent enough to recognize artifice when it was presented to him.[26] Therefore, when Oliver Mowat contacted Thompson six months after he became minister of justice and requested federal acquiescence in Ontario's newly minted Factories Act, Thompson realized that the game was afoot. Rather than play at Mowat's bidding, Thompson merely informed the Ontario premier that if he felt such legislation was within the jurisdiction of the province, it hardly needed federal confirmation. Deftly turning the tables on Mowat, Thompson then queried the premier as to why he evidently thought the legislation was beyond the province's authority. In effect, Thompson was uninterested in becoming embroiled in a fracas of Mowat's construction, evidently for the premier's benefit. As Margaret Evans concludes, Thompson "was not disputing the provincial authority to pass a factory act and need take no action if the act was intra vires," whereas Mowat was attempting to obtain a resolution with the federal government over a matter it had claimed jurisdiction and thus wished to settle the question in avoidance of subsequent litigation.[27] Obviously, Thompson was of a very different stripe than was Macdonald.

Although a strained interaction, this first exchange between Thompson and Mowat marked the eventual resumption of the unofficial exchanges that had occurred before the escheats and forfeitures difficulties of 1875. And as Peter Waite notes, "Despite the opening gambit over factory legislation, their cordiality grew."[28] Indeed, Waite quite rightly gives Thompson credit for a significant decrease in the combativeness and ill will between the department and Ontario. Not only was there a "steep diminution in the volume and acerbity of the correspondence," but Thompson steadfastly avoided arbitrary or vindictive interference with provincial legislation, in part also to smoothing out relations with Ontario. Waite continues: "This was a result of Thompson's informal talks with Oliver Mowat, the great champion of provincial causes. These began in 1886, and their general effect was to render unnecessary, as far as Ontario was concerned, the formal apparatus of disallowance. The tone of this correspondence was one of mutual respect, even friendliness."[29] With Thompson, the relationship between the Department of Justice and the provinces had come full circle; nation building, like the completion of Confederation, could not be achieved by internecine warfare between the federal government and the provinces. Flexibility and a willingness to construct understandings between gentlemen politicians was, it was learned, a necessity and not a luxury in the art of statecraft. A lesson hard learned by the federal government during these years of constitutional strife, it still resonates as a truth of effective governance in Canada.

The Department and the Completion of Confederation

Shaped by a philosophical make-up combining the ideology of law with a deeply held scepticism of the ability of law or legal remedy to effect thoroughgoing reform, the demands placed upon the Canadian minister of justice, attorney general, and Department of Justice mirrored the confluence of law and politics. Neither completely good nor bad, this fusion was a realistic product of Canada's colonial history and the evolution of its political and legal institutions arrayed against a series of widely subscribed expectations and assumptions about law and its practitioners. Distinct from the English portrayal of an apolitical advisor to the crown and government, the British North American attorney general assumed an expanding range of duties, from conducting criminal assize to drafting legislation and, by the 1830s and 1840s, donning the mantle of political and governmental leadership in local assemblies. Indeed, by 1867 and the British North America Act, the office of attorney general had become synonymous with legislative and political power at both the provincial and federal level of governance in the new dominion.

Notwithstanding this accumulated influence, Confederation provided an opportunity for re-creating the office of attorney general in Canada. Consistent with the federal nature of the union, functions vested previously in a single attorney general were divided between federal and provincial spheres. The new federal attorney general and minister of justice shouldered the task of advising the federal government and various department of state, while provincial attorney generals continued to perform many of their colonial-era duties. At the federal level, this shift in emphasis meant that the provision of counsel in relation to the government's mandate increasingly dominated the attorney general's work, no matter how slight or abstract the actual legal content of the referrals. Further, once the Department of Justice was created in 1868 to support the minister of justice and attorney general, it assumed responsibility for an assortment of law-related concerns; a development consistent with the ideology of law and its corollary that those trained in the law were apolitical and possessed a cache of specialized insight or knowledge. Specifically, not only did the department provide the federal government with legal advice, but administrating the royal prerogative of mercy, creating a national penitentiary system, and managing of the judiciary were quickly portrayed as natural extensions of the legal advisors' mandate in the newly minted Confederation scheme. In effect, the ideology of law rationalized the continued prominence of legally trained people within a variety of governmental and bureaucratic roles, while at the same time, lending weight and legitimacy to the subsequent practices and decisions. As a consequence, law and accommodations grounded in the confluence of law and politics assumed a central role in working out the administrative implications flowing from the union, a task that was well in hand by 1878.

Not surprisingly, for those burdened with the provision of legal counsel to the federal government, the Conservative resurgence of that year and the battles that followed did not alter the daily routine. The continuity provided by Lash's presence in 1878 ensured that while the tumult of a change in government was all about, departmental business continued unabated. As such, the usual assortment of queries required attention. Petitions for remissions of sentences needed to be weighed, penitentiary reports prepared, tribunals for controverted elections struck, all while entreaties from hopeful candidates for judicial vacancies arrived in the daily mail. More pressing was the resignation of Jean-Thomas Taschereau from the Supreme Court, a seat that needed to be filled quickly to bolster the Court's already sagging reputation. Although the expected resignation of Chief Justice Richards also loomed large on the horizon, given the challenges faced during the completion of Confederation, such eventualities were well within the department's compass.

That business continued apace was an easily overlooked indication that, in countless ways, the union scheme had hardened into shape. The constitution and its governmental superstructure had been completed, and now the task turned to discerning how the two elements would function in practice. One part of that structure had been the Department of Justice and its attendant responsibilities for providing the federal government with legal advice. So too was the department's mandate to review Dominion and provincial legislation, advise on the royal prerogative, administer federal penitentiaries, and supervise the nation's judiciary. Through this process, the department developed an approach to governance reflecting an unsettled and changing set of responses "to the continual interaction among men, forces, ideas and institutions."[30] Further, this pattern was the product of "thousands of tiny contingent practices" that, in turn, created a way of thinking resident in the department as a whole.[31] In essence, the functioning of the Department of Justice reflected the emergence of a governmentality wherein it employed tactics rather than law and even used law, and its interpretation, as tactics.[32] Or, put another way, the department practised the art of statecraft and did so in accordance with federal interests and, it was assumed, for the benefit of the Canadian nation-state. It was, of course, this conflation of federal interests with the national well-being that emerged as a fundamental weakness of the federal approach to the constitutional battles of the post-1878 era.

In the end, a central question arising from the department's role in completing Confederation concerns the department's success in portraying its preferred "images and legal categories" as the only rational ones for Canada as a whole.[33] Success was relative. Within the context of the department's proscribed role of steering the federal government away from, and when necessary through, legal entanglements, it usually succeeded in portraying these manoeuvres as "sound pragmatic common sense."[34] Further, the advice tendered to the federal government was artfully depicted as constituting apolitical legal counsel. Yet neither the success nor the apolitical veneer would be maintained after 1878 for all the reasons the federal cause floundered in the constitutional battles with Ontario. Not only was the federal government's interpretation of the law revealed to be overtly politicized, but the department, emboldened by the success of participating in the completion of Confederation, was ill prepared for legal contests where the opponent refused to be intimidated by the apparent might of the federal government.

On other fronts, the department's success was more long-lived. Its advisory role regarding the royal prerogative of mercy, the construction and administration of a national penitentiaries system, and the supervision of the Canadian judiciary were all orchestrated in a manner reasserting the fiction of the attorney general as an apolitical counsel to the government. In all of these areas, the veneer was successfully maintained despite ample evidence to the contrary. Not only was the prerogative of mercy managed so as to indicate a rationality and reasonableness in how these fateful decisions were rendered, but also the task was accomplished while reinforcing the notion that the attorney general was best suited to provide such advice. Canadian penitentiaries were supervised in a similar fashion, demonstrating the federal government's ability to protect the Dominion's citizenry by allegedly reforming the criminal class and, in so doing, reifying this new relationship between the public and the government. Finally, through the complicated and subtle task of appointing members to the Canadian bench, the department navigated the straits of political favour, professional skill, and party obligation. At the same time, it aided the launch of the Canadian Supreme Court but fell short of creating an autonomous tribunal befitting the new dominion.

Ultimately, through the pursuit of its mandate and the attendant attempts to govern the law, the department's activities demonstrated the inherent congruence of law and politics in the completion of Confederation. This congruence, of course, was not limited to the eleven years after union but was an inescapable reality for a political world so completely imbued with the ideology of law. What marked these years as distinct was not only the degree to which the department was able to champion its notions but, conversely, its almost total failure to do so in the constitutional battles of the post-1878 era. The change in fortune was stunning and ought not to be swept away in favour of the traditional constructions of post-Confederation history. For in detailing the subtleties of the years between 1867 and 1878, we not only move closer to a fuller understanding of the dynamics of that which transpired in the subsequent era of constitutional strife, but we are able to discern the complexities of statecraft and governmentality practised by the Department of Justice, disguised as the government's apolitical legal advisor.

Notes

Chapter 1: Introduction

1 George W. Brega to John A. Macdonald, 30 December 1867, National Archives of Canada [NAC], Manuscript Group [MG] 26A, vol. 146, 59376-7. On Brega's uneven career as an agent and lobbyist, see James G. Snell, "A Foreign Agent in Washington: George W. Brega, Canada's Lobbyist, 1867-1870," in *Civil War History* 26, 1 (1980): 53-70; and Ben Forster, *A Conjunction of Interests: Business, Politics, and Tariffs, 1825-1879* (Toronto: University of Toronto Press, 1986), 69-71.

2 An Act respecting the Department of Justice, 31 Victoria, chapter 39. On the American legislation, see Cornell W. Clayton, *The Politics of Justice: The Attorney General and the Making of Legal Policy* (New York: M.E. Sharpe, 1992), 25-6; and Nancy V. Baker, *Conflicting Loyalties: Law and Politics in the Attorney General's Office, 1789-1990* (Lawrence: University of Kansas Press, 1992), 62-3.

3 On "making the constitution," see Paul W. Kahn, *Legitimacy and History: Self-Government in American Constitutional Theory* (New Haven: Yale University Press, 1992), 5, 9-31.

4 Ged Martin, *Britain and the Origins of Canadian Confederation, 1837-67* (Vancouver: University of British Columbia Press, 1995).

5 One facet of this process is detailed in Ben Forster's discussions of the Liberal Party's attitude towards tariffs; see Forster, supra note 1 at 147-64.

6 See generally A.A. den Otter, *The Philosophy of Railways: The Transcontinental Railway Idea in British North America* (Toronto: University of Toronto Press, 1997).

7 Second reading of "The Receiver-General and Attorney General Bill" took place on 2 April 1878 and the third reading eight days later on 10 April 1878. See Canada, House of Commons, *Debates,* 5th Session, 2 April 1878, vol. 5, 1584-624 and 1811-4.

8 The bill passed in amended form but was defeated in the Conservative-dominated Senate. See "Toussaint-Antoine-Rodolphe Laflamme," in Sir Charles G.D. Roberts and Arthur L. Tunnell, eds., *A Standard Dictionary of Canadian Biography* (Toronto: Trans-Canada Press, 1938), 225.

9 See Bruce W. Hodgins, *John Sandfield Macdonald* (Toronto: University of Toronto Press, 1971), 100; and Hodgins, "Disagreement at the Commencement: Divergent Ontarian Views of Federalism, 1867-1871," in Donald Swainson, ed., *Oliver Mowat's Ontario* (Toronto: Macmillan of Canada, 1972), 61.

10 Robert C. Vipond, *Liberty and Community: Canadian Federalism and the Failure of the Constitution* (Albany: State University of New York Press, 1991), 124.

11 Garth Stevenson, *Ex Uno Plures: Federal-Provincial Relations in Canada, 1867-1896* (Montreal and Kingston: McGill-Queen's University Press, 1993), 234.

12 Report of Attorney General Oliver Mowat, 22 February 1875, in W.E. Hodgins, ed., *Correspondence, Reports of the Ministers of Justice and Order in Council upon the subject of Dominion and Provincial Legislation, 1867-1895* (Ottawa: Queen's Printer, 1896), 118.

13 Oliver Mowat to Edward Blake, 23 June 1875, Archives of Ontario, [AO] M-242, no. 1.

14 Vipond, *Liberty and Community*, supra note 10 at 156.

15 Ibid., 182-90.

16 Stevenson, *Ex Uno Plures,* supra note 11 at 75, 201-2. The most pressing reason for replacing Campbell with Thompson was to provide the latter with a prominent place as part of the overall plan to strengthen Conservative chances in the election of 1887. See P.B. Waite, *The Man from Halifax: Sir John Thompson, Prime Minister* (Toronto: University of Toronto Press, 1985), 131-3.

17 Michel Foucault, "Governmentality," in G. Bruchell, C. Gordon, and P. Miller, eds., *The Foucault Effect: Studies in Governmentality* (Chicago: University of Chicago Press, 1991), 95.

18 Rod Preece, "The Political Wisdom of John A. Macdonald," *Canadian Journal of Political Science* 17, 3 (September 1984): 459-502.

19 "Inasmuch as the Minister is politically responsible for everything done in his department, he is given supreme authority, and he therefore has the power to overrule any of his civil servants at any time." Robert MacGregor Dawson, *The Government of Canada* (Toronto: University of Toronto Press, 1963), 240.

20 See Judith Fingard, *Jack in Port: Sailortowns of Eastern Canada* (Toronto: University of Toronto Press, 1982), 194-243.

21 An excellent examination of how the line between claims and results becomes blurred is Dorothy E. Chunn, *From Punishment to Doing Good: Family Courts and Socialised Justice in Ontario, 1880-1940* (Toronto: University of Toronto Press, 1992).

22 J.E. Hodgetts, *Pioneer Public Service: An Administrative History of the United Canadas, 1841-1867* (Toronto: University of Toronto Press, 1955), 35.

23 Statement of G.W. Wicksteed, law clerk, 10 April 1880, House of Commons, *Journals of the Senate,* 1 May 1880, vol. 14 (1880), 227. There is some question as to what exactly Wicksteed meant by his reference to the preparation of bills. His official duties did not include drafting bills, but he unofficially filled this role when required.

24 British North America Act, 1867, ss. 96, 99, and 100.

25 Cindy Sondik Aron, *Ladies and Gentlemen of the Civil Service: Middle-Class Workers in Victorian America* (New York: Oxford University Press, 1987). The pursuit of stability is noted by W.A. Calder in reference to prison guards; see W.A. Calder, "The Federal Penitentiary System in Canada, 1867-1899:A Social and Institutional History" (PhD diss., University of Toronto, 1979), 94-6.

26 Dawson, *The Government of Canada,* supra note 19 at 294-6.

27 See generally, Sondik Aron, *Ladies and Gentlemen of the Civil Service,* supra note 25.

28 Desmond H. Brown, ed., *The Birth of a Criminal Code: The Evolution of Canada's Justice System* (Toronto: University of Toronto Press, 1995), 3-4. Also see Desmond H. Brown, *The Genesis of the Canadian Criminal Code of 1892* (Toronto: Osgoode Society, 1989).

29 Hodgetts, *Pioneer Public Service,* supra note 22 at 36.

30 Memorandum for the minister of justice from Z.A. Lash, December 1878, NAC, RG 13, vol. 419.

31 See Jonathan Swainger, "A Bench in Disarray: The Quebec Judiciary and the Federal Department of Justice, 1867-1878," *Les Cahiers de Droit* 34, 1 (March 1993): 59-92.

32 For a small sampling, see Peter Oliver, *"Terror to Evil-Doers": Prisons and Punishments in Nineteenth-Century Ontario* (Toronto: Osgoode Society for Canadian Legal History, 1998); Calder, "The Federal Penitentiary System in Canada," supra note 25; Russell Smandych, "Tory Paternalism and the Politics of Penal Reform in Upper Canada, 1830-34: A 'Neo-revisionist' Account of the Kingston Penitentiary," *Criminal Justice History: An International Annual* 12 (1991): 57-84; Russell Smandych, "Beware of the 'Evil American Monster': Upper Canadian Views on the Need for a Penitentiary, 1830-1834," *Canadian Journal of Criminology* 33, 2 (1991): 125-47; Peter Oliver, "From Jails to Penitentiary: The Demise of Community Corrections in early Ontario," *Correctional Options* 4 (1984): 4-10; Peter Oliver, "A Terror to Evil-Doers: The Central Prison and the 'Criminal Class' in Late Nineteenth-Century Ontario" in Roger Hall, William Westfall, and Laurel A. MacDowell, eds., *Patterns of the Past: Interpreting Ontario's History* (Toronto: Dundurn Press, 1988), 221-50; C.J. Taylor, "The Kingston, Ontario Penitentiary and Moral Architecture," *Histoire sociale/Social History* 12, 24 (1979): 385-408; Rainer Baehre, "Prison as Factory, Convict as Worker: A Study of the Mid-Victorian St. John Penitentiary, 1841-1880," in Jim Phillips, Tina Loo, and Susan Lewthwaite, eds., *Essays in the History of Canadian Law: Crime and Criminal Justice* (Toronto:

Osgoode Society for Canadian Legal History, 1994), 439-77; and Baehre, "From Bridewell to Federal Penitentiary: Prisons and Punishment in Nova Scotia before 1880," in Philip Girard and Jim Phillips, eds., *Essays in the History of Canadian Law: Nova Scotia* (Toronto: The Osgoode Society, 1990), 163-99.

33 Calder, "The Federal Penitentiary System in Canada," supra note 25 at 65-144.

34 Karl Mannheim, *Ideology and Utopia: An Introduction to the Sociology of Knowledge* (New York: Harcourt, Brace and World, 1936), 57.

35 David Sugarman, "Law, Economy and the State in England, 1750-1914: Some Major Issues," in David Sugarman, ed., *Legality, Ideology, and the State* (London: Academic Press, 1983), 231.

36 Carolyn Strange, "The Lottery of Death: Capital Punishment, 1867-1976," *Manitoba Law Journal* 23, 3 (January 1996): 594-619.

37 Edward Blake to Alexander Mackenzie, 25 September 1875, supra note 13, reel 5, no. 177.

38 See generally, Strange, "The Lottery of Death," supra note 36; and Strange, ed., *Qualities of Mercy: Justice, Punishment, and Discretion* (Vancouver: University of British Columbia Press, 1996).

39 Benedict Anderson, *Imagined Communities: Reflections on the Origins and Spread of Nationalism* (London: Verso, 1991), 6-7.

Chapter 2: An Apolitical Advisor

1 Edmund S. Morgan, *Inventing the People: The Rise of Popular Sovereignty in England and America* (New York: W.W. Norton and Company, 1988), 13.

2 Ibid., 14.

3 Natalie Zemon Davis, *Fiction in the Archives: Pardon Tales and Their Tellers in Sixteenth-Century France* (Stanford: Stanford University Press, 1987), 3.

4 Morgan, *Inventing the People,* supra note 1 at 14.

5 H.W. Arthurs, *"Without the Law": Administrative Justice and Legal Pluralism in Nineteenth-Century England* (Toronto: University of Toronto Press, 1985), 1.

6 David Sugarman, "Law, Economy and the State in England, 1750-1914: Some Major Issues," in David Sugarman, ed., *Legality, Ideology, and the State* (London: Academic Press, 1983), 231.

7 Robert W. Gordon, "'The Ideal and the Actual in the Law': Fantasies and Practices of New York City Lawyers, 1870-1910," in G.W. Gawalt, ed., *The New High Priests: Lawyers in Post Civil War America* (Westport, CT: Greenwood Press, 1984), 53.

8 Sugarman, "Law, Economy and the State in England," supra note 6 at 230-1.

9 Arthurs, "Without the Law," supra note 5 at 1.

10 Robert Gordon, "Introduction: J. Willard Hurst and the Common Law Tradition in American Legal Historiography," *Law and Society Review* 20 (Fall 1975): 31.

11 Robert Gordon, "Critical Legal Histories," *Stanford Law Review* 36 (1984): 100-1.

12 On the origins of the English attorney general, see John L.J. Edwards, *The Law Officers of the Crown: A Study of the Offices of the Attorney-General and Solicitor-General of England with an Account of the Office of the Director of Public Prosecutions of England* (London: Sweet and Maxwell, 1964); and James William Norton-Kyshe, *The Law and Privileges Relating to the Attorney-General and Solicitor-General of England, with a History from the Earliest Periods and a Series of King's Attorneys and Solicitors-General from the Reign of Henry III to the 60th of Queen Victoria* (London: Stevens and Haynes, 1897).

13 See generally, Robert Gordon, "The Independence of Lawyers," *Boston University Law Review* 68 (1988): 1-83.

14 Mark Tushnet, "Perspectives on the Development of American Law: A Critical Review of Friedman's A History of American Law," *Wisconsin Law Review* 1 (1977): 100.

15 See generally, Paul Romney, "Responsibility and Independence," in *Mr. Attorney: The Attorney-General for Ontario in Court, Cabinet, and Legislature, 1791-1899* (Toronto: Osgoode Society, 1986), 158-200.

16 T.D. McGee, Report of T.D. McGee on the Public Departments, 1863, National Archives of Canada [NAC], Record Group [RG] 1, E7, vol. 59A, 32-4.

17 Elizabeth Arthur, "Francis Maseres," in *Dictionary of Canadian Biography,* vol. 6 (Toronto: University of Toronto Press, 1987), 491-5; James H. Lambert, "Sir James Monk," ibid.,

511-5; Patrick Brode, *Sir John Beverley Robinson: Bone and Sinew of the Compact* (Toronto: Osgoode Society, 1984); Romney, *Mr. Attorney,* supra note 15; Brian Cuthbertson, *The Old Attorney General: A Biography of Richard John Uniacke* (Halifax: Nimbus, 1980); and John Doull, *Sketches of Attorney Generals of Nova Scotia, 1750-1926* (Halifax: 1964), 26-34.

18 Romney, *Mr. Attorney,* supra note 15 at 159.

19 Ibid., 160.

20 Gerald Craig, ed., *Lord Durham's Report* (Toronto: McClelland and Stewart, 1963), 55.

21 Ibid., 64.

22 Ibid., 65.

23 The plural reference reflects the fact that after 1841 there were two attorney generals in the united province.

24 This peculiarity did not go unnoticed. See Canada, National Archives of Canada [NAC], Report of a Committee of the Honourable the Executive Council, 12 November 1846, NAC, RG 1, E8, vol. 16, Executive Council at 21.

25 See Ian Radford, "Sydenham and Utilitarian Reform," in Allan Greer and Ian Radford, eds., *Colonial Leviathan: State Formation in Mid-Nineteenth Century Canada* (Toronto: University of Toronto Press, 1992), 81.

26 J.E. Hodgetts, *Pioneer Public Service: An Administrative History of the United Canadas, 1841-1867* (Toronto: University of Toronto Press, 1955), 26. Also see Donald Creighton, *John A. Macdonald: The Young Politician* (Toronto: Macmillan Company of Canada, 1952), 70-1.

27 Ibid., 27.

28 Report of T.D. McGee on the Public Departments, 1863, NAC, RG 1, E7, vol. 59A, 32-3.

29 Romney, *Mr. Attorney,* supra note 15 at 159-60.

30 Hodgetts, *Pioneer Civil Service,* supra note 26 at 272-3. My emphasis.

31 Canada, NAC, Report of a Committee of the Honourable the Executive Council, supra note 24 at 21-3.

32 Romney, *Mr. Attorney,* supra note 15 at 176-88.

33 Ibid., 183-5. Also see John Hillyard Cameron, question 40, Appendix to Canada, *Journals of the Legislative Assembly of the Province of Canada,* 1850, vol. 9., appendix BB.

34 Ibid.

35 Robert Baldwin, question 105, ibid.

36 Ibid.

37 Hodgetts, *Pioneer Civil Service,* supra note 26 at 83.

38 McGee, Report of T.D. McGee on the Public Departments, supra note 28 at 32-4.

39 Ibid., 32.

40 An Act respecting the Department of Justice, 31 Victoria, chapter 39. The bill received second reading on 6 May 1868 and third reading on the following day when it went into Committee of the Whole. See Canada, House of Commons, *Debates,* 1st Parliament, 1st session, 1868, 643 and 646.

41 John L.J. Edwards, *Ministerial Responsibility for National Security as it Relates to the Offices of Prime Minister, Attorney General and Solicitor General of Canada* (Ottawa: Queen's Printer, 1980), 8.

42 An Act respecting the Department of Justice, s. 1.

43 Ibid., s. 2.

44 Ibid., s. 3.

45 On the Colonial Office, see David M.L. Farr, *The Colonial Office and Canada, 1867-1887* (Toronto: University of Toronto Press, 1955).

46 See Department of Justice Mail Registers, 1868, NAC, RG 13, A1, vol. 435, no. 924; and Colonial Office 42/672, NAC, reel B489, no. 11668, 531-6.

47 The following is based upon the Memorandum concerning the powers of disallowance, 8 June 1868, NAC, RG 13, vol. 419. Also see Department of Justice letter book, 8 June 1868, RG 13, A3, vol. 554, 696-9.

48 Daily Journal, 4 May 1868, University of Western Ontario, University of Western Ontario Regional Room, David Mills Papers, box 4285, no. 244. The entry made more than a month before the memorandum was released suggests that Macdonald circulated a draft

among prominent lawyers for commentary before completing the final version. Mills' entry notes that Macdonald had initially proposed two grounds for disallowance; an act being contrary to public policy and its being ultra vires.

49 Ibid.

50 The following is based upon Department of Justice Circular, 11 June 1868, NAC, RG 13, accession 86-7/361, box 2, no. 13/1868.

51 Governor General Lord Dufferin to John A. Macdonald, 19 October 1873, NAC, MG 26A, vol. 79, 30965-78. My emphasis.

52 On Blake, see Benjamin Forster and Jonathan Swainger, "Edward Blake" in *Dictionary of Canadian Biography,* vol. 13 (Toronto: University of Toronto Press, 1998), 74-85.

53 "Speech of Charles Tupper at Halifax" in C.H. Mackintosh, ed., *Grits in Office: Profession and Practice Contrasted* (Ottawa: Conservative Association of the Dominion, 1876), 41-2. Also see Macdonald Papers, NAC, MG 26A, vol. 158, 64419-20.

54 "Sir John A. Macdonald's Speech at Thomas White Banquet," ibid., 22. Also see Macdonald Papers, NAC, MG 26A, vol. 158, 64400.

55 Edward Blake to Alexander Mackenzie, 26 November 1875, private, NAC, MG 26B, reel M-198. For a sample of press commentary, see *Nation,* 19 November 1875, 541; "Independence of the Judiciary," *London Free Press,* 22 November 1875; "The Minister of Justice and the Mail," *Toronto Globe,* 24 November 1875; "Doubtful Justice," *London Free Press,* 25 November 1875; "Ministers and Ex-Ministers," *Toronto Globe,* 1 December 1875; Toronto Mail, 1 December 1875; "The Blake Controversy," *London Free Press,* 3 December 1875; and Editorial, *Nation,* 21 January 1876.

56 Blake to Mackenzie, NAC, MG 26B, reel M-198.

57 Alexander Mackenzie to Edward Blake, 27 November 1875, Archives of Ontario [AO], MS 20 (5), no. 85.

58 Robert C. Vipond, *Liberty and Community: Canadian Federalism and the Failure of the Constitution* (Albany: State University of New York Press, 1991), 188.

59 Alexander Mackenzie to Edward Blake, 25 September 1876, AO, MS 20 (5) no. 180.

60 Confidential memorandum on the arrangement of cabinet offices and emoluments, 23 January 1877, AO, MS 20 (24).

61 House of Commons, *Debates,* 5th Session, 2 April 1878, vol. 5, 1584-624.

62 Mr. Mitchell, ibid., 1585.

63 Sir John A. Macdonald, ibid., 1589.

64 Ibid., 1588.

65 Ibid., 1624.

66 Alexander Mackenzie, ibid., 1591.

67 Ibid.

68 Edward Blake, ibid., 1599.

69 "Toussaint-Antoine-Rodolphe Laflamme," in Sir Charles G.D. Roberts and Arthur L. Tunnell, eds., *A Standard Dictionary of Canadian Biography* (Toronto: Trans-Canada Press, 1938), 225.

Chapter 3: The Department of Justice and the Business of Governance

1 Hewitt Bernard to James Robert Gowan, 15 August 1867, James Robert Gowan Papers, Manuscript Group [MG] 27 I E 31, National Archives of Canada [NAC].

2 Ibid. Two weeks earlier, Bernard had written: "I fancy I shall remain where I am now, at the fountain of Justice with perhaps some better title, and I hope more pay than hitherto." Hewitt Bernard to T.C. Patteson, 1 August 1867, Archives of Ontario, [AO] MU 2306.

3 Hallam's New Dominion Churn and Washer was granted its letters patent in September 1868. See Department of Justice Register, 1868, NAC, RG 13, A1, vol. 437, no. 196.

4 On this last point, see Jonathan Swainger, "A Distant Edge of Authority: Capital Punishment and the Prerogative of Mercy in British Columbia, 1872-1880," in Hamar Foster and John McLaren eds., *Essays in the History of Canadian Law: British Columbia and the Yukon* (Toronto: Osgoode Society for Legal History, 1995), 204-41.

5 John W. Cell, *British Colonial Administration in the Mid-Nineteenth Century: The Policy-Making*

Process (New Haven and London: Yale University Press, 1970), xi.

6 Robert W. Gordon, "Critical Legal Histories, *Stanford Law Review* 36 (1984): 84-5 and footnote 80, 90.

7 Michel Foucault, "Governmentality," in G. Bruchell, C. Gordon, and P. Miller, eds., *The Foucault Effect: Studies in Governmentality* (Chicago: University of Chicago Press, 1991), 95.

8 As cited in ibid., 112.

9 J.E. Hodgetts, *The Canadian Public Service: A Physiology of Government, 1867-1970* (Toronto: University of Toronto Press, 1973), 49.

10 R. MacGregor Dawson, "The Canadian Civil Service, 1867-1880," *Canadian Historical Review* 7 (1926): 34-45.

11 J.K. Johnson, ed., *The Letters of Sir John A. Macdonald, 1836-1857*, vol. 2 (Ottawa: Queen's Printer, 1968), 51, 126-7; order-in-council no. 534/1868, 29 May 1868, NAC, RG 2. For biographical detail on Bernard, see *Canada Law Journal* 29 (1893): 130-1 and 149-50; and P.B. Waite, "Hewitt Bernard," in *Dictionary of Canadian Biography,* vol. 12 (Toronto: University of Toronto Press, 1990), 97-8; and W. Stewart Wallace, ed., "Hewitt Bernard," in *Dictionary of Canadian Biography,* vol. 1 (Toronto: Macmillan Company of Canada, 1945), 45.

12 George Maclean Rose, ed., "Zebulon Aiton Lash," in *Cyclopaedia of Canadian Biography: Being Chiefly Men of the Time* (Toronto: Rose Publishing Company, 1886), 657. Also see Henry James Morgan, *The Canadian Men and Women of the Time: A Handbook of Canadian Biography of Living Characters* (Toronto: William Briggs, 1912), 638-9; C.W. Parker, *Who's Who and Why*, vol. 6 and 7 (Toronto: International Press, 1914), 1361; and W. Stewart Wallace, ed., *Dictionary of Canadian Biography*, vol. 2 (Toronto: Macmillan Company of Canada, 1945), 344.

13 Edward Blake to Z.A. Lash, private correspondence, 18 April 1876, AO, MS 20 (19), 211-2.

14 Lash to Blake, 19 April 1876, NAC, MG 27, I D2, reel M244.

15 Lash to Blake, ibid., 26 April 1876. A written acceptance was mailed the following day; see Lash to Blake, ibid., 27 April 1876.

16 Order-in-council no. 493/1876, 19 May 1876, NAC, RG 2.

17 Hewitt Bernard to James Robert Gowan, 13 April 1876, NAC, MG 27, I E 31, 73.

18 Order-in-council no. 1190/1882, 23 May 1881, NAC, RG 2.

19 Order-in-council no. 984/1872, 26 October 1872, NAC, RG 2. Bernard's memorandum of 8 October 1872 requesting addition help began with the assertion that "for some time past it has been found impossible, with the present staff of the Department of Justice, to keep up anything approaching to the efficient discharge of the daily business referred to it." See Hewitt Bernard to the Privy Council, 8 October 1872, in order-in-council no. 976/1872, 12 October 1872, NAC, RG 2.

20 See John A. Macdonald to John Barwick, Woodstock, confidential memorandum, 5 March 1872, NAC, MG 26A, vol. 575, 317, and order-in-council no. 984/1872, 26 October 1872, NAC, RG 2.

21 Order-in-council no. 977/1874, 28 July 1874, NAC, RG 2.

22 Order-in-council no. 1532/1874, 18 December 1874, NAC, RG 2; and Memorandum of Télesphore Fournier, 18 December 1874, NAC, RG 13, A4, vol. 1382. For the original order, see order-in-council no. 976/1872, 12 October 1872, NAC, RG 2, and Hewitt Bernard's memorandum of 8 October 1872.

23 Power's initial appointment to the civil service was on 7 December 1874; he was subsequently transferred to the Department of Justice on 1 July 1875. See Canada, *The Civil Service List of Canada, 1887* (Ottawa: Queen's Printer, 1888), 2.

24 See "Augustus Power" in Morgan, *The Canadian Men and Women of the Time,* supra note 12 at 914.

25 See "Hugh Richardson," ibid., 939 and order-in-council no. 836/1876, 18 September 1876, NAC, RG 2.

26 John Hillyard Cameron, question 40, Appendix to Canada, *Journals of the Legislative Assembly of the Province of Canada*, vol. 9, 1850, appendix BB. For a contemporary American description, see Opinion from Caleb Cushing to the president, 8 March 1854, *Official Opinions of the Attorneys General of the United States Advising the President and Heads of Departments, in Relation to their Official Duties: And Expounding the Constitution, Subsisting Treaties with Foreign Governments and With Indian Tribes, and the Public Laws of the Country,* edited

by Benjamin F. Hall (Washington: 1852), vol. 11, 347-55.

27 T.D. McGee, *Report of T.D. McGee on the Public Departments,* 1863, NAC, RG 1, E7, vol. 59A, 28-30.

28 "Department of Justice," first report of the Civil Service Commission, *Sessional Papers,* 1869, no. 19, 15.

29 David Sugarman, "Law, Economy and the State in England, 1750-1914: Some Major Issues," in David Sugarman, ed., *Legality, Ideology, and the State* (London: Academic Press, 1983), 216.

30 See Desmond Brown, ed., *The Birth of a Criminal Code: The Evolution of Canada's Justice System* (Toronto: University of Toronto Press, 1995), 12.

31 See Department of Justice Opinion Re Rideau Hall Estate, 23 November 1868, NAC, RG 13, A3, vol. 555, 384-9; 10 December 1868, 414-7; and 16 December 1868, 426-8; Department of Justice Opinion Re Windsor-Annapolis Railway, NAC, RG 13, A3, vol. 555, 131-6; and RG 13, accession 86-87/084, no. 14/1874 Re Windsor-Annapolis Railway, 30 November 1878.

32 Edward Blake, "The Teeswater Demonstration," in *Reform Government in the Dominion. The Pic-Nic Speeches* (Toronto: Globe Steam Book and Job Press, 1878), 135; and Rodolphe Laflamme, House of Commons *Debates,* 3rd Parliament, 5th Session, 2 April 1878, vol. 5, 1585.

33 See Eugene Forsey, "Meetings of the Queen's Privy Council for Canada, 1867-1882," *Canadian Journal of Economics and Political Science* 32 (February-November 1966), 489-98.

34 Report of G.W. Wicksteed and Hewitt Bernard, 24 February 1868, NAC, RG 13, Accession 86-87/361, no. 16/1868, 3.

35 Department of Justice Register, 1868, RG 13, A1, vol. 437.

36 Judith Tilloch, *The Rideau Canal: Defense, Transport and Recreation* (Ottawa: Parks Canada, 1981), 5-16.

37 Ibid., 12.

38 *An Act for transferring to one of Her Majesty's Principal Secretaries of State the powers and estates and property therein described, now vested in the Principal Officers of Her Majesty's Ordnance, and for vesting other part of the Ordnance Estates and Property therein described in Her Majesty the Queen, for the benefit, use and purposes of this Province,* 19 Victoria, chapter 45.

39 J.B. Slater to Mr. Braun, undersecretary, Department of Public Works, 14 June 1869, cited in Tilloch, *The Rideau Canal,* supra note 36 in note 10 at 19.

40 J.B. Slater to the Department of Public Works, 8 February 1872, NAC, RG 13, vol. 1860, no. 278/1872.

41 Ibid.

42 See Michael S. Cross, "Nicholas Sparks," in *Dictionary of Canadian Biography,* vol. 9 (Toronto: University of Toronto Press, 1976), 733-5.

43 See Desmond Morton, "William Foster Coffin," in *Dictionary of Canadian Biography,* vol. 10 (Toronto: University of Toronto Press, 1972), 180-2.

44 Hewitt Bernard, Department of Justice Opinion, 14 September 1872, NAC, RG 13, vol. 1860, no. 278/1872.

45 Ibid.

46 Hewitt Bernard to Alexander Mackenzie, 12 June 1874, NAC, RG 13, A3, vol. 566, 730-3. The statute to which Bernard referred was *An Act to explain provisions of the Ordnance Vesting Act and to remove certain difficulties which have occurred in carrying the said provision into effect,* 9 Victoria, chapter 42. His quotation from the statute was somewhat selective in that the land was granted by Sparks "for the purposes of the said Canal, provided no buildings be erected thereon." Not only had the provision concerning canal purposes been interpreted broadly but also buildings had in fact been constructed within the reserve.

47 Department of Justice to Department of Public Works, 16 June 1874, ibid., 770.

48 Marine and Fisheries Department to Department of Justice, 29 September 1872, NAC, RG 13, vol. 2138, no. 31/1872.

49 William Frederick Whitcher, for the Minister of Marine and Fisheries, to Hewitt Bernard, 27 September 1872, ibid.

50 Ibid.

51 N.d., Hewitt Bernard, Draft opinion re Burlington Beach, ibid.

52 Ibid. Also see *An Act for the Organisation of the Department of Marine and Fisheries of Canada,* 31 Victoria, chapter 57; and *An Act to amend chapter sixty-two of the Consolidated Statutes of Canada, and to provide for the better regulation of Fishing and the protection of Fisheries,* 29 Victoria, chapter 11, s. 3.
53 Bernard, Draft opinion re Burlington Bench, supra note 48.
54 Edward Blake, Department of Justice Opinion, 1 April 1876, NAC, RG 13, A3, vol. 576, 467-8.
55 The summary of this cases is based on Zebulon Lash, Department of Justice Memorandum to Edward Blake, 4 January 1877; and Rodolphe Laflamme, Department of Justice Opinion, 29 January 1877, RG 13, accession 86-87/084, no. 55/1876.
56 Spiles are large timbers used to support or stabilize heavy objects. It would appear that jackscrews were devices that were attached to the spiles and then used to elevate the hull.
57 Zebulon Lash, Department of Justice Memorandum, to Edward Blake, 4 January 1877; and Edward Blake to secretary of state, 5 January 1877, NAC, RG 13, accession 86-87/084, no. 55/1878. Although correct in noting that a claim for damages against the government had to be filed in Exchequer, Lash confused "The Petition of Right Act" with "The Supreme and Exchequer Court Act, which specifies that the Exchequer Court of Canada "shall have exclusive original jurisdiction in all cases" in which a monetary claim is made against the Dominion of Canada. See "The Supreme and Exchequer Court Act, 1875," chapter 11, s. 58, and "The Petition of Right Act, 1875," chapter 12.
58 Zebulon Lash, Department of Justice Memorandum to Rodolphe Laflamme, 29 January 1877, ibid.
59 E.V. Bothwell, Superintendent of Welland Canal to F. Braun, Secretary of Public Works, 19 March 1877, ibid.
60 Lord Blackburn, *David Geddes* v. *The Proprietors of the Bann Reservoir, Appeal Cases,* vol. 3 (1877-8), 456.
61 Hewitt Bernard, Memorandum re William F. Coffin's memorandum as to Ordnance lands, 31 January 1876, NAC, RG 13, accession 86-87/084, no. 9/1876.
62 Hewitt Bernard, Department of Justice Memorandum, 31 July 1876, NAC, RG 13, accession 86-87/084, vol. 2, no. 9/1876.
63 *An Act respecting Ordnance and Admiralty Lands in the Provinces of Ontario and Quebec,* 40 Victoria, chapter 8; and *An Act respecting certain Ordnance and Admiralty Lands in the Provinces of New Brunswick and Nova Scotia,* 42 Victoria, chapter 33. Also see "Annual Report of the Secretary of State for the year 1868," *Sessional Papers,* 1869, no. 14, 35-49.
64 See Robin B. Burns, "Thomas D'Arcy McGee," in *Dictionary of Canadian Biography,* vol. 9 (Toronto: University of Toronto Press, 1976), 489-94.
65 On the accusation against Bernard, see Department of Justice report, 7 January 1870, NAC, RG 13, A3, vol. 558, 284-7; and Department of Justice letter, 2 March 1870, 468.
66 See Petition of Alexander Turner to Lord Lisgar, 24 April 1869, and W.H. Fall to Hon. Secretary of State for Canada, 29 April 1869, NAC, RG 6, A1, vol. 6, no. 1000; Hewitt Bernard to Hugh Allan, private, NAC, RG 13, A3, vol. 556, 659-62; Bernard to Allan, 15 May 1870, 673; Bernard to Allan, 19 May 1869, 687-9; Bernard to Allan, 25 May 1870, 700; Department of Justice Report, NAC, RG 13, A3, vol. 557, 438-41. John Jordan, another key witness in the McGee assassination case, eventually ran afoul of the law in British Columbia. See Judge H.P.P. Crease to Hon. Minister of Justice, 7 June 1878, NAC, RG 13, vol. 2036, no. 1878/903.
67 See Lester D. Langley, "The Republican and Cuba: The Ten Years' War," in *The Cuban Policy of the United States: A Brief History* (New York: John Wiley and Sons, 1968), 53-81; John Edwin Fagg, *Cuba, Haiti, and the Dominion Republic* (Englewood Cliffs: Prentice Hall, 1965), 38-41; Allan Nevis, *Hamilton Fish: An Inner History of the Grant Administration* (New York: Frederick Ungar Publishing, 1936 and 1957), 667-94; and Harry Guggenheim, *The United States and Cuba: A Study in International Relations* (New York: Macmillan Company, 1934), 23-9.
68 For the general outline of the insurrection and its place in international relations, see Christopher J. Bartlett, "British Reaction to the Cuban Insurrection of 1868-1878," *Hispanic American Historical Review* 37, 3 (August 1957): 296-312.
69 Telegraphed report of Spanish Consul at Quebec, 31 August 1869, NAC, RG 13, A3, vol.

439, no. 1171. Also see Department of Justice memorandum to E.A. Meredith, undersecretary of state, 9 September 1869, NAC, RG 13, A3, vol. 557, 332-5.

70 Report from C.J. Coursol, Montreal, concerning reports from Mr. G.A. Munroe and Spanish vice-consul re recruiting in Montreal, 12 August 1871, NAC, RG 13, A3, vol. 446.

71 Neutrality towards Spain and Cuba, 13 July 1869, NAC, RG 13, A3, vol. 439, no. 1165.

72 See Department of Justice report on Canadian neutrality, 5 March 1870, NAC, RG 13, A3, vol. 558, 492-4; and Department of Justice report on Cuban situation, 16 March 1870, 573-4.

73 Department of Justice report, 14 August 1872, NAC, RG 13, A3, vol. 562, 192-4.

74 Department of Justice memorandum, 14 August 1872, ibid., 195-6.

75 Department of Justice memorandum, 23 August 1872, ibid., 247-8.

76 Department of Justice letter, 26 August 1872, ibid., 260-4. Evidently the *Southern* was swamped in the Sydney harbour.

77 See "Alleged enlistment of men for service in Cuba," 23 January 1873, NAC, Colonial Office [CO] 42/715, no. 1120, 161-77.

78 George Stanley, *The Birth of Western Canada: A History of the Riel Rebellions* (Toronto: University of Toronto Press, 1961), 180-2; George Woodcock, *Gabriel Dumont* (Edmonton: Hurtig Publishers, 1975), 93-102; and Bob Beal and Rod Macleod, *Prairie Fire: The North-West Rebellion* (Toronto: McClelland and Stewart, 1984), 43.

79 See "Case of Gabriel Dumont," NAC, CO 42/737, no. 12709, 312-61a. Also see Stanley Gordon, "Lawrence Clarke," in *Dictionary of Canadian Biography*, vol. 11 (Toronto: University of Toronto Press, 1982), 194-5, and Richard Mackie, "James A. Grahame," in *Dictionary of Canadian Biography*, vol. 13 (Toronto: University of Toronto Press, 1994), 398-400.

80 Department of Justice memorandum, 9 October 1875, AO, M-242, letter book 2, 327 and continued on 449.

81 Confidential Department of Justice memorandum, n.d. (probably 10 October or 11 October 1875), AO, M-249, letter book 2, 376.

82 Edward Blake to A.T. Wood, 12 October 1875, AO, reel M-249, letter book 2, 393.

83 "Case of Gabriel Dumont," NAC, CO 42/737, no. 12709, 329a.

Chapter 4: Advisors to the Crown and the Prerogative of Mercy

1 *British North America Act, 1867,* 30 and 31 Victoria, chapter 3, 91 (27) and 92 (14).

2 Ibid., s. 12. On the Colonial Office position, see pp. 57-8.

3 Carolyn Strange, "The Lottery of Death: Capital Punishment, 1867-1976," *Manitoba Law Journal* 23, 3 (January 1996): 594-619.

4 John A. Macdonald to Hon. J.W. Trutch, lieutenant governor, British Columbia, 19 January 1872, National Archives of Canada [NAC], Manuscript Group [MG] 26A, vol. 575, letter book 17A, 105-9.

5 John A. Macdonald to Hon. Oliver Mowat, attorney general, Ontario, 28 August 1873, NAC, MG 26A, vol. 576A, letter book 20, 533-5.

6 Dispatch from Edward Cardwell to Governor Viscount Monck, 3 December 1864, NAC, MG 26A, vol. 50, 19781.

7 See Attorney General Martin Wilkins to Captain H. Moody, 21 May 1868, NAC, Colonial Office [CO] no. 42, vol. 671, 397-400; Department of Justice Memorandum, NAC, RG 13, A3, vol. 555, 437-8 and 443-7; *Attorney General for Canada* v. *Attorney General of Ontario, Ontario Appeal Reports,* 19 (1892): 31-40; and Edward Blake, *The Executive Power Case* (Toronto: Press of the Budget, 1892); and Paul Romney, *Mr. Attorney: The Attorney General for Ontario in Court, Cabinet, and Legislature 1791-1899* (Toronto: Osgoode Society, 1986), 258-9.

8 For an insightful examination of how petitions were crafted, see Natalie Zemon Davis, *Fiction in the Archives: Pardon Tales and Their Tellers in Sixteenth-Century France* (Stanford: Stanford University Press, 1987).

9 The following is based on Re James McGarry, NAC, RG 13, A1, vol. 435, no. 365.

10 Report of Minister of Justice, 26 December 1867, ibid. McGarry's sentence is eventually remitted in 1871; see Re James McGarry, NAC, RG 13, A1, vol. 444, no. 870.

11 Re John C. Clifford, NAC, RG 13, A1, vol. 450, no. 1299.

12 See Report of Hewitt Bernard re convict Gideon Grotleau, 15 June 1876, NAC, RG 13, A3,

vol. 578, 39-40.

13 Report of Hewitt Bernard re convict Eusète Foutaine, 18 June 1878, ibid., 37.

14 *An Act respecting Penitentiaries, and the Directors thereof, and for other purposes,* 31 Victoria, chapter 75, s. 62.

15 W.A. Calder, "The Federal Penitentiary System in Canada, 1867-1899: A Social and Institutional History" (PhD diss., University of Toronto, 1979), 158.

16 For example, see Re Thomas Swanton, NAC, RG 13, A1, vol. 440, no. 214; Re Jonathan George, ibid., vol. 444, no. 168; Re John McGinnis, ibid., vol. 448, no. 1007; Re Michael Hoolahan, ibid., vol. 450, no. 349; and Re Owen Keenan, ibid., no. 689.

17 Re Entichianne Boucher, NAC, RG 13, A1, vol. 435, no. 44; and RG 6, A1, vol. 1, no. 57.

18 Report of Z.A. Lash re convict James Tallon, 17 August 1876, RG 13, A3, vol. 579, 446-8. Lash was supported in his report by the trial judge, who wrote that, "The ends of justice may be regarded as satisfied in his case by imprisonment for three or four months."

19 George Daxon, RG 13, A1, vol. 454, no. 773.

20 Report of Z.A. Lash on convict George Daxon, 28 June 1876, ibid., 304-6.

21 George was sentenced to death initially for the rape of Hannah Brown but had his sentence commuted to life imprisonment. When asked to comment on the length of time served, Judge Morrison, who tried the case, stated that seven years' imprisonment was a just sentence. See RG 13, C1, vol. 1407. Report of Hewitt Bernard, 7 July 1874, concurred in Téle-sphore Fournier, re convict Jonathan George. Also see RG 2, vol. 255, no. 29. For a similar request regarding prisoner Honore Trudelle, see Hector Langevin to John A. Macdonald, 1 September 1873, NAC, MG 26A, vol. 226, 96882-3.

22 Report of Z.A. Lash, 12 September 1876, NAC, RG 13, A3, vol. 579, 844-5. Also see Department of Justice report re John H. Dunning, 28 June 1876, ibid., 396-401.

23 J.W. King, F.X. Prieur, and J.G. Moylan, "Seventh Annual Report of the Directors of Penitentiaries of the Dominion of Canada for the year 1874," *Sessional Papers,* 1875, no. 87, 2.

24 Re Ann Connolly, RG 13, A1, vol. 440, no. 1411.

25 Re Henry Smith, RG 13 A1, vol. 444, no. 64; re George Gustaff, ibid., no. 772; re John O'Toole, ibid., no. 1255; and re S. Cunningham alias William Howard, vol. 450, no. 1106.

26 Re Thomas Connolly, RG 13 A1, vol. 444, no. 757.

27 Re Henry Allen, RG 13, A1, vol. 450, no. 803.

28 Re Onzième St. Pierre, Joseph Lizotte, Honoré Pin and Edouard Thibaud, NAC, RG 6, vol. 8, no. 1955.

29 It had been specified by 1875 that prisoners could obtain remission for up to one-sixth off their entire sentence. See James G. Moylan, "First Annual Report of the Inspector of Penitentiaries of the Dominion of Canada, for the year 1875," *Sessional Papers,* 1876, no. 14, 8.

30 My sincere thanks to Evelyn Spanner for her wise counsel in handling these remission statistics.

31 Re R.B. Lynch, NAC, RG 73c, vol. 430, letters no. 707, 730, 749; RG 13, A1, vol. 440, no. 1020 and 1308 and vol. 444, no. 443.

32 Re John Smith, NAC, RG 13, A1, vol. 458, no. 730 and re James Ryan, ibid., no. 967.

33 J.M. Ferris, "Warden's Report of Kingston Penitentiary, for 1869," *Sessional Papers,* 1870, no. 5, 9. For similar comments, see John Flanigan, "Report of the Acting Warden of the Kingston Penitentiary, for the year ending 31st December 1870," *Sessional Papers,* 1871, no. 60, 8-9; Terence J. O'Neill, James W. King, and F.X. Prieur, "Fourth Annual Report of the Directors of Penitentiaries of the Dominion of Canada for the year 1871," *Sessional Papers,* 1872, no. 27, 2; John Creighton, "Report of the Warden of the Kingston Penitentiary, for the year ending 31st December, 1871," *Sessional Papers,* 1872, no. 27, 19.

34 John Creighton, "Kingston Penitentiary, Annual Report of the Warden for 1874," *Sessional Papers,* 1875, no. 87, 11.

35 Edward Blake to Alexander Mackenzie, 25 September 1876, Archives of Ontario [AO], MS 20, reel 5, no. 177.

36 For the British Columbia cases of piracy, see Jonathan Swainger, "A Distant Edge of Authority: Capital Punishment and the Prerogative of Mercy, 1872-1880," Hamar Foster and John McLaren, eds., *Essays in the History of Canadian Law: British Columbia and Yukon* (Toronto: Osgoode Society, 1995), 204-41. Lauchlon McKinnon, Charles McKinnon, and John McNevin were found guilty of burglary on Prince Edward Island in 1875 and sentenced to

death. The sentences were commuted quickly. See re McKinnon, McKinnon and McNevin, NAC, RG 13, C1, vol. 1414.

37 John A. Macdonald to Lord Lisgar, 8 November 1869, NAC, MG 26A, vol. 76, 29702-5.

38 John A. Macdonald to J.W. Ritchie, 8 June 1868, NAC, MG 26A, letter book 11, 854.

39 See report of Chief Justice W.B. Richards, 7 October 1872, in Re William Reed, NAC, RG 13, C1, vol. 1410. Also see report of Judge Adam Wilson, 27 November 1872, in re John McGinnis, ibid.

40 Passed in 1873, the act to ameliorate the severity of the law provided judges with the power to pass the sentence of death, life imprisonment, or a sentence of not less than seven years in cases of rape. A second act in 1877 reduced the punishment for attempted murder and carnal knowledge of a female under ten years of age to life imprisonment. See 36 Victoria, chapter 50 and 51, and 40 Victoria, chapter 28.

41 See Strange, "The Lottery of Death," supra note 3.

42 Report of A.A. Dorion re convict James Fox alias Brenton, 6 December 1873, NAC, RG 13, C1, vol. 1411, re James Fox alias Brenton.

43 Dr. Workman to Edward Blake, 28 May 1876, in re Christopher Ward, NAC, RG 13, C1, vol. 1414. For other examples, see the case of Timothy Topping, who murdered his wife and four children, and Erastus Hotchkiss, who murdered his mother with an axe. See re Timothy Topping vol. 1411, and vol. 1414 re Erastus Hotchkiss ibid. Also see Dr. Joseph Workman, "Case of Erastus Hotchkiss," *American Journal of Insanity* 32 (1875-6): 405-19.

44 Re David Robbins and re Michael McConnell, NAC, RG 13, C1, vol. 1414.

45 See Report of W.B. Richards, C.J., 14 November 1870, in Re John Graham alias Armstrong, NAC, RG 13, C1, vol. 1408; Report of Judge Adam Wilson, 15 May 1871, in Re John McGinnis, ibid., vol. 1410; Re Elizabeth Workman, in vol. 1410; Report of Judge Adam Wilson, 14 May 1874, in Re John Sullivan, vol. 1411; Re Christopher Ward, ibid., vol. 1414; and Re James Smith, ibid., vol. 1411.

46 Michael Stephen Hindus, *Prison and Plantation: Crime, Justice, and Authority in Massachusetts and South Carolina, 1767-1878* (Chapel Hill: University of North Carolina Press, 1980), 104.

47 The following is based on Re Elizabeth Workman, NAC, RG 13, C1, vol. 1410.

48 Judge Adam Wilson to Sir John A. Macdonald, 21 March 1873, ibid.

49 Judge Adam Wilson to the secretary of state, 8 May 1873, ibid. Butler was released for lack of evidence implicating him in the beating death.

50 Alexander Mackenzie to John A. Macdonald, 28 May 1873, ibid.

51 John A. Macdonald to Lord Dufferin, 31 May 1873, NAC, MG 26A, vol. 78, 30628.

52 Ibid., 30629-30.

53 "A Sad, Sad Story," *Christian Guardian,* 11 August 1875.

54 Both Toronto dailies had extensive coverage from 6 August to 7 August 1875, and 14 October to 18 October 1875. For the circumstances of Gilmour's death, see Re A.P. Davis and Alice Davis, NAC, RG 13, C1, vol. 1414. Regarding Gilmour's motives in seeking the Davises, see the confession of Alice Davis in Re A.P. Davis and Alice Davis.

55 Summarizing the case, the *Globe* wrote that, "The unpleasant duty devolving upon the jury was rendered as easy as possible. Never did a more complete chain of circumstantial testimony send a murderer to the gallows." See "The Davis Case," *Toronto Globe,* 18 October 1875.

56 "The Davis Case," *Toronto Mail,* 18 October 1875.

57 "'Dr' Paul Davis Again," *Toronto Globe,* 7 August 1875.

58 "The Davis Case," ibid., 18 October 1875; and editorials, *Toronto Globe,* 18 October 1875.

59 "The Davis Case," *London Free Press,* 20 October 1875.

60 "The Davis Case," *Toronto Globe,* 18 October 1875.

61 Ibid. In its column of 11 August 1875, *Christian Guardian* stated, "This tragic affair teaches all, in startling tones, that those who take the first step in the way of folly and sin cannot know to what depths of sorrow, shame, and ruin it may lead." See "A Sad, Sad Story," *Christian Guardian,* 11 August 1875.

62 "The Davis Case," *Toronto Globe,* 18 October 1875.

63 "The Assizes: The Gilmour Abortion Case," *Toronto Mail,* 15 October 1875.

64 "Abortion Murders," ibid., 5 August 1875.

65 "The Abortion Case," *Toronto Mail,* 7 August 1875. Also see "Capital Punishment," ibid., 22

October 1875.

66 "Capital Punishment," ibid., 20 October 1872, and "The Sentence in the Davis Case," ibid., 21 October 1872.

67 The distinction between murder and manslaughter is to be found in *Offences against the person,* 32 and 33 Victoria, chapter 20, s. 6.

68 Confidential memorandum, n.d., Edward Blake Papers, AO, MG 27, I D2, reel M-250, letter book 3, 65.

69 Ibid., 66.

70 See Re Eric Benzel Sparham and William H. Graves, NAC, RG 13, C1, vol. 1413. The Sparham case, in which a ninety-page pamphlet was published in Sparham's defence, is testament to the undeveloped state of medical evidence in nineteenth-century Canada. See Canada, National Archives of Canada, *A Defence of Dr. Eric Benzel Sparham, Charged and Convicted of the Crime of Murder, Being a Medico-Legal Inquiry into the Cause of the Death of Miss Sophia Elizabeth Burnham, His Supposed Victim* (Brockville: Leavitt and Southworth, 1876), ibid. Also see Constance Backhouse, *Petticoats and Prejudice: Women and Law in Nineteenth-Century Canada* (Toronto: Osgoode Society, 1991), 162.

71 John A. Macdonald to Hon. James Cockburn, 4 January 1871, NAC, MG 26A, vol. 574, letter book 15, 20-1. Macdonald was referring to an application for remission for a McCrea who had been found guilty of procurement.

72 Lord Dufferin to Edward Blake, 26 November 1875, supra note 65, reel M-235, no. 5.

73 "Supplementary and confidential memorandum in the case of the Davises," November 1875, NAC, reel M-250, letter book 3, 151-9.

74 Alexander Mackenzie to Edward Blake, 27 November 1875, AO, MS 20 (5), no. 86.

75 Ibid.

76 Edward Blake to Alexander Mackenzie, private correspondence, 27 November 1875, supra note 68, reel M-250, letter book 3, 193-4.

77 "Latest From Ottawa: Davis' Sentence commuted," *Toronto Globe,* 30 November 1875.

78 "The Fate of the Davises," *Toronto Globe,* 1 December 1875.

79 Ibid.

80 "The Davis Case," *Toronto Mail,* 1 December 1875.

81 "The Clements Trial, ibid., 24 January 1876.

82 "The Verdict in the Clements Case," *Toronto Globe,* 24 January 1876.

Chapter 5: Canadian Penitentiaries

1 Creighton assumed the position of warden on 3 January 1871, having been gazetted on 31 December 1870. See Kingston Penitentiary, warden's daily journal, RG 73, vol. 425, 40-2.

2 John A. Macdonald to John Creighton, private correspondence, 31 October 1871, National Archives of Canada [NAC], Manuscript Group [MG] 26A, vol. 575, letter book 16, 409-11. Creighton's entry in the warden's journal for 5 October 1871 documents his frustration with the quality of the penitentiary staff and the sense that he was obligated to look after almost all aspects of the institution. See 5 October 1871, RG 73, vol. 425, 126-7.

3 W.A. Calder, "The Federal Penitentiary System in Canada, 1867-1899: A Social and Institutional History" (PhD diss., University of Toronto: 1979), 145.

4 Macdonald to Creighton, supra note 2.

5 Ibid. See "I am shown two interesting Penitents," in *David Copperfield* (New York: New American Library, 1962), 838-45.

6 "Seventh Annual Report of the Directors of Penitentiaries of the Dominion of Canada for the year 1874," *Sessional Papers,* 1875, no. 87, 2.

7 "Warden's Annual Report for the year 1872," *Sessional Papers,* 1873, no. 75, 11. Creighton's emphasis.

8 Calder notes this disagreement between most ministers and the inspectors or director; see Calder, "The Federal Penitentiary System in Canada," supra note 3 at 265-6.

9 The unwillingness of the department to send a Canadian representative to international meetings addressing penal issues was a source of complaint. When Creighton visited a number of American penitentiaries to witness their operation, he did so on his holidays. See "Kingston Penitentiary, Annual Report of the Warden for the year 1873," *Sessional Papers,* 1873, no. 42, 22. On Canadian nonattendance at international congresses, see

"Third Annual Report of the Inspector of Penitentiaries of the Dominion of Canada for the year 1878," *Sessional Papers,* 1879, no. 27, 6.

10 David Garland, *Punishment and Modern Society: A Study in Social Theory* (Oxford: Clarendon Press, 1990), 51-2.

11 Compare "Annual Report of Donald Aneas MacDonell, warden of the Kingston Penitentiary, for the year 1868," *Sessional Papers,* 1869, no. 5, 16, with "Second Annual Report of the Directors of Penitentiaries of the Dominion of Canada for the year 1869," *Sessional Papers,* 1870, no. 5, 2.

12 "Second Annual Report of the Inspector of Penitentiaries of the Dominion of Canada, for the year 1877," *Sessional Papers,* 1878, no. 12, 13. See pp. 83-4 and pp. 89-93 for a description of the Crofton system and its reception in Canada.

13 Calder, "The Federal Penitentiary System in Canada," supra note 3 at 101-25; and Peter Oliver, *"Terror to Evil-Doers": Prisons and Punishments in Nineteenth-Century Ontario* (Toronto: Osgoode Society for Canadian Legal History, 1998), 313.

14 Calder, "The Federal Penitentiary System in Canada," supra note 3 at 100-1.

15 Ibid., 163-85.

16 David J. Rothman, "Perfecting the Prison: United States, 1789-1865," in Norval Morris and David J. Rothman, eds., *The Oxford History of the Prison: The Practice of Punishment in Western Society* (Oxford: Oxford University Press, 1995), 125.

17 See Garland, *Punishment and Modern Society,* supra note 10 at 257.

18 Ibid., 269-70.

19 Randall McGowan, "The Well-Ordered Prison," in Morris and Rothman, eds., *The Oxford History of the Prison,* supra note 16 at 103.

20 "Warden's Report of Kingston Penitentiary," *Sessional Papers,* 1870, no. 5, 4.

21 John Creighton to T.J. O'Neill, 3 January 1872, NAC, RG 73, vol. 432, 714. The schoolmaster, Mr. Delaney, had been warned by Creighton to stop drinking on 11 October 1871. See warden's daily journal, 11 October 1871, NAC, RG 73, vol. 425, 128-9.

22 Calder, "The Federal Penitentiary System in Canada," supra note 3 at 98.

23 Garland, *Punishment and Modern Society,* supra note 10 at 287.

24 Benedict Anderson, *Imagined Communities: Reflections on the Origins and Spread of Nationalism* (London: Verso, 1991), 6-7.

25 See An Act respecting Penitentiaries, and the Directors thereof, and for other purposes, 31 Victoria, chapter 75, s. 11, for a confirmation of this transfer.

26 Sir W.F. Williams to H.E. Governor General, 22 August 1867, NAC, MG 26A, vol. 75, 29095-6. Also see Lord Monck to John A. Macdonald, 20 August 1867, ibid., 29092-4; John A. Macdonald to E.A. Meredith, 3 September 1867, ibid., 29097; and Hewitt Bernard to Lord Monck, 7 September 1867, ibid., 29098-9.

27 Rainer Baehre, "From Bridewell to Federal Penitentiary: Prisons and Punishment in Nova Scotia before 1880," in Philip Girard and Jim Phillips, eds., *Essays in the History of Canadian Law – Nova Scotia,* vol. 3 (Toronto: Osgoode Society, 1990), 187.

28 On MacDonell, see J.W. Johnson, "Donald Aeneas MacDonell," in *Dictionary of Canadian Biography,* vol. 10 (Toronto: University of Toronto Press, 1972), 469-70.

29 See John A. Macdonald to A.H. Myers, Trenton, 14 October 1867, NAC, MG 26A, vol. 514, pt. 1, 162; J.M. Ferres to D.A.E. MacDonell, 29 October 1867, ibid., vol. 300, pt. 1, 137091-5; D.A.E. MacDonell to J.M. Ferres, 30 October 1867, ibid., 137096-7; James Neish to D.A.E. MacDonell, 11 January 1868, ibid., 137100; D.A.E. MacDonell to John A. Macdonald, 13 January 1868, ibid., 137098-9; D.A.E. MacDonell to Sir John A. Macdonald, 16 January 1868, 137102-3; J.M Ferres, Extract for Inspector's Memorandum Book, 16 October 1865, ibid., 137104; J.M. Ferres and T.J. O'Neill, 15 December 1865, Extract from Inspector's Minute Book; John A. Macdonald to D.A.E. MacDonell, private correspondence, ibid., vol. 514, pt. 2, 407; D.A.E. MacDonell to John A. Macdonald, 20 January 1868, ibid., vol. 300, pt. 1, 137110; D.A.E. MacDonell to John A. Macdonald, 27 January 1868, ibid., 137111; D.A.E. MacDonell to Sir John A. Macdonald, 10 February 1868, ibid., 137113; D.A.E. MacDonell to Sir John A. Macdonald, 24 March 1868, ibid., 137114-5; D.A.E. MacDonell to Sir John A. Macdonald, 29 April 1868, confidential memorandum, ibid., 137118; D.A.E. MacDonell to John A, Macdonald, 27 April 1868, confidential memorandum, ibid., 137119; D.A.E. MacDonell to Alexander Campbell, 6 May 1868, ibid., 137120-1; D.A.E. MacDonell

to Sir John A. Macdonald, 26 September 1868, ibid., vol. 341, 156133-4; and John A. Macdonald to J.M. Ferres, private correspondence, 31 December 1868, ibid., vol. 515, pt. 2, 332.

30 *An Act respecting Penitentiaries, and the Directors thereof, and for other purposes,* 31 Victoria, chapter 75.

31 The following description of the Crofton system is based on Calder, "The Federal Penitentiary System in Canada," supra note 3 at 31-52 and Oliver, *"A Terror to Evil Doers,"* supra note 13, at 295-9. Also see Robert G. Waite, "From Penitentiary to Reformatory: Alexander Maconochie, Walter Crofton, Zebulon Brockway, and the Road to Prison Reform – New South Wales, Ireland, and Elmire, New York, 1840-70" in *Criminal Justice History – An International Annual* 12 (1991): 85-105.

32 On Meredith's role in drafting the legislation, see Calder, "The Federal Penitentiary System in Canada," supra note 3 at 50. On Meredith, see Peter Oliver, "Edmund Allen Meredith," in *Dictionary of Canadian Biography,* vol. 12 (Toronto: University of Toronto Press, 1990), 728-31; and Oliver, *"A Terror to Evil Doers,"* supra note 13, passim. For a more general discussion of Meredith's life and career, see Sandra Gwyn, *The Private Capital – Ambition and Love in the Age of Macdonald and Laurier* (Toronto: McClelland and Stewart, 1984).

33 D.A.E. MacDonell to Sir John A. Macdonald, 24 March 1868, NAC, MG 26A, vol. 300, pt. 1, 137114-5.

34 Garland, *Punishment and Modern Society,* supra note 10 at 181.

35 J.G. Moylan to Sir John A. Macdonald, 15 May 1868, NAC, MG 26A, vol. 60, 24448-52.

36 See generally, "Warden's Report of Kingston Penitentiary, for 1869," in Second Annual Report of the Directors of Penitentiaries of the Dominion of Canada, for the year 1869, *Sessional Papers,* 1870, no. 5, 3-12. Also see J.M. Ferris to Hewitt Bernard, NAC, RG 73, vol. 431, 192. On Ferris generally, see Lorne Ste. Croix, "James Moir Ferres," in *Dictionary of Canadian Biography,* vol. 9 (Toronto: University of Toronto Press, 1976), 257-8.

37 J.M. Ferres to Hewitt Bernard, 10 February 1870, ibid., 704-7.

38 Kingston Penitentiary, warden's daily journal, NAC, RG 73, vol. 424, 777.

39 See H. Pearson Gundy, "John Creighton," in *Dictionary of Canadian Biography,* vol. 9 (Toronto: University of Toronto Press, 1976), 216-7.

40 "Report of the Warden of Kingston Penitentiary, for the year ending 31st December, 1871," *Sessional Papers,* 1872, no. 27, 17.

41 Warden's daily journal, 3 January 1871, NAC, RG 73, vol. 425, 40-2.

42 "Report of Warden of Saint John Penitentiary for the year 1868," *Sessional Papers,* 1870, no. 5, 52.

43 "First Annual Report of the Directors of Penitentiaries of Dominion of Canada, for the year 1868," ibid., 5-6.

44 "St. John Penitentiary Warden's Report," *Sessional Papers,* 1875, no. 87, 67.

45 Baehre, "From Bridewell to Federal Penitentiary," supra note 27 at 188. Also see "First Annual Report of the Directors of Penitentiaries of Dominion of Canada, for the year 1868," ibid., 7.

46 "First Annual Report of the Directors of Penitentiaries of Dominion of Canada, for the year 1868," supra note 42 at 8.

47 "Halifax, Nova Scotia, Penitentiary, Warden's Report," *Sessional Papers,* 1871, no. 60, 67; and "First Annual Report of the Inspector of Penitentiaries of the Dominion of Canada for the year, 1875," *Sessional Papers,* 1876, no. 14, 22 and 125.

48 "Halifax, N.S., Penitentiary, Warden's Report for 1870," *Sessional Papers,* 1871, no. 60, 67.

49 "Report of the Warden of the Kingston Penitentiary, for the year ending 31st December, 1871," *Sessional Papers,* 1873, no. 27, 17.

50 Gal. 6:7: "For whatsoever a man soweth, that shall he also reap."

51 "Warden's Report for the Year ending 31st December 1873," *Sessional Papers,* 1873, no. 42.

52 "Halifax Penitentiary," *Sessional Papers,* 1876, no. 14, 125.

53 See Garland, *Punishment and Modern Society,* supra note 10 at 249-76.

54 *An Act respecting Penitentiaries and the Inspection thereof, and for other purposes,* 38 Victoria, chapter 44.

55 Ibid., ss. 3 and 4.

56 Ibid., s. 10, ss. 1.

57 On statistics and proving penitentiary efficiency, see "First Annual Report of the Inspector of Penitentiaries of the Dominion of Canada, for the year 1875," *Sessional Papers,* 1876, no. 14, 10.
58 "Kingston Penitentiary, Annual Report of the Warden for 1874," *Sessional Papers,* 1874, no. 87, 12.
59 John Creighton to J.G. Moylan, 1 April 1874, NAC, RG 73, vol. 433, 200-1. Creighton's emphasis.
60 "First Annual Report of the Inspector of Penitentiaries of the Dominion of Canada," *Sessional Papers,* 1876, no. 14, 6.
61 St. John Penitentiary, Warden's Report for the year 1872," *Sessional Papers,* 1873, no. 75, 61.
62 "Kingston Penitentiary, Report of the Warden for Six Months ending 30th June 1877," *Sessional Papers,* 1878, no. 12, 16.
63 Ibid., 13.
64 "Report of the Warden of the Penitentiary of St. Vincent de Paul, for the year ending the 31st December 1874," *Sessional Papers,* 1875, no. 87, 47.
65 "Third Annual Report of the Inspector of Penitentiaries of the Dominion of Canada for the year 1878," *Sessional Papers,* 1879, no. 27, 13.
66 See "St. John Penitentiary," *Sessional Papers,* 1877, no. 15, 18; "Kingston Penitentiary, Report of the Warden for Six Months Ending 30th June 1877," *Sessional Papers,* 1878, no. 12, 18; "Third Annual Report of the Inspector of Penitentiaries of the Dominion of Canada," *Sessional Papers,* 1879, no. 27, 7.
67 "Sixth Annual Report of the Directors of Penitentiaries of the Dominion of Canada, for the year 1873," *Sessional Papers,* 1873, no. 42, 14. Also see Peter Oliver, "A Terror to Evil-Doers: The Central Prison and the 'Criminal Class' in Late Nineteenth-Century Ontario," in Roger Hall, William Westfall, and Laurel A. MacDowell, eds., *Patterns of the Past: Interpreting Ontario's History* (Toronto: Dundurn Press, 1988), 211-50; and Oliver, *"A Terror to Evil Doers,"* supra note 13 at 399-463.
68 "Sixth Annual Report of the Directors of Penitentiaries," 8.
69 "Kingston Penitentiary, Annual Report of the Warden for the year 1873," *Sessional Papers,* 1874, no. 42, 22.
70 "First Annual Report of the Inspector of Penitentiaries of the Dominion of Canada, for the year 1875," *Sessional Papers,* 1876, no. 14, 7.
71 "Second Annual Report of the Inspector of Penitentiaries as to Dominion of Canada, for the year 1876," *Sessional Papers,* 1877, no. 15, 7-8.
72 "Sixth Annual Report of the Directors of Penitentiaries of the Dominion of Canada, for the year 1873," ibid., 3-4.
73 "Second Annual Report for the Inspector of Penitentiaries as to Dominion of Canada for the year 1876," *Sessional Papers,* 1877, no. 15, 6-7.
74 "Third Annual Report of the Inspector of Penitentiaries of the Dominion of Canada for the year 1878," *Sessional Papers,* 1879, no. 27, 7.
75 "First Annual Report of the Inspector of Penitentiaries of the Dominion of Canada, for the year 1875," *Sessional Papers,* 1876, no. 14, 6.
76 "Second Annual Report of the Inspector of Penitentiaries," supra note 71 at 12.
77 Ibid., 14.
78 Ibid., 15.
79 Criminal Law Reform, 2 September 1869, NAC, RG 13, A1, vol. 439, no. 439.
80 Criminal Law Reform, 9 March 1870, NAC, RG 13, A1, vol. 441, no. 281.
81 Criminal Law Reform, 2 June 1871, NAC, RG 13, A1, vol. 444, no. 696; and E.C. Wines New York Prison Association to F. Turville, 3 October 1871, NAC, MG 26A, vol. 76, 29907-10.
82 Lawrence Friedman, *Crime and Punishment in American History* (New York: Basic Books, 1993), 159-60.
83 Penitentiary Congress, 8 April 1872, NAC, RG 13, A1, vol. 446, no. 467.
84 "Second Annual Report of the Inspector of Penitentiaries as to Dominion of Canada for the year 1876," *Sessional Papers,* 1877, no. 15, 8.
85 "Third Annual Report of the Inspector of Penitentiaries of the Dominion of Canada for the Year 1878," *Sessional Papers,* 1879, no. 27, 7.

86 Calder, "The Federal Penitentiary System in Canada," supra note 3 at 200.
87 "Fifth Annual Report of the Directors of Penitentiaries of the Dominion of Canada for the year 1872," *Sessional Papers,* 1873, no. 75, 4.
88 "First Annual Report of the Inspector of Penitentiaries of the Dominion of Canada for the year 1875," *Sessional Papers,* 1876, no. 14, 7.
89 Ibid., 9.
90 Ibid., 10.
91 "Second Annual Report of the Inspector of Penitentiary as to Dominion of Canada for the year 1876," *Sessional Papers,* 1877, no. 15, 12.
92 "Second [sic] Annual Report of the Inspector of Penitentiaries of the Dominion of Canada for the year 1877," *Sessional Papers,* 1878, no. 12, 13.
93 Garland, *Punishment and Modern Society,* supra note 10 at 187.
94 "Fourth Annual report of the Directors of Penitentiaries of the Dominion of Canada for the year 1871," *Sessional Papers,* 1872, no. 27, 4.
95 Ibid., 5
96 "First Annual Report of the Inspector of Penitentiaries of the Dominion of Canada for the year 1875," *Sessional Papers,* 1876, no. 13, 6 and 10.
97 Ibid., 22.
98 "First Annual Report of the Inspector of Penitentiaries of the Dominion of Canada for the year 1875," *Sessional Papers,* 1876, no. 13, 24.
99 Report of the Minister of Justice as to Penitentiaries in Canada for the year ended 31st December 1876," *Sessional Papers,* 1877, no. 15, 20.
100 Seän McConville, "The Victorian Prison: England, 1865-1965" in Morris and Rothman, eds., *The Oxford History of the Prison,* supra note 16 at 145.
101 Garland, *Punishment and Modern Society,* supra note 10 at 257.

Chapter 6: The Department of Justice and the Judiciary

1 J.A.G. Griffith, *The Politics of the Judiciary* (Cornwall: Fontana Press, 1987), 193.
2 Ibid., 194
3 David G. Bell, "Judicial Crisis in Post-Confederation New Brunswick," in W. Wesley Pue and Dale Gibson, eds., *Glimpses of Canadian Legal History* (Winnipeg: Legal Research Institute, 1991), 199. On the New Brunswick Bench, see David G. Bell, "Introduction," in Joseph William Lawrence, ed., *Judges of New Brunswick* (Saint John: Acadiensis Press, 1985).
4 The phrase is Sir John A. Macdonald's; see Macdonald to Hon. Joseph Curran Morrison, 26 November 1869, National Archives of Canada [NAC], Manuscript Group [MG] 26A, vol. 573, 580-1.
5 See Rodolphe Laflamme, Canada, House of Commons, *Debates,* 3rd Parliament, 2nd Session, 27 March 1875, 936.
6 For a small sample of the correspondence the Winter case generated, see Address to the House of Commons, 30 March 1868, *Journal of the House of Commons,* vol. 1, 167; *Sessional Papers,* 1870, vol. 6, no. 67; Report of George-Etienne Cartier, acting for the Minister of Justice, 4 April 1871, NAC, RG 13, A3, vol. 599, 888-90; Report of Hewitt Bernard, 25 September 1871, ibid., vol. 560, 886-8, and Department of Justice Register, 1871, no. 1156, RG 13, A1, vol. 444. On Monk's application, see the correspondence between A.A. Dorion to Telésphore Fournier, 4 October 1875, Archives of Ontario [AO], MS 20 (3), no. 2; and Dorion to Edward Blake, from 7 October -29 October 1875, NAC, MG 27, I D2, reel M-239, no. 3-6.
7 See Gordon T. Stewart, *The Origins of Canadian Politics: A Comparative Approach* (Vancouver: University of British Columbia Press, 1986), 75-82.
8 See Jonathan Swainger, A Rhetorical Division: The Minister of Justice and the Judiciary, 1867-1878, in "Governing the Law: The Canadian Department of Justice in the early Confederation Era" (PhD diss., University of Western Ontario, 1992), 283-90.
9 See Jonathan Swainger, "A Bench in Disarray: The Quebec Judiciary and the Federal Department of Justice, 1867-1878," *Les Cahiers de Droit* 34, 1 (March 1993): 78-9.
10 Ibid., 83-9. See Judge Robert MacKay to Luther Holton, 27 January 1876, AO, MS 20 (3), no. 13; Holton to Blake, 2 February 1876, ibid., no. 15; MacKay to Holton, 3 February 1876, ibid., no. 17; and Holton to Blake, 6 February 1876, ibid., no. 18.

11 C.E. Church to Alexander Mackenzie, n.d., AO, MS 20 (5), no. 127. See a similar entreaty written by Chas. A. Sadlier on his own behalf and directed to A.A. Dorion, Sadlier to Dorion, 13 December 1873, RG 13, A1, no. 2095; and James H. Peter to A.A. Dorion, 21 December 1873, ibid., no. 2159.

12 John A. Macdonald to Hon. H. Blanchard, private correspondence, 27 January 1872, NAC, MG 26A, vol. 522, 670-1. Also see Macdonald to Alfred W. Savary, private correspondence, 21 October 1872, ibid., vol. 521, 754-5.

13 John A. Macdonald to Mackenzie Bowell, 24 October 1872, NAC, MG 26A, vol. 522, 22-3. Also see Macdonald to Bowell, 25 October 1872, ibid., vol. 189, 78706-8.

14 John A. Macdonald to Mackenzie Bowell, 4 December 1872, ibid., vol. 189, 78709-10. For the appointment, see *Canada Gazette,* vol. 6, 507, (1872-3).

15 John A. Macdonald to Lt. Governor Hastings Doyle, 22 February 1870, NAC, MG 26A, vol. 574, 10-3.

16 John A. Macdonald to Hon. T.W. Anglin, 10 January 1871, NAC, MG 26A, vol. 574, 70-1.

17 W.H. Draper to John A. Macdonald, 18 February 1868, NAC, MG 26A, vol. 160, 65008-11. Draper's official request for a six-month leave was received on 12 February 1868. See Department of Justice Register, 1868, NAC, RG 13A, vol. 435a, no. 174. His eventual resignation was received on 14 October; see ibid., no. 872.

18 Draper to Macdonald, ibid.

19 Draper to Macdonald, 12 March 1868, ibid., 65014-6.

20 Hon. Joseph Curran Morrison to John A. Macdonald, 20 April 1868, ibid., 65019-20.

21 VanKoughnet to Macdonald, 26 July 1868, ibid., 65031-2.

22 John A. Macdonald to John S. Macdonald, 15 September 1868, NAC, MG 26A, vol. 572, 1078-9. The source of Sir John's interpretation of events appears to have been W.H. Draper; see Draper to Macdonald, 7 September 1868, NAC, MG 26A, vol. 160, 65035.

23 John A. Macdonald to Hon. P.M. VanKoughnet, 21 October 1868, NAC, MG 26A, vol. 160, 65045-6.

24 John A. Macdonald to Edward Blake, 9 November 1868, NAC, MG 26A, vol. 573, 116-7.

25 Department of Justice Register, 1868, NAC, RG 13, A1, vol. 437, no. 391 and 393-6.

26 John A. Macdonald to Hon. Joseph Curran Morrison, 26 November 1869, NAC, MG 26A, vol. 573, 580-1. Also see W.L. Morton, "Philip Michael Matthew Scott VanKoughnet," in *Dictionary of Canadian Biography*, vol. 9 (Toronto: University of Toronto Press, 1976), 803-4.

27 John A. Macdonald to Hon. John Hillyard Cameron, 15 November 1869, NAC, MG 26A, vol. 573, 425-6.

28 Ibid.

29 John A. Macdonald to Hon. Joseph Curran Morrison, 26 November 1869, NAC, MG 26A, vol. 573, 580-1.

30 Ibid.

31 John A. Macdonald to Joseph Curran Morrison, 2 December 1869, MG 26A, vol. 573, 640-1.

32 John A. Macdonald to Joseph Curran Morrison, 17 December 1869, MG 26A, vol. 576, 754-a.

33 John A. Macdonald to John Hillyard Cameron, 15 November 1869, NAC, MG 26A, vol. 573, 425-6, and ibid., 24 December 1869, 791-2.

34 John A. Macdonald to John S. Macdonald, 27 December 1869, NAC, MG 26A, vol. 573, 801-6. Spragge's elevation and Strong's appointment are registered in the Department of Justice Register, 1869, NAC, RG 13, A1, vol. 439, no. 1660 and 1661.

35 John A. Macdonald to Joseph Curran Morrison, 27 December 1869, NAC, MG 26A, vol. 573, 797-8. Also see John A. Macdonald to John Hillyard Cameron, 24 December 1869, ibid., 791-2.

36 Oliver Mowat to John A. Macdonald, 24 October 1872; and Macdonald to Mowat, 25 October 1872, NAC, MG 26A, vol. 253, 114949-50.

37 John A. Macdonald to Oliver Mowat, 25 October 1872, ibid., 114957-8.

38 John A. Macdonald to Hon. J.G. Spragge, 25 October 1872, NAC, MG 26A, vol. 576, 26. The theme of Americanization was repeated to Chief Justice Draper, Chief Justice Morris, and Judge Gowan. See MG 26A, vol. 576, 27-8, 149-50, and 180. Sir John suggested that Mowat's "going into politics again has met with general condemnation by all thinking

men of all parties." John A. Macdonald to Chief Justice Morris, 8 November 1872, ibid., 149-50.

39 Ibid., Macdonald to Spragge, 25 October 1872, 26, and Macdonald to Draper, 25 October 1872, 27-8.

40 John A. Macdonald to John Coyne, 30 November 1872, NAC, MG 26A, vol. 576, 207; and Macdonald to Draper, 25 October 1872, 27-8. Moss and Crooks are among the names noted by *Canada Law Journal* 8, New Series (November 1872): 267-8.

41 John A. Macdonald to John Hillyard Cameron, 27 November 1872, MG 26A, vol. 576, 181a.

42 Department of Justice Register, 1872, NAC, RG 13, A1, no. 1359 and 1597.

43 John A. Macdonald to T.C. Patteson, 7 December 1872, NAC, Macdonald Papers, MG 26A, vol. 576, 256-7.

44 John A. Macdonald to Chief Justice Morris, 4 December 1972, NAC, MG 26A, vol. 576, 244-5.

45 Ibid. Sir John also expressed this sentiment to Mr. Justice Gray of the British Columbia Supreme Court: John A. Macdonald to Mr. Justice Gray, 30 November 1872, MG 26A, vol. 576, 214-5.

46 John A. Macdonald to D'Arcy Boulton, 12 December 1872, NAC, MG 26A, vol. 576, 315-6.

47 J.K. Johnson and P.B. Waite, "Macdonald, Sir John Alexander," in *Dictionary of Canadian Biography,* vol. 12 (Toronto: University of Toronto Press, 1990), 611. Also see P.B. Waite, "Sir John A. Macdonald: The Man," in Harvey L. Dyck and H. Peter Krosby, eds., *Empire and Nation: Essays in Honour of Frederic H. Soward* (Vancouver: University of British Columbia Press, 1969), 37.

48 Edward Blake to F. Bechard, 27 January 1876, AO, MS 20 (16), 92-3.

49 Edward Blake, "The Teeswater Demonstration," in *Reform Government in the Dominion. The Pic-Nic Speeches* (Toronto: Globe Steam Book and Job Press, 1878), 138-9.

50 Gordon T. Stewart, *The Origins of Canadian Politics*, 71.

51 Ibid.

52 Alexander Mackenzie to Edward Blake, 29 May 1874, AO, MS 20 (5), no. 10.

53 Ibid.

54 Hon. Antoine A. Dorion, 9 March 1865, in Canada, *Parliamentary Debates on the subject of the Confederation of the British North American Provinces* (Quebec City: Hunter, Rose, Parliamentary Printers, 1865), 860.

55 L.H. Holton to Alexander Mackenzie, 5 June 1874, NAC, reel M-197, 488-91; and A.J. Smith to Edward Blake, 16 July 1874, AO, MS 20 (6), no. 2.

56 Dale C. Thomson, *Alexander Mackenzie: Clear Grit* (Toronto: Macmillan Company of Canada, 1960), 199.

57 Edward Blake to Luther Holton, 11 September 1875, AO, MS 20 (3), no. 6.

58 Luther Holton to Edward Blake, 12 September 1875, ibid., no. 7.

59 Ibid.

60 Lucius Huntington to Edward Blake, mid-September 1875, NAC, MG 27, I D2, reel M-248, 468-74.

61 Ibid.

62 Rodolphe Laflamme to Alexander Mackenzie, 22 September 1875, NAC, reel M-197, 630.

63 Rodolphe Laflamme to Alexander Mackenzie, 1 October 1878, NAC, reel M-199, 2219-20.

64 See Ian Bushnell, *The Captive Court: A Study of the Supreme Court of Canada* (Montreal and Kingston: McGill-Queen's University Press, 1992); James G. Snell and Frederick Vaughan, *The Supreme Court of Canada – History of the Institution* (Toronto: University of Toronto Press, 1985); Peter H. Russell, *The Supreme Court of Canada as a Bilingual and Bicultural Institution* (Ottawa: Queen's Printer, 1969); Frank H. Underhill, "Edward Blake, the Supreme Court Act and the Appeal to the Privy Council, 1876-6," *Canadian Historical Review* 19 (1938); and Frank McKinnon, "The Establishment of the Supreme Court of Canada," *Canadian Historical Review* 26 (1946).

65 Sir John A. Macdonald to Hon. A.G. Archibald, 18 October 1871, private and confidential memorandum, NAC, MG 26A, vol. 575, 327-30.

66 Bushnell incorrectly states that Strong was a member of Ontario's Chancery Court when he drafted the bill. Strong was appointed vice-chancellor seven months after Macdonald

introduced the Supreme Court bill to the House of Commons. See Bushnell, *The Captive Court,* supra note 64 at 6.

67 "Bill 80," s. 53, NAC, MG 26A, vol. 159, 64799.

68 Ibid., s. 56, 64800.

69 Sir John A. Macdonald, Canada, House of Commons, *Debates,* 1st Parliament, 3rd Session, 18 March 1870, 523.

70 Bushnell, *The Captive Court,* supra note 64 at 9.

71 Donald Creighton, *John A. Macdonald: The Old Chieftain* (Toronto: Macmillan Company of Canada, 1955), 33-56.

72 Supreme Court of Canada, 1 June 1869, circular letter to judges of all the courts in the Dominion enclosing copy of Act constituting this Court and asking their respective opinion thereupon, NAC, RG 13, A1, vol. 439, no. 858. Macdonald invited Strong to Ottawa to go over the replies once they arrived at the capital; see Macdonald to Samuel H. Strong, NAC, MG 26A, vol. 573, 36.

73 Oliver Mowat to John A. Macdonald, 3 September 1869, NAC, MG 26A, vol. 159, 64623. Also see J.G. Spragge to John A. Macdonald, 13 September 1869, ibid., 64855.

74 J.G. Spragge to John A. Macdonald, 13 September 1869, ibid., 64857. Spragge's emphasis.

75 W.J. Ritchie, *Observations of the Chief Justice of New Brunswick on a Bill entitled "An Act to Establish a Supreme Court for the Dominion of Canada"* (Fredericton: Queen's Printer, 1870), 15. A copy of Ritchie's address can be found in Edward Blake's paper, AO, MU 266, box 128, enclosure 127, and in Gordon Bale, *Chief Justice William Johnstone Ritchie: Responsible Government and Judicial Review* (Ottawa: Carleton University Press, 1991), 340-71. Also see Judge Meredith to Hewitt Bernard, 24 February 1870, NAC, MG 26A, vol. 159, 64697; W.B. Richards to John A. Macdonald, 16 March 1870, ibid., 64703-4, and 15 May 1870, 64705-6; and Adam Wilson to John A. Macdonald, 5 April 1870, NAC, MG 26A, vol. 159, 64754.

76 Also see Judge Adam Wilson to John A. Macdonald, 5 April 1870, ibid., 64754-5.

77 "Bill 48," MG 26A, vol. 159, ss. 47, 50, and 51.

78 Sir John A. Macdonald, House of Commons, *Debates,* 1st Parliament, 3rd Session, 18 March 1870, 523.

79 John A. Macdonald to Chief Justice William Draper, 19 April 1870, NAC, MG 26A, vol. 577, 154-5. For a description of Macdonald's collapse, see Hewitt Bernard to Judge James Robert Gowan, NAC, MG 27, I E 31, vol. 1, 10 May 1870, 47-51, and 14 May 1870, 52-3; Dr. J.Y. Bown, House of Commons, *Debates,* 1st Parliament, 3rd Session, 7 May 1870, 1411-2; and Creighton, *John A. Macdonald,* supra note 71 at 68-72.

80 George-E. Cartier, 27 February 1865, *Parliamentary Debates on the Subject of Confederation,* supra note 54 at 576-7; Joseph Cauchon, 27 February 1865, ibid., 575-6; A.A. Dorion, 6 March 1865, ibid., 690; Henri Taschereau, 10 March 1865, ibid., 896-7; and G.W. Wicksteed to John A. Macdonald, n.d., NAC, MG 26A, vol. 159, 64595-7, 64600-2, and 64606-13. Also see Russell, *The Supreme Court of Canada as a Bilingual and Bicultural Institution,* supra note 64 at 7-9; and Underhill, "Edward Blake, the Supreme Court Act and the Appeal to the Privy Council," supra note 64 at 245-6.

81 George-E. Cartier, House of Commons, *Debates,* 1st Parliament, 3rd Session, 10 May 1870 and 11 May 1870, 1498 and 1520.

82 Macdonald identified Quebec and "the majority of the Maritimes" as being unfriendly to the Supreme Court bill. See John A. Macdonald to Hon. J.H. Cameron, confidential memorandum, 21 January 1871, NAC, MG 26A, vol. 574, 144.

83 On Mills, see Robert Vipond's fascinating study *Liberty and Community: Canadian Federalism and the Failure of the Constitution* (Albany: State University of New York Press, 1991). Also see Vipond, "David Mills," in *Dictionary of Canadian Biography,* vol. 13 (Toronto: University of Toronto Press, 1994), 707-12.

84 David Mills to John A. Macdonald, 17 March 1870, NAC, MG 26A, vol. 159, 64709.

85 Ibid., 64709-10.

86 Ibid., 64710.

87 John A. Macdonald, 6 February 1865, in Canada, *Parliamentary Debates on the subject of the Confederation of the British North American Provinces,* supra note 54 at 42. Also see John A. Macdonald to Matthew C. Cameron, 19 December 1864, NAC, MG 26A, vol. 571, 74-7; and Macdonald to S.H. Strong, cited in Snell and Vaughan, *The Supreme Court of Canada,*

supra note 64 at 6, note 5. "My opinion is that the General Gov't or Parliament should pay no more attention to the status or position of the Local Governments than they would to the prospects of the ruling party in the Corporation of Quebec or Montreal." Sir John A. Macdonald to Brown Chamberlin, 26 October 1868, NAC, vol. 573, 41-3.

88 Mills to Macdonald, supra note 84 at 64711.

89 Bushnell, *The Captive Court,* supra note 64 at 10.

90 Sir John A. Macdonald to Hon. A.G. Archibald, 18 October 1871, private and confidential memorandum, NAC, MG 26A, vol. 575, 327-30.

91 *An Act to Establish a Supreme Court, and a Court of Exchequer, for the Dominion of Canada (1875),* 38 Victoria, chapter 11. Télesphore Fournier, House of Commons, *Debates,* 3rd Parliament, 2nd Session, 23 February 1875, 285. Also see Underhill, "Edward Blake, The Supreme Court Act and the Appeal to the Privy Council," 246; Russell, *The Supreme Court of Canada as a Bilingual and Bicultural Institution,* 11; and Snell and Vaughan, *The Supreme Court of Canada,* 10-1, supra note 64.

92 Télesphore Fournier, House of Commons, *Debates,* 3rd Parliament, 2nd Session, 23 February 1875, 266.

93 Ibid., 286-7.

94 Rodolphe Laflamme, 27 March 1875, ibid., 936.

95 Télesphore Fournier, 23 February 1875, ibid., 286.

96 This legislation transferring the responsibilities of the JCPC, a prerogative court, to the Supreme Court of Judicature, a court of law, would provide the Canadians with an excuse to limit appeals to nonprerogative courts. While an appeal to the foot of the throne would be maintained, it would be directly to the monarch and not an English court. See Underhill, "Edward Blake, the Supreme Court Act and the Appeal to the Privy Council," supra note 64 at 253-5.

97 Sir John A. Macdonald, House of Commons, *Debates,* 3rd Parliament, 2nd Session, 22 February 1875, 289.

98 John A. Macdonald to Lord Dufferin, 4 October 1872, NAC, MG 26A, vol. 576, 626-7.

99 Aemilius Irving, in House of Commons, *Debates,* 3rd Parliament, 2nd Session, 30 March 1875, 976.

100 Sir John A. Macdonald, ibid. Also see Macdonald's speech at the Thomas White banquet in Montreal; C.H. Mackintosh, ed., *Liberal Conservative Handbook. Grits in Office – Profession and Practice Contrasted* (Ottawa: Conservative Association of the Dominion, 1876), 20.

101 See "What is the Truth?" *Toronto Mail,* 30 November 1874; "Bacchus in High Places," *Ottawa Daily Citizen,* 1 December 1874; Luther H. Holton to Alexander Mackenzie, 4 December 1874, NAC, Mackenzie Papers, MG 26B, reel M-197, 684-5; and Mackenzie to Télesphore Fournier, 7 December 1874, ibid., Mackenzie letter book, vol. 1, 243-4.

102 See "Bill for establishing a Supreme Court and a Court of Exchequer," 9 April 1875, NAC, Colonial Office [CO] 42/736, 55-116; "Act to establish a Supreme Court and a Court of Exchequer for the Dominion," 10 August 1875, NAC, CO 42/738, 103-46b; "Supreme Court Act," 15 September 1875, NAC, CO 42/737, 151-3; "Supreme Court Act proclaimed," 22 September 1875, ibid., 210-1; "Canadian Supreme Court Act," 29 September 1875, ibid., 214-8a; "Canadian Supreme Court Act, 29 September 1875, NAC, CO 42/740, 525-7a; "Canadian Supreme Court Act," 528-9; and "The Supreme and Exchequer Court Act," 15 October 1875, NAC, CO 42/738, 300-28a.

103 Alexander Mackenzie to Edward Blake, 25 September 1875, AO, MS 20 (5), no. 52, and Edward Blake to Alexander Mackenzie, 25 September 1875, ibid., no. 53.

104 The various letters offering positions to the original members of the Supreme Court can found in the Blake papers, supra note 60, reel M-248, 395-402 and 551-2.

105 For Blake's offer to Henry and his acceptance, see Edward Blake to W.A. Henry, 4 September 1875, ibid., reel M-248, 395-6; and Henry to Blake, 16 September 1875, ibid., reel M-243, no. 252.

106 On Nova Scotian judicial patronage, see p.100.

107 See pp. 107-8.

108 For the peculiar exchanges between Mackenize and Blake on the possibility of Blake assuming the chief justiceship, see Edward Blake to Alexander Mackenzie, 22 April 1875, AO, MS 20 (5), no. 27; ibid., 6 May 1875, no. 31; and Mackenzie to Blake, ibid., 10 May

1875, no. 32.

109 Glimpses of the personality clashes that existed can be seen in Macdonald's papers, NAC, MG 26A, vol. 160. For Mackenzie and Blake's exchange concerning a fracas between J.C. Morrison of Ontario's Queen's Bench and Richards, see Alexander Mackenzie to Edward Blake, 10 November 1875, confidential memorandum, supra note 60 at reel M-242, no. 73.

110 For Blake's offer to Richards and his acceptance, see Blake to Richards, 11 September 1875, supra note 60 at reel M-248, 397-8; and Richards to Blake, 14 September 1875, ibid., reel M-243, no. 234.

111 For Blake's offer to Strong and his acceptance, see Blake to Strong, 11 September 1875, ibid., reel M-248, 399-400; and Strong to Blake, 15 September 1875, ibid., reel M-243, no. 242.

112 On Strong's personality, see Snell and Vaughan, *The Supreme Court of Canada,* supra note 64 at 36-40; and Bale, *Chief Justice William Johnstone Ritchie,* supra note 75 at 206-7.

113 See pp. 112-13.

114 For Blake's offer to Ritchie, see Blake to Ritchie, 11 September 1875, supra note 60, reel M-248, 401-2.

115 On the discussions concerning the second Quebec seat, see Edward Blake to Lucius Huntington, mid-September 1875, supra note 60, reel M-248, 468-74; Blake to Huntington, 16 September 1875, ibid., 477; and Alexander Mackenzie to Edward Blake, 25 September 1875, AO, MS 20 (5), no. 52. See Andrée Désilets, "Sicotte (Cicot), Louis-Victor" in *Dictionary of Canadian Biography*, vol. 11 (Toronto: University of Toronto Press, 1982), 821-4.

116 For Blake's offer to Taschereau, see Blake to Taschereau, 22 September 1875, supra note 60, reel M-248, 551-2, and for Taschereau's hesitancy in accepting the nomination, see Snell and Vaughan, *The Supreme Court of Canada,* supra note 64 at 14.

117 Luther Holton to Alexander Mackenzie, 10 November 1875, NAC, reel M-198, 1040. Holton was evidently unaware that Moss, following the advice of friends, decided that the appointment to the Ontario Bench was a better fit. See J.D. Edgar to Edward Blake, 17 September 1875, supra note 60 at reel M-249, no. 5.

118 Russell, *The Supreme Court of Canada and a Bilingual and Bicultural Institution,* supra note 64 at 17-8.

119 Bale, *Chief Justice William Johnstone Ritchie,* supra note 75 at 154.

120 The phrase "author its own supremacy" is a paraphrase of Governor General Lord Dufferin, as cited in Bushnell, *The Captive Court,* supra note 64 at 38. For the criticism of the court, see Snell and Vaughan, *The Supreme Court of Canada,* supra note 64 at 28-51 and Bushnell, *The Captive Court,* supra note 64 at 91-6.

121 See Bushnell, *The Captive Court,* supra note 64 at 28-37.

122 Memorandum regarding the Supreme Court Act, 6 October 1875, supra note 60 at reel M-249, 590-2.

123 Edward Blake to Richard Cartwright, 7 October 1875, ibid., 215.

124 On the variety of issues shouldered by Blake on this mission, see David M.L. Farr, *The Colonial Office and Canada, 1867-1887* (Toronto: University of Toronto Press, 1955), 107-65.

125 Frank H. Underhill, "Edward Blake's Interview with Lord Cairns on the Supreme Court Act, July 5, 1876," *Canadian Historical Review* vol. 19 (1938), 293.

126 Underhill, "Edward Blake, the Supreme Court Act and Appeal to the Privy Council," supra note 64 at 260.

127 See W.H. Draper to John A. Macdonald, 12 March 1868, NAC, MG 26A, vol. 160, 65016.

128 As cited in Cynthia M. Smith and Jack McLeod, eds., *Sir John A. – An Anecdotal Life of John A. Macdonald* (Toronto: Oxford University Press, 1989), 61.

129 J.K. Johnson and P.B. Waite, "Macdonald, Sir John Alexander," supra note 47 at 603.

130 P.B. Waite, *The Man from Halifax: Sir John Thompson, Prime Minister* (Toronto: University of Toronto Press, 1985), 126-38.

Chapter 7: Conclusion

1 Donald Creighton, *John A. Macdonald: The Old Chieftain* (Toronto: Macmillan Company of Canada, 1955), 237.

2 Ibid., 254.

3 P.B. Waite, *Macdonald: His Life and World* (Toronto: McGraw-Hill Ryerson, 1975), 135.

4 Creighton, *John A. Macdonald,* supra note 1 at 322.
5 A. Margaret Evans, *Sir Oliver Mowat* (Toronto: University of Toronto Press, 1992), 169.
6 Ibid., 324 and 377.
7 Waite, *Macdonald: His Life and World,* supra note 3 at 22.
8 Oliver Mowat to Edward Blake, 23 June 1875, National Archives of Canada [NAC], reel M-242.
9 Ontario, *An Act to amend the Law respecting Escheats and Forfeitures,* 37 Victoria, chapter 8.
10 Creighton, *John A. Macdonald,* supra note 1 at 336.
11 For the "little tyrant" comments, see ibid., 377, and Evans, *Sir Oliver Mowat,* supra note 5 at 162. On the chops comment, see Waite, *Macdonald: His Life and World,* supra note 3 at 13.
12 Paul Romney, *Mr. Attorney – The Attorney General for Ontario in Court, Cabinet, and Legislature* (Toronto: Osgoode Society, 1986), 248.
13 Report of Attorney General Oliver Mowat, 22 February 1875, in W.E. Hodgins, ed., *Correspondence, Reports of the Ministers of Justice and Orders in Council upon the subject of Dominion and Provincial Legislation, 1867-1895* (Ottawa: Queen's Printer, 1896), 113.
14 Romney, *Mr. Attorney,* supra note 12 at 249. Evans follows Romney's lead on this view; see Evans, supra note 5 at 149. Also see Garth Stevenson, *Ex Uno Plures: Federal-Provincial Relations in Canada, 1867-1896* (Montreal and Kingston: McGill-Queen's University Press, 1993), 200-1.
15 Edward Blake, *Argument in the Privy Council, The St. Catherine's Milling and Lumber Company v. The Queen* (Toronto: Press of the Budget, 1888), 5. For a similar statement, see Blake, *Escheats for Want of Heir; The Provinces are entitled to Them, The Argument for the Provincial View, in the Mercer Escheat Case* (Toronto: C. Blackett Robinson, 1881), 5.
16 Evans, *Sir Oliver Mowat,* supra note 5 at 159.
17 P.B. Waite, *Canada 1874-1896 – Arduous Destiny* (Toronto: McClelland and Stewart, 1971), 96, and P.B. Waite, *The Man from Halifax: Sir John Thompson, Prime Minister* (Toronto: University of Toronto Press, 1985), 102. The spelling of MacDonald's name also appears as McDonald and Macdonald.
18 Donald Swainson, "Sir Alexander Campbell," in *Dictionary of Canadian Biography,* vol. 12 (Toronto: University of Toronto Press, 1990), 150-4.
19 R. Laflamme to Z.A. Lash, n.d., NAC, RG 13, vol. 419; and Report of James Macdonald, order-in-council no. 914/1879, 18 June 1879, NAC, RG 2. The appointment was confirmed on 25 June 1879.
20 The Attorney General of Ontario and Andrew F. Mercer, *The House of Lords and Privy Council,* vol. 8 (1883), 767. Also see Romney, *Mr. Attorney,* supra note 12 at 252-5.
21 See memorandum of Z.A. Lash to Minister of Justice, RG 13, NAC, vole 419. James MacDonald left the Department of Justice on 19 May 1881.
22 On McCarthy, see Larry L. Kulisek, "McCarthy, Dalton," in *Dictionary of Canadian Biography,* vol. 12 (Toronto: University of Toronto Press, 1990), 578-88.
23 Evans, *Sir Oliver Mowat,* supra note 5 at 173.
24 Stevenson, *Ex Uno Plures,* supra note 14 at 201.
25 On Thompson's arrival, see Creighton, *Sir John A. Macdonald,* supra note 1 at 429-30 and Waite, *The Man from Halifax,* supra note 17 at 130-3.
26 The following is based on Evans, *Sir Oliver Mowat,* supra note 5 at 192-3 and Waite, *The Man from Halifax,* supra note 17 at 197-8.
27 Evans, *Sir Oliver Mowat,* supra note 5 at 193.
28 Waite, *The Man from Halifax,* supra note 17 at 198.
29 Ibid., 230-1.
30 John W. Cell, *British Colonial Administration in the Mid-Nineteenth Century: The Policy-Making Process* (New Haven and London: Yale University Press, 1970), xi.
31 Robert W. Gordon, "Critical Legal Histories," *Stanford Law Review,* vol. 36 (1984), 84-5 and footnote 80, 90.
32 Michel Foucault, "Governmentality," in G. Bruchell, C. Gordon, and P. Miller, eds., *The Foucault Effect: Studies in Governmentality* (Chicago: University of Chicago Press, 1991), 95.
33 Gordon, supra note 31 at 109.
34 As cited in Gordon, ibid., 112.

Selected Bibliography

Primary Sources

Canada. An Act for the Organisation of the Department of Marine and Fisheries of Canada, 31 Victoria, chapter 57.

–. An Act for transferring to one of Her Majesty's Principal Secretaries of State the powers and estates and property therein described, now vested in the Principal Officers of Her Majesty's Ordnance, and for vesting other part of the Ordnance Estates and Property therein described in Her Majesty the Queen, for the benefit, use and purposes of this Province, 19 Victoria, chapter 45.

–. An Act respecting certain Ordnance and Admiralty Lands in the Provinces of New Brunswick and Nova Scotia, 42 Victoria, chapter 33.

–. An Act respecting Ordnance and Admiralty Lands in the Provinces of Ontario and Quebec, 40 Victoria, chapter 8.

–. An Act respecting Penitentiaries, and the Directors thereof, and for other purposes, 31 Victoria, chapter 75.

–. An Act respecting Penitentiaries and the Inspection thereof, and for other purposes, 38 Victoria, chapter 44.

–. An Act respecting the Department of Justice, 31 Victoria, chapter 39.

–. An Act to amend chapter sixty-two of the Consolidated Statutes of Canada, and to provide for the better regulation of Fishing and the protection of Fisheries, 29 Victoria, chapter 11.

–. An Act to Establish a Supreme Court, and a Court of Exchequer, for the Dominion of Canada (1875), 38 Victoria, chapter 11.

–. *The Blue Book; or, Statement of the Public Service of the Former province of Canada for the Half-Year Ended 30th June 1867*. Ottawa: Hunter, Rose and Co., 1868.

–. British North America Act, 1867, 30 and 31 Victoria, chapter 3.

–. *Canada Gazette*. Vol. 1-12. Ottawa: Queen's Printer, 1867-78.

–. *The Civil Service List of Canada*, 1867-78. Ottawa: Queen's Printer, 1868-79.

–. *Journals of the Legislative Assembly of the Province of Canada*, 1850.

–. *Offences against the person*, 32 and 33 Victoria, chapter 20.

–. *Parliamentary Debates on the subject of the Confederation of the British North American Provinces*. Quebec City: Hunter, Rose, Parliamentary Printers, 1865.

–. *Sessional Papers*, 1866-78.

–. House of Commons. *Debates*, 1867-78.

–. National Archives of Canada. *A Defence of Dr. Eric Benzel Sparham, Charged and Convicted of the Crime of Murder, Being a Medico-Legal Inquiry into the Cause of the Death of Miss Sophia Elizabeth Burnham, His Supposed Victim*. Record Group 13, C1, vol. 1413. (Brockville, 1876.)

–. Department of Justice Records. Record Group 13.

–. Orders-in-Council. Record Group 2.

–. Report of a Committee of the Honourable the Executive Committee, 12 November 1846. Record Group 1, E8, vol. 16.

Canada Law Journal, 1868-78.
Great Britain. Colonial Office Records 42.
Lower Canada Law Journal, 1866.
McGee, T.D. *Report of T.D. McGee on the Public Departments*, 1863. Record Group 1, E7, vol. 59A.
Morgan, Henry James. *The Canadian Men and Women of the Time: A Handbook of Canadian Biography*. Toronto: W. Briggs, 1898.
–. *The Canadian Men and Women of the Time: A Handbook of Canadian Biography of Living Characters*. Toronto: W. Briggs, 1912.
–, ed. *The Canadian Legal Directory: A Guide to the Bench and Bar of the Dominion of Canada*. Toronto: R. Carswell, 1878.
Parker, C.W. *Who's Who and Why*, vol. 6 and 7. Toronto: International Press, 1914.
Reform Government in the Dominion. The Pic-Nic Speeches. Toronto: Globe Steam Book and Job Press, 1878.
Rose, George Maclean, ed. *Cyclopeadia of Canadian Biography: Being Chiefly Men of the Time*. Toronto: Rose Publishing Company, 1886.

Newspapers

London Free Press.
Montreal Gazette.
Nation.
Ottawa Daily Citizen.
Toronto Globe.
Toronto Mail.
Victoria Daily British Colonist.
Victoria Daily Standard.

Personal Papers

Canada. National Archives of Canada. James Robert Gowan Papers. Manuscript Group 27, I E 31.
–. Sir John A. Macdonald Papers. Manuscript Group 26A.
–. Alexander Mackenzie Papers. Manuscript Group 26B.
Ontario. Archives of Ontario. Edward Blake Papers, Manuscript series 20.
–. Alexander Campbell Papers, Manuscript unit 469.
–. T.C. Patteson Papers, Manuscript unit 2306.
University of Western Ontario. University of Western Ontario Regional Room. David Mills Papers.

Secondary Sources

Armstong, Christopher. "The Mowat Heritage in Federal Provincial Relations." In *Oliver Mowat's Ontario*, edited by Donald Swainson, 93-118. Toronto: Macmillan Company of Canada, 1972.
Arthurs, H.W. *"Without the Law": Administrative Justice and Legal Pluralism in Nineteenth-Century England*. Toronto: University of Toronto Press, 1985.
Audet, Francis-J. "Les juges en chef de la Province de Québec: William Gregory." *La Revue du Droit* 3 (April 1925): 351-6.
Backhouse, Constance. *Petticoats and Prejudice: Woman and Law in Nineteenth-Century Canada*. Toronto: Osgoode Society, 1991.
Baehre, Rainer. "From Bridewell to Federal Penitentiary: Prisons and Punishment in Nova Scotia before 1880." In *Essays in the History of Canadian Law: Nova Scotia*, edited by Philip Girard and Jim Phillips. Toronto: Osgoode Society, 1990.
–. "Prison as Factory, Convict as Worker: A Study of the Mid-Victorian St. John Penitentiary, 1841-1880." In *Essays in the History of Canadian Law: Crime and Criminal Justice*, edited by Jim Phillips, Tina Loo, and Susan Lewthwaite. Toronto: Osgoode Society for Canadian Legal History, 1994.
Baker, G. Blaine. "The Juvenile Advocate Society, 1821-1826: Self-Proclaimed Schoolroom

for Upper Canada's Governing Class." In *Canadian Historical Association Historical Papers*, 74-101. N.p., 1986.

–. "'So Elegant a Web': Providential Order and the Rule of Secular Law in Early Nineteenth-Century Upper Canada." *University of Toronto Law Journal* 38 (Spring 1988): 184-205.

Baker, Nancy V. *Conflicting Loyalties: Law and Politics in the Attorney General's Office, 1789-1990*. Lawrence: University of Kansas Press, 1992.

Bale, Gordon. *Chief Justice William Johnstone Ritchie: Responsible Government and Judicial Review*. Ottawa: Carleton University Press, 1991.

Beattie, John. "The Royal Pardon and Criminal Procedure in Early Modern England." *Canadian Historical Association Historical Papers*, 9-22. N.p., 1987.

–. *Crime and the Courts in England*. New Haven: Yale University Press, 1989.

Bell, David G. "Judicial Crisis in Post-Confederation New Brunswick." In *Glimpses of Canadian Legal History*, edited by W. Wesley Pue and Dale Gibson. Winnipeg: Legal Research Institute, 1991.

Bellomo, J. Jerald. "Upper Canadian Attitudes Towards Crime and Punishment." *Ontario History* 64 (March 1972): 11-26.

Blake, Edward. "The Teeswater Demonstration." *Reform Government in the Dominion. The Pic-Nic Speeches*. Toronto: Globe Steam Book and Job Press, 1878.

Brode, Patrick. *Sir John Beverley Robinson: Bone and Sinew of the Compact*. Toronto: Osgoode Society, 1984.

Brown, Desmond H. *The Genesis of the Canadian Criminal Code of 1892*. Toronto: Osgoode Society, 1989.

–. *The Birth of a Criminal Code: The Evolution of Canada's Justice System*. Toronto: University of Toronto Press, 1995.

Burke, Sister Teresa Avila. "Mackenzie and His Cabinet, 1873-1878." *Canadian Historical Review* 41 (1960): 128-48.

Bushnell, Ian. *The Captive Court: A Study of the Supreme Court of Canada*. Montreal and Kingston: McGill-Queen's University Press, 1992.

Calder, W.A. "The Federal Penitentiary System in Canada, 1867-1899: A Social and Institutional History." PhD diss., University of Toronto, 1979.

Cell, John W. *British Colonial Administration in the Mid-Nineteenth Century: The Policy-Making Process*. New Haven and London: Yale University Press, 1970.

Chunn, Dorothy. *From Punishment to Doing Good: Family Courts and Socialised Justice in Ontario, 1880-1940*. Toronto: University of Toronto Press, 1992.

Clayton, Cornell W. *The Politics of Justice: The Attorney General and the Making of Legal Policy*. New York: M.E. Sharpe, 1992.

Craig, Gerald, ed. *Lord Durham's Report*. Toronto: McClelland and Stewart, 1963.

Creighton, Donald. *John A. Macdonald: The Young Politician*. Toronto: Macmillan Company of Canada, 1952.

–. *John A. Macdonald: The Old Chieftain*. Toronto: Macmillan Company of Canada, 1955.

Cuthbertson, Brian. *The Old Attorney General: A Biography of Richard John Uniacke*. Halifax: Nimbus, 1980.

Davis, Natalie Zemon. *Fiction in the Archives: Pardon Tales and Their Tellers in Sixteenth-Century France*. Stanford: Stanford University Press, 1987.

Dawson, R. MacGregor. "Canadian Civil Services Before Confederation," *Canadian Historical Review* 5 (1924): 118-31.

–. "The Canadian Civil Service, 1867-1880." *Canadian Historical Review* 7 (1926): 34-45.

–. *The Government of Canada*. Toronto: University of Toronto Press, 1963.

Den Otter, A.A. *The Philosophy of Railways: The Transcontinental Railway Idea in British North America*. Toronto: University of Toronto Press, 1997.

Dictionary of Canadian Biography, vols. 1, 2. Toronto: Macmillan Company of Canada, 1945.

Dictionary of Canadian Biography, vols. 3, 4, 6, 9, 10, 11, 12, 13. Toronto: University of Toronto Press, 1972, 1976, 1979, 1982, 1987, 1990, 1994.

Doull, John. *Sketches of Attorney Generals of Nova Scotia*. Halifax: n.p., 1964.

Edwards, John Ll.J. *The Law Officers of the Crown: A Study of the offices of the Attorney-General and Solicitor-General of England with an account of the Office of the Director of Public Prosecutions of England.* London: Sweet and Maxwell, 1964.

–. *Ministerial Responsibility for National Security as it Relates to the Offices of Prime Minister, Attorney General and Solicitor General of Canada.* Ottawa: Queen's Printer, 1980.

Evans, A. Margaret. "Oliver Mowat: Vice-Chancellor of Upper Canada, 1864-72." *Ontario History* 71, 2 (June 1979): 75-82.

–. *Sir Oliver Mowat.* Toronto: University of Toronto Press, 1992.

Evans, M. Keith. "The Prerogative of Pardon in Canada, Its Development 1864-1894." Master's thesis, Carleton University, 1971.

Farr, David M.L. *The Colonial Office and Canada, 1867-1887.* Toronto: University of Toronto Press, 1955.

Fingard, Judith. *Jack in Port: Sailortowns of Eastern Canada.* Toronto: University of Toronto Press, 1982.

–. *The Dark Side of Life in Victorian Halifax.* Porter's Lake: Pottersfield Press, 1989.

Flaherty, David H., ed. *Essays in the History of Early American Law.* Chapel Hill: University of North Carolina Press, 1969.

Forsey, Eugene. "Meetings of the Queen's Privy Council for Canada, 1867-1882." *Canadian Journal of Economics and Political Science* 32 (February-November 1966): 489-98.

Forster, Ben. *A Conjunction of Interests: Business, Politics, and Tariffs, 1825-1879.* Toronto: University of Toronto Press, 1986.

Foucault, Michel. "Governmentality." In *The Foucault Effect: Studies in Governmentality,* edited by G. Bruchell, C. Gordon, and P. Miller. Chicago: University of Chicago Press, 1991.

Friedman, Lawrence. *Crime and Punishment in American History.* New York: Basic Books, 1993.

Garland, David. *Punishment and Modern Society: A Study in Social Theory.* Oxford: Clarendon Press, 1990.

Girard, Philip, and Jim Phillips. *Essays in the History of Canadian Law: Nova Scotia.* Toronto: Osgoode Society, 1990.

Gordon, Robert W. "Introduction: J. Williard Hurst and the Common Law Tradition in American Legal Historiography." *Law and Society Review* 20 (Fall 1975): 9-55.

–. "Critical Legal Histories." *Stanford Law Review* 36 (1983-1984): 57-125.

–. "'The Ideal and the Actual in the Law': Fantasies and Practices of New York City Lawyers, 1870-1910." In *The New High Priests: Lawyers in Post Civil War America,* edited by G.W. Gawalt. Westport, CT: Greenwood Press, 1984.

–. "The Independence of Lawyers." *Boston University Law Review* 68 (1988): 1-83.

Griffiths, J.A.G. *The Politics of the Judiciary.* Cornwall: Fontana Press, 1987.

Hodgetts, J.E. *Pioneer Public Service: An Administrative History of the United Canadas, 1841-1867.* Toronto: University of Toronto Press, 1955.

Hodgins, Bruce W. *John Sandfield Macdonald.* Toronto: University of Toronto Press, 1971.

–. "Disagreement at the Commencement: Divergent Ontarian Views of Federalism, 1867-1871." In *Oliver Mowat's Ontario,* edited by Donald Swainson. Toronto: Macmillan of Canada, 1972, 52-68.

Hodgins, W.E., ed. *Correspondence, Reports of the Ministers of Justice and Order in Council upon the subject of Dominion and Provincial Legislation, 1867-1895.* Ottawa: Queen's Printer, 1896.

Hoffer, Peter Charles. *The Law's Conscience: Equitable Constitutionalism in America.* Chapel Hill: University of North Carolina Press, 1990.

Ignatieff, Michael. *A Just Measure of Pain: The Penitentiary in the Industrial Revolution, 1750-1850.* London: Penguin Books, 1978.

Johnson, J.K., ed. *The Letters of Sir John A. Macdonald, 1836-1857,* vol. 2. Ottawa: Queen's Printer, 1968.

Kahn, Paul W. *Legitimacy and History: Self-Government in American Constitutional Theory.* New Haven: Yale University Press, 1992.

Knafla, Louis A., and Terry Chapman. "Criminal Justice in Canada: A Comparative Study of the Maritimes and Lower Canada, 1760-1812." *Osgoode Hall Law Journal* 21, 2 (June 1983): 245-74.

La Forest, G.V. *Disallowance and Reservation of Provincial Legislation.* Ottawa: Department of Justice, 1955.

Laurier, Wilfrid. "Sir Antoine-Aimé Dorion." *The Week* 3, 48 (26 September 1890): 677, 679.

Mackintosh, C.H., ed. *Grits in Office: Profession and Practice Contrasted.* Ottawa: Conservative Association of the Dominion, 1876.

Martin, Ged. *Britain and the Origins of Canadian Confederation, 1837-67.* Vancouver: University of British Columbia Press, 1995.

Masur, Louis P. *Rites of Execution: Capital Punishment and the Transformation of American Culture, 1776-1865.* Oxford: Oxford University Press, 1989.

McKinnon, Frank. "The Establishment of the Supreme Court of Canada." *Canadian Historical Review* 26 (1946): 258-74.

Morgan, Edmund S. *Inventing the People: The Rise of Popular Sovereignty in England and America.* New York: W.W. Norton and Company, 1988.

Morris, Norval, and David J. Rothman, eds. *The Oxford History of the Prison.* Oxford: Oxford University Press, 1995.

Morton, W.L. "The Conservative Principle in Confederation." *Queen's Quarterly* 61 (Winter 1965): 528-46.

–. "Confederation, 1870-1896." In *Contexts of Canada's Past: Selected Essays of W.L. Morton,* edited by A.B. McKillop. Toronto: Carleton Library, 1980.

Norton-Kyshe, James William. *The Law and Privileges relating to the Attorney-General and Solicitor-General of England, with a history from the earliest periods and a series of King's Attorneys and Solicitors-General from the reign of Henry III to the 60th of Queen Victoria.* London: Stevens and Haynes, 1897.

Oliver, Peter. "From Jails to Penitentiary: The Demise of Community Corrections in early Ontario." *Correctional Options* 4 (1984): 4-10.

–. "A Terror to Evil Doers: The Central Prison and the 'Criminal Class' in Late Nineteenth-Century Ontario." In *Patterns of the Past: Interpreting Ontario's History,* edited by Roger Hall et al. Toronto: Dundurn Press, 1988.

–. *"Terror to Evil-Doers": Prisons and Punishments in Nineteenth-Century Ontario.* Toronto: Osgoode Society for Canadian Legal History, 1998.

Preece, Rod. "The Political Wisdom of John A. Macdonald." *Canadian Journal of Political Science* 17, 3 (September 1984): 459-502.

Radford, Ian. "Sydenham and Utilitarian Reform." In *Colonial Leviathan: State Formation in Mid-Nineteenth Century Canada,* edited by Allan Greer and Ian Radford. Toronto: University of Toronto Press, 1992.

Ritchie, W.J. *Observations of the Chief Justice of New Brunswick on a Bill entitled "An Act to Establish a Supreme Court for the Dominion of Canada."* Fredericton: Queen's Printer, 1870.

Roberts, Sir Charles G.D., and Arthur L. Tunnell, eds. *A Standard Dictionary of Canadian Biography.* Toronto: Trans-Canada Press, 1938.

Romney, Paul. *Mr. Attorney: The Attorney-General for Ontario in Court, Cabinet, and Legislature, 1791-1899.* Toronto: Osgoode Society, 1986.

–. "From the Types Riot to the Rebellion: Elite Ideology, Anti-Legal Sentiment, Political Violence, and the Rule of Law in Upper Canada." *Ontario History* 79 (June 1987): 113-44.

–. "Very Late Loyalist Fantasies: Nostalgic Tory 'History' and the Rule of Law in Upper Canada." In *Canadian Perspectives on Law and Society: Issues in Legal History,* edited by W. Wesley Pue and Barry Wright. Ottawa: Carleton University Press, 1988.

Rothman, David J. *The Discovery of the Asylum: Social Order and Disorder in the New Republic.* Boston: Little, Brown and Company, 1971.

Russell, Peter H. *The Supreme Court of Canada as a Bilingual and Bicultural Institution.* Ottawa: Queen's Printer, 1969.

Smandych, Russell. "Beware of the 'Evil American Monster': Upper Canadian Views on the Need for a Penitentiary, 1830-1834." *Canadian Journal of Criminology* 133, 2 (1991): 125-47.

–. "Tory Paternalism and the Politics of Penal Reform in Upper Canada, 1830-34: A 'Neo-Revisionist' Account of the Kingston Penitentiary." *Criminal Justice History: An International Annual* 12 (1991): 57-84.

Snell, James G., and Frederick Vaughan. *The Supreme Court of Canada: History of the Institution.* Toronto: University of Toronto Press, 1985.
Sondik Aron, Cindy. *Ladies and Gentlemen of the Civil Service: Middle-Class Workers in Victorian America.* New York: Oxford University Press, 1987.
Strange, Carolyn. "The Lottery of Death: Capital Punishment, 1867-1976." *Manitoba Law Journal* 23, 3 (January 1996): 594-619.
–, ed. *Qualities of Mercy: Justice, Punishment, and Discretion.* Vancouver: University of British Columbia Press, 1996.
Stevenson, Garth. *Ex Uno Plures: Federal-Provincial Relations in Canada, 1867-1896.* Montreal and Kingston: McGill-Queen's University Press, 1993.
Stewart, Gordon T. *The Origins of Canadian Politics: A Comparative Approach.* Vancouver: University of British Columbia Press, 1986.
Sugarman, David. "Law, Economy and the State in England, 1750-1914: Some Major Issues." In *Legality, Ideology, and the State,* edited by David Sugarman. London: Academic Press, 1983.
Swainger, Jonathan. "A Bench in Disarray: The Quebec Judiciary and the Federal Department of Justice, 1867-1878." *Les Cahiers de Droit* 34, 1 (March 1993): 59-92.
–. "A Distant Edge of Authority: Capital Punishment and the Prerogative of Mercy in British Columbia, 1872-1880." In *Essays in the History of Canadian Law: British Columbia and the Yukon,* edited by Hamar Foster and John McLaren. Toronto: Osgoode Society for Legal History, 1995.
Taylor, C.J. "The Kingston, Ontario Penitentiary and Moral Architecture." *Histoire sociale/Social History* 24, 12 (1979): 385-408.
Thomson, Dale C. *Alexander Mackenzie: Clear Grit.* Toronto: Macmillan Company of Canada, 1960.
Tilloch, Judith. *The Rideau Canal: Defense, Transport and Recreation.* Ottawa: Parks Canada, 1981.
Torrance, F.W. *A Letter to the Attorney General of the Province of Quebec on the Administration of Justice.* Montreal: J. Lovell, 1873. University of Western Ontario Pamphlet Collection.
Underhill, Frank H. "Edward Blake, The Supreme Court Act, and the Appeal to the Privy Council, 1876-6." *Canadian Historical Review* 19 (1938): 245-63.
Upton, L.F.S., ed. *The Diary and Selected Papers of Chief Justice William Smith, 1784-1793.* Toronto: Champlain Society, 1963.
Vipond, Robert C. *Liberty and Community: Canadian Federalism and the Failure of the Constitution.* Albany: State University of New York Press, 1991.
Waite, Peter B. "Sir John A. Macdonald: The Man." In *Empire and Nations: Essays in Honour of Frederich H. Soward,* edited by Harvey L. Dyck and H. Peter Krosby. Vancouver: University of British Columbia Press, 1969, 36-53.
Waite, P.B. *Canada 1874-1896: Arduous Destiny.* Toronto: McClelland and Stewart, 1971.
–. *Macdonald: His Life and World.* Toronto: McGraw-Hill Ryerson, 1975.
–. *The Man from Halifax: Sir John Thompson, Prime Minister.* Toronto: University of Toronto Press, 1985.
Whitelaw, W. Menzies. "Reconstructing the Quebec Conference." *Canadian Historical Review* 19 (June 1938): 123-37.
Wilton, Carol, ed. *Essays in the History of Canadian Law – Beyond the Law: Lawyers and Business in Canada, 1830 to 1930.* Toronto: Osgoode Society Press, 1990.
Workman, Dr. Joseph. "Case of Erastus Hotchkiss." *American Journal of Insanity* 32 (1876): 405-19.
Young, Brian. *George-Etienne Cartier: A Montreal Bourgeois.* Montreal and Kingston: McGill-Queen's University Press, 1981.
Zubrycki, Richard M. *The Establishment of Canada's Penitentiary System: Federal Correctional Policy 1867-1900.* Toronto: University of Toronto: Faculty of Social Work, 1980.

Index

Set in Stone by Darlene Remus
Printed and bound in Canada by Friesens
Copy editor: Judy Phillips
Proofreader: Lauren Ollsin
Indexer: Annette Lorek